MYTHOLOGIZING NORVAL MORRISSEAU

MYTHOLOGIZING NORVAL MORRISSEAU

ART AND THE COLONIAL NARRATIVE IN THE CANADIAN MEDIA

CARMEN L. ROBERTSON

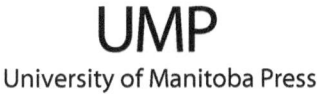

UMP

University of Manitoba Press

University of Manitoba Press
Winnipeg, Manitoba
Canada R3T 2M5
uofmpress.ca

20 19 18 17 16   1 2 3 4 5

Cover design: Kirk Warren
Interior design: Karen Armstrong Graphic Design
Cover photo: Dick Loek/GetStock.com

Library and Archives Canada Cataloguing in Publication

Robertson, Carmen L., 1962–, author
Mythologizing Norval Morrisseau : art and the colonial narrative
in the Canadian media / Carmen L. Robertson.

Includes bibliographical references and index.
Issued in print and electronic formats.
ISBN 978-0-88755-810-8 (pbk).
ISBN 978-0-88755-501-5 (pdf).
ISBN 978-0-88755-499-5 (epub)

1. Morrisseau, Norval, 1931-2007—Public opinion. 2. Morrisseau, Norval,
1931-2007—In mass media. 3. Morrisseau, Norval, 1931-2007—Appreciation.
4. Native artists—Canada--Public opinion. 5. Native artists—Press coverage—Canada.
6. Native art—Press coverage—Canada. 7. Native peoples—Press coverage—Canada.
I. Title.

ND249.M66R6 2016   759.11   C2015-907999-3
                                                  C2015-908000-2

The University of Manitoba Press gratefully acknowledges the financial support
for its publication program provided by the Government of Canada through the Canada
Book Fund, the Canada Council for the Arts, the Manitoba Department
of Culture, Heritage, Tourism, the Manitoba Arts Council,
and the Manitoba Book Publishing Tax Credit.

CONTENTS

ILLUSTRATIONS

MYTHOLOGIZING
NORVAL
MORRISSEAU

Discipline, Performativity, and Morrisseau

Native artists had to know how to play the white man's game, they had to be able to work the media and the market, or they weren't going anywhere.

Sarah Milroy, *Globe and Mail*, 7 February 2006

With the 2006 opening of *Norval Morrisseau: Shaman Artist* at the National Gallery of Canada in Ottawa, Ontario, two of Canada's leading newspapers, the *Globe and Mail* and the *Ottawa Citizen*, characterized the Anishinaabe artist's retrospective as a "taming of demons."[1] While each paper acknowledged Morrisseau as a pivotal artist in Canadian art history, both stories attributed demons to Morrisseau, when in actuality it was the Canadian nation and its colonial arm of nationalism, the media, that were the primary source of the many demons attributed to Morrisseau. As the first Indigenous[2] artist in Canada to break into the mainstream art world, Morrisseau had entered an exclusive and elitist club with an exhibition of his work at Toronto's Pollock Gallery in September 1962. Yet while Morrisseau was feted and fawned upon, he struggled to be taken seriously as an artist. With the first media coverage of his art opening in Toronto, Morrisseau came under intense scrutiny by Canada's media. The press found the seemingly exotic and authentic Morrisseau hard to resist: *Indian*[3] first, artist second.

In a recent essay for the National Museum of the American Indian's exhibition *Before and After the Horizon: Anishinaabe Artists of the Great Lakes*, curator Gerald McMaster acknowledges that Norval Morrisseau's "rise in the early 1960s gave significant voice to later generations of First Nations artists across the country." McMaster describes how "Morrisseau quickly became an iconic, tragicomic artist—a role frequently reinforced by the art world—and, to his credit, he was often more than happy to oblige. At the same time, his character and strategies were quite different because, while he may have been characterized as a primitive, he was also extremely serious about the decrepit conditions in which most Aboriginal peoples lived."[4] Labelling him a "latter day neo-primitivist," McMaster explains that Morrisseau can be defined by his "deep attachment to his traditional Anishinaabe heritage" and by his "elevated stature in an art world where difference is not just accepted but encouraged."[5] McMaster's analysis of Morrisseau is based on forty years of study and analysis, and he clearly identifies the artist's deep understanding of Canadian colonial culture. I disagree with McMaster, however, when he says that the art world not only accepted difference but encouraged it. The media, and newspaper art critics in particular, did not, for the most part, approve of Morrisseau's difference. While titillated by his exoticism, the press largely disparaged his difference, scorned his performative gestures, and often positioned his art as primitive. Much finger wagging followed the artist, who was mostly interested in painting his unique visual stories and pushing boundaries—boundaries that shifted because of the artist's trailblazing efforts.

As Canada's first Indigenous art star, Morrisseau served as a test case of sorts for the media to teach readers about artistic expressions of identity and difference. His racialized identity remained key to this lesson. The educative role of media in relation to race is a relatively understudied topic yet clearly, as described in the literature, the media does more than simply report the news. Political scientist Paul Kellstedt argues that although understandings of how the press has covered race are "largely ignored by scholars," the press's influence in matters of race is a form of "social learning."[6] Historian Carlos E. Cortes similarly contends that mass media powerfully and persuasively teaches children about diversity.[7] The press, when covering Morrisseau, adopted disciplining racial discourses already promoted in Canadian newspaper coverage of Indigenous peoples. Because of the skewed media reporting, Morrisseau often came to stand in for all Indigenous peoples—a monolithic object, an Imaginary Indian.[8] Many stories, then, revealed less about Morrisseau and more about Canadian society. And as *Globe and Mail* art critic Sarah Milroy astutely noted, Morrisseau quickly learned to play the game, working the media and the market, to make readings of the myth surrounding the artist more complex and nuanced.[9]

This study is not simply about the role of the media in constructing a racialized identity for the artist. It also investigates Morrisseau's own performative gestures in questioning and resisting the confining box of stereotypical tropes into which the press so easily plunked him. Often, media narratives and Morrisseau's own commentary stood at odds. At times Morrisseau confronted the press, challenging reporters to cover his artistic achievements rather than focus on his personal life. Yet Morrisseau also manipulated his shaman persona, spoon-feeding the media a construction not so different from what they craved.

The mythology surrounding Morrisseau is not easily unpacked. Fraught with identity politics, colonial misconceptions, racialized tropes, and Morrisseau's own implicated ways of framing himself, intertwined signifiers cross-pollinate in complex ways. Meaning is always in process and as a result is unstable because readers bring multiple meanings to texts. My reading of the texts and images in this study is a product of my positioning as an Indigenous female, as an academic, and as someone who grew up in rural Saskatchewan in the 1960s and 1970s constituted, constrained, and enabled in a criss-crossing of discourses. Drawing on press coverage, Morrisseau's engagement with media sources, and a variety of other sources, I have gathered together a narrative that considers not only the man and his art, but also Canada's role in forging the story of Morrisseau.

In this way, Morrisseau can be understood as a discourse, a myth, a fantasy; part of a larger colonial narrative that helps explain the Canadian nation. Roland Barthes explained myth as a particular type of discourse: "Myth is depoliticized speech ... [It] does not deny things, on the contrary, its function is to talk about them; simply, it purifies them, it makes them innocent, it gives them a natural and eternal justification."[10] By naturalizing something, according to Barthes, a depoliticizing occurs that strips it of its history. Mythology surrounding Morrisseau strips him of his history and of the history of Canadian colonialism. Mythology inserts him into an innocent and naturalized narrative through which the nation attempts to hide its colonial legacy. Concealment is at the centre of myth. Various kinds of manipulation are enacted on Morrisseau by popular cultural sources in constructing myth, though I reject any simple dichotomy or binary in untangling these myths or hierarchal power structure. Foucault points out "where there is power there is resistance" and it is in discourses that "power and knowledge are joined together."[11] No one domain deserves explanatory value over another. Utilizing a wide range of media sources and other texts, I hope to illuminate the complex interaction of discourses, made legible in particular moments that maintain the mythology surrounding this artist.

In a process of naturalization, Canada has sought to erase its colonial past. At a G20 summit news conference in Pittsburg, Pennsylvania, in 2009,

Prime Minister Stephen Harper naively stated, "We have no history of colonialism."[12] That said, many have written extensively about Canada's colonial past and present, and scholarship has shown that colonialism is tied up with notions of knowledge and power.[13] With Morrisseau as an object of study, a nexus of colonialism, the gaze, and the politics of performance emerges that is not a simple thing, but which draws attention to the complications of such an examination. Gathering the strands of this analysis does not lead to a single, monolithic interpretation but rather highlights the many ways in which Canada tries to absolve itself from complicity with its colonial past and present.

Canada's Story

Building a national creation myth came easily to the United States. The frontier myth endures and unites the nation.[14] Anthropologist Pauline Turner Strong's recent study on cultural representations of American Indians and the American Imaginary, outlines for the United States the ways in which simulations, a term she borrows from Anishinaabe literary scholar Gerald Vizenor, such as, "calculating 'Indian Blood,' adopting 'Indian' mascots, assuming 'Indian' names, and 'playing Indian'—work to establish and maintain colonial dominance."[15] As a colonial entity, Canada's story has not emerged so readily and much has been penned regarding why Canada has not been able to formulate a fitting narrative to inspire its citizens nationally. Mythologies surrounding Morrisseau have been entangled with collectively held images that make up the Canadian national imaginary.

Benedict Anderson's *Imagined Communities,* first published in 1983, forced a reconsideration of the concept of nation with his challenge that a nation constitutes an imagined community, "imagined because the members of even the smallest nation will never know most of their fellow-members, meet them, or even hear of them, yet in the minds of each lives the image of their communion."[16] The constructedness of national identity, he argues, relies heavily on imagined narratives to weave together a nation's birth story. Stuart Hall argues that nationalist discourse constructs meanings that "are contained in the stories told about it, memories which connect its present with its past, and images which are constructed of it."[17]

Former Canadian Prime Minister Stephen Harper stepped up mythology production, attempting to convince Canadians that the problematic War of 1812 and Canada's part in the bloody World War I Battle of Vimy Ridge should be celebrated as defining moments that shape the nation. As part of this symbolic rhetoric, the imagery on the Canadian twenty-dollar bill was updated to reflect Harper's attempt at national identity building: in 2011 the Canadian Mint replaced the image of Haida artist Bill Reid's *Spirit of Haida Gwaii*, a former effort to acknowledge First Nations contributions to Canada's narrative, with an image of the newly built Canadian Vimy Ridge Memorial. At the same time, this effort at reshaping national identity remains hampered by Canadians' general disinterest in such memorials. Many Canadians have misidentified the latest twenty-dollar bill image as the New York City World Trade Towers destroyed in 2001, or a naked woman—so much for mythmaking.[18] The recent discovery of one of the ships from the 1845 Franklin expedition to Canada's Arctic has been interpreted by the media and also described by Prime Minister Harper as "a key moment in our country's history."[19] That a British expedition seeking to chart the Northwest Passage decades prior to Confederation can be claimed as a key moment in Canada's collective story requires an imagination that is squarely situated in the ongoing practice of Canadian nation-building.

Aboriginal peoples complicate national stories. The United States, in its frontier myth, made the cowboy and Indian narrative into a war story and easily put the issue of settling the west to rest. Cowboys won that cultural war, and expansion was embraced and glorified. Still, as Vizenor points out, in the United States, "nationalism ... [is] the most monotonous simulation of dominance" because "some tribes are simulated as national cultural emblems."[20] Turner Strong agrees that in her survey of images of political sovereignty of the nation-state and Indigenous sovereignty "the collectively held images that make up the American national imaginary are complex and contested."[21]

Canada has also grappled with its sense of the imaginary, finding the crafting of a national identity an ongoing and difficult task similar to challenges found in other settler nations such as New Zealand, in part because of Indigenous presence. Sport scholar Mark Falcous argues that in New Zealand, as part of an effort to promulgate an outwardly inclusive national narrative that brought Māori and settler narratives together to distinguish it as distinct from Britain, their former colonial master, the media promoted the nation's All Black rugby team and their performance of the Māori haka as a symbol of national unity. Falcous finds that while such signification can be read in multiple ways, "this imagery symbolizes a politically neutered reading of the effects of colonialism in that it conveys a romanticized vision—reduced to humour—that omits the cultural, political, and military realities of colonial domination in Aotearoa."[22] Still, he also highlights the potential for resistant agency within media readings. Art historian Nicolas

Thomas argues, for example, that characterizations of Māori tradition, spirituality, and mythology promoted in relation to international art exhibitions mounted during the 1970s and 1980s "were probably more significant than the drawbacks arising from the recapitulation of restrictive primitivism."[23]

Canada has long used a pan-Aboriginal narrative that presents a contrived homogenization of diverse Indigenous cultures in an effort to exploit the nation's uniqueness, to distinguish itself from Britain, making the matter a messy one. In 1993, literary scholar Terry Goldie described Canada's quandary when considering Indigenous peoples: "The white Canadian looks at the Indian. The Indian is Other and therefore alien. But the Indian is indigenous and therefore cannot be alien. So the Canadian must be alien. But how can the Canadian be alien within Canada?"[24] A culture of denial about Canada's colonial past has been key to Canada's image as peacekeepers.[25] Historian Ken Coates challenges notions of the rosy national tale of settlers as benevolent peacekeepers, asking non-Indigenous readers to "imagine the story of Canada, the Maritimes, and Aboriginal policy as an indigenous person might see it."[26] He frankly asserts, "First Nations live with the consequences of a brutal, dehumanizing history in a way that non-Aboriginal people simply do not."[27] Historian J.R. Miller has written extensively about Canada's historic treatment of Native peoples, and in *Lethal Legacy* he finds that Canada's colonial history has been overlooked in Canadian public policy making.[28] This colonial dilemma continues in many cultural forums throughout Canadian culture today. The history of the treaties, residential schools, and ongoing systemic racism plagues Canada's attempts at a unifying national story.

Aboriginal art has offered Australia and New Zealand, two other countries colonized by the British, options for manipulating their national mythologies and crafting a story separate from that of European nations. Thomas agrees that Indigenous identity has problematized nation-building efforts, yet finds that Aboriginal art solves some of these issues.[29] Outlining the settler artist's incorporation of Indigenous motifs in an effort to craft a national image and also charting how Indigenous arts have been utilized to assert sovereignty and rights, Thomas concedes that an admixture of race and art creates a complex dynamic.[30] Art provides colonial nations such as Australia or New Zealand opportunities to create an identity distinct from its mother country. Yet it also reminds those settler nations of their Indigenous past (and present), which troubles an otherwise glorifying narrative. Canada has also viewed Indigenous art as one way to proffer a national identity.

Covering Morrisseau

The media provides us with much of what we know about the world in which we live. I've never visited the Middle East or attended a G20 summit, yet I have opinions on these events and ideas, some based on what the media has presented. Conceptions of media, its purpose, its effects, its technologies, have changed dramatically in the twenty-first century. With the Internet, access to information has exploded and changed the ways we learn. That the press serves a "disciplinary" function that feeds and reflects a variety of needs and sources, including those deemed hegemonic, has been well established through discourse analysis that draws on theoretical frames advanced by Foucault.[31] Decades ago, humanists such as Stuart Hall, Edward Said, and Noam Chomsky began to argue that press content regurgitates the prevailing hegemonic order in any given Western society.[32] Social scientists likewise have drawn conclusions about the nature and influence of media content. Agenda-setting theory, in simple terms, has shown that the media has the power not merely to frame stories but also to tell readers and viewers what to think. This theoretical work dates from the 1970s and was pioneered by Maxwell McCombs and Donald Shaw.[33]

In this investigation of Morrisseau, I am interested in how media sources have framed Morrisseau and helped manipulate the mythology that surrounds the artist. This discourse analysis includes analysis of news coverage in print media and magazines, the artist's representation in two National Film Board documentaries, and in a later CBC documentary. Morrisseau's behaviour, of most interest to the media, became increasingly problematic and open for discussion over the decades. During a period in the late 1980s, for example, the press frenzy surrounding his alcoholism could be likened to the media circus in 2013–14 surrounding then Toronto Mayor Rob Ford.[34]

Canada's media served up an unruly Morrisseau in an effort to both discipline Indigenous bodies and "teach" Canadians about Indigenous peoples. Arguably, his behaviour as much as his art, as reported in documentaries, magazines, and newspapers throughout Canada for over five decades, presented a confining narrative with little space for consideration outside a narrow racialized sphere. Morrisseau's resistance to the constructed racial fixity imposed by Canadian cultural norms refreshingly ruptures the discourse in ways that amount to an ongoing critical revision of the disciplinary authority of race.

Disciplinary actions and performative imperatives confine notions of race. However, in his struggle against subjection, Morrisseau attempted to forge new modes of identity that challenge essentialized claims, manipulating the restrictive tropes also present in press reports. This theoretical direction is examined throughout this study. The media continually worked to control its messages related to Morrisseau, but as I have aimed to document, the savvy artist used the press to his advantage when possible, complicating this mythology.

Morrisseau's own reflexive interventions shifted racial significations in subtle ways even as the press maintained entrenched constructions. The artist's story, as told by the media, offers instances of fixity but also illustrates, at times, how racial bodies are not natural but are instead socially formed and thus open to agency. As Foucault concludes, "we are always in a position of beginning again."[35]

Foucault also argues that discipline "makes" individuals, explaining in *Discipline and Punish* that disciplinary power emerged in eighteenth-century Europe to modify and manipulate the body so as to control the individual body and create a docile and productive national subject.[36] The complexities of this concept gain momentum when interpreted through the colonial lens of Canadian Indigenous-settler relations. Legislation, education, and cultural policy undermined Indigenous identities in favour of a national discourse of whiteness. Canada's press played an integral role in the shaping and maintaining of Indigenous bodies in Canada by feeding mainstream readers a steady diet of stereotypical constructions that confirmed other popular cultural representations while denying inequities existed. Media analyst Teun Van Dijk states, "One of the main strategies of the ideological framework keeping white dominance in place is precisely to deny or to play down the prevalence of racism and to blame victims for the persistent inequalities that are its outcome."[37]

And while clearly readers can and do make their own meanings from what the media feeds them in ways that can be complex, few sources of information were available when Morrisseau arrived on the scene in the 1960s, exacerbating the power of the press. Yasmin Jiwani agrees that the media implicitly reproduces racism, constituting "a monopoly of knowledge, and through ... practices of selection, editing, and production determine the kinds of information we receive about our culture, nation, and the rest of the world."[38] As Mark Anderson and I demonstrate in *Seeing Red: A History of Natives in Canadian Newspapers*, Canadian English-language newspapers from the 1860s through to the present promoted and continue to promote the colonial imaginary, framing and constructing bodies that conformed to essentialized and negative images that constantly shape the Imaginary Indian.[39] Historian Lyle Dick concludes that "since Confederation the national media based in central Canada have been oriented to historical representations aligned to expansionist imperatives."[40]

Nadine Ehlers, in *Racial Imperatives*, employs the term "racial discipline" to describe a network of relations that together formulate racial identity.[41] A form of racialized discipline was enacted on Morrisseau by the media. While reports about his art were less confining, skirting primitivist discourse, his racial identity could not escape being disciplined by the press. In "The Ethics of Care for the Self as a Practice of Freedom," Foucault observes that subjects serve as the objects of discourse and that press reports acknowledge this notion.[42] Complicity between the press, racism, and colonialism result.

Coverage of Morrisseau's life by the media spanned his career and has continued since his death in 2007. Reports of the struggles over who laid claim to his body and of more recent court cases related to the many forgeries sold as Morrisseau originals demonstrate an unwavering fascination with the man. Such interest stems not only from Morrisseau's pivotal art but also from his engaging nature that captivated the media. Writing in *Maclean's* magazine in 1979, Christopher Hume suggested that "nobody enjoys Morrisseau more than Morrisseau ... When he talks, others listen; where he goes, people follow."[43] Yet even taking into account Hume's particular characterization of Morrisseau as a self-promoter, it remains difficult to fully comprehend the man and his work despite more than forty years of press attention. Trying to pin him down has been complicated by Canada's colonial need to essentialize him within the narrow but bifurcated roles available. In the media's coverage of Morrisseau, peppered with interviews and quotes by his gallery dealers, art critics, columnists, concerned citizens, and Morrisseau himself, the artist's own aims are at times difficult to recognize. Recently, artist and writer Barry Ace asserted that Morrisseau worked to fashion a mythic public persona as an exotic yet primitive artist to appease his collectors. Morrisseau, according to Ace, offered the art-buying public "a rare opportunity to own a fragmentary glimpse of a mythical past."[44] Art historian Ruth B. Phillips agrees that reporters postulating about Morrisseau's character became a pattern through his life: "Journalists devoted as much space to the novelty of the occasion and exotic appearance of the artist as they did to the art itself."[45] Curator Greg Hill titled the 2006 retrospective exhibition of Morrisseau's oeuvre *Norval Morrisseau: Shaman Artist*, acknowledging the importance of the problematic shamanistic role to Morrisseau, his art, and to the public.[46] As the press and the art world attempted to figure him out, Morrisseau fashioned his own compelling persona that at times soberly resisted media frames and at other times played with these same signifiers.

A Short Biography

Born in 1931, Anishinaabe artist Norval Morrisseau entered the world at a hospital in Port Arthur (Thunder Bay), Ontario, and was raised on the Sand Point Reserve near Lake Nipigon in the Canadian Shield of northwestern Ontario, a landscape dotted with rock, lakes, and rivers. Born at a time in Canadian history when Indigenous peoples struggled under a series of oppressive laws and practices, Morrisseau's upbringing was influenced by assimilationist governmental policies. Indian residential school attendance was a requirement, ceremonial activities were outlawed as dictated by Canada's Indian Act, and other non-legislated practices such as the "pass system" shaped reserve life.[47] These external forces affected Morrisseau but were tempered by his access to a rich repository of closely guarded cultural knowledge, imparted through story and ceremony. His parents, Grace Theresa Nanakonagos and Abel Morrisseau, followed Anishinaabe protocol by sending their oldest son to live with his grandparents Moses "Potan" and Veronique Nanakonagos at Sandy Lake Reserve on Lake Nipigon. There, he benefitted from a traditional education steeped in stories and cultural proto- cols conveyed to him by his grandfather, an acknowledged powerful shaman trained within the Medewiwin spiritual traditions. Morrisseau's grandmother Veronique, also a force in his life, was a devout Catholic who further shaped his upbringing. Schooled in the stories, protocols, and ceremonies of the Anishinaabe by his grandfather, tempered by a syncretic relationship with Roman Catholicism from his grandmother, Morrisseau grew up with a keen awareness of the sacredness of all life.

However, like all First Nations children at that time, Morrisseau's family life was disrupted when he was sent to the Catholic St. Joseph's Residential School in Fort William at age six. Morrisseau, like many who attended such government-controlled schools, found it impossible to escape emotional and sexual abuse that left deep scars.[48] After four years away, he returned to Sandy Lake and continued his cultural schooling, receiving formal education only to the fourth grade at the public school in Beardmore, Ontario.

As part of Morrisseau's traditional teachings he experienced a vision quest in his youth under the direction of his grandfather, which he candidly describes in the 1973 National Film Board of Canada documentary, *The Paradox of Norval Morrisseau*.[49] His encounter on that occasion with a sacred bear influenced his life, and the bear serves as a common subject in his art. Another significant event in the form of a healing ceremony also shaped his art practice. While critically ill at age nineteen, Morrisseau received the name Miskwaabik Animiiki (Copper Thunderbird) from a medicine woman.

As Morrisseau explained, "She gave me a new name, the name of Copper Thunderbird. That was a very, very powerful new name; and it cured me."[50] His name becomes integral to his mythology, especially in the twenty-first century.

While in a sanatorium in Fort William in the mid-1950s receiving treatment for tuberculosis (TB), Morrisseau met his future wife, Harriet Kakegamic, a Cree woman from Sandy Lake Reserve north of Red Lake, Ontario, who was visiting her father, David Kakegamic, who also had TB. A disease that spread throughout the Indigenous population beginning in the mid-nineteenth century, tuberculosis was linked to sudden economic, ecological, and political change, and presaged morbidity and mortality among First Nations, according to James Daschuk in *Clearing the Plains*.[51] It was common for those inflicted with TB to spend extended lengths of time in a sanatorium, as was the case for Morrisseau. He and Harriet married upon his release and lived in Beardmore and then in Red Lake, where Morrisseau experimented as an artist while working to support his wife. In the mid to late 1950s his art production was a mix of traditional and contemporary art. He often drew on birch bark, a traditional Anishinaabe medium. Morrisseau began to sign his works as Copper Thunderbird written in Cree syllabics, an alphabet designed by Protestant church minister and missionary James Evans in 1840 to teach the Bible to Cree speakers. Morrisseau's Cree wife Harriet taught him syllabics.

Besides being steeped in traditional Anishinaabe arts and cultural practices and maintaining a commitment to preserving traditional Anishinaabe knowledge in pictorial form, Morrisseau was strongly influenced in his artistic development by key people. Ruth B. Phillips argues that encounters between "strangers and native artists" led to "counter-modern" interventions.[52] She notes that meeting Dr. Joseph Weinstein, a doctor with ties to Paris and the Modern art scene, and his wife Esther, was instrumental in shaping Morrisseau's art practice. This nascent artistic influence opened Morrisseau to a wider conception of art that challenged and inspired him. His connection to the Weinsteins is also the seed of his link to Picasso and his later construction as Picasso of the North.

An Ontario artist, Susan Ross of Thunder Bay, met Morrisseau while sketching in the Beardmore area and they, too, became friends. Morrisseau's correspondence with Ross in the early 1960s reveals his reliance on her for artistic supplies and responses to art questions.[53] Their relationship similarly motivated Morrisseau to explore new ideas and markets for his art. The letters reveal Morriseau's personal awareness of himself as artist and dispel the myth that he was a so-called tabula rasa when it came to art—unaware of Western concepts of art. Clearly the Weinsteins and Ross made a strong artistic impression on him.

Anthropologist Selwyn Dewdney also supported Morrisseau in his early artistic development. Dewdney was conducting research into Anishinaabe rock art on behalf of the Royal Ontario Museum when a local Ontario Provincial Police constable wrote to him about Morrisseau, who had a rich knowledge that might be helpful to Dewdney. On a trip to the Red Lake area, Morrisseau shared his cultural knowledge of rock art with Dewdney, who studied and wrote on the subject. Dewdney saw Morrisseau as a collaborator in his research, and later helped Morrisseau by editing *Legends of My People* (1965).[54] Like Weinstein and Ross, Dewdney was also an artist. However, unlike these other two, Dewdney initially encouraged Morrisseau to work in traditional mediums such as birchbark and leather, though later supported his shift to early experimentation in oils.[55] Curator Greg Hill argues that it was probably Dewdney who encouraged Morrisseau to sign his work as Copper Thunderbird in syllabics.[56] Dewdney became a strong advocate for Morrisseau, clearly evidenced by their rich and personal correspondence.[57] However, Barry Ace believes that Dewdney's advice to Morrisseau to paint in ways that appeared more stereotypically "authentic" and to paint on moosehide using colours similar to those used by "prehistoric Indians" demonstrates his anthropological perspective rather than artistic direction.[58]

Morrisseau's life changed dramatically when he met gallery owner Jack Pollock, who had heard about the artist from Susan Ross and visited him in Beardmore in 1962. Pollock described his first impressions of Morrisseau as an "artist with vision" who lived an isolated existence in squalor, in a "makeshift shack erected on the garbage dump outside of town."[59] Still, it was Pollock's offer of an art exhibition at the Pollock Gallery in Toronto in September 1962 that shifted the course of Morrisseau's life. As the first Indigenous artist to show his work in a contemporary art gallery in Canada, Morrisseau's debut created a stir in the media and the exhibition sold out the first day. While his art hailed a new development in Canadian art, it was the artist who garnered the most interest.

The September 1962 exhibition at the Pollock Gallery in Toronto changed Norval Morrisseau's life. Recognized as an artist and a public figure, both his art and his private life were caught in an enduring spotlight. The 1960s were a whirlwind of activity for Morrisseau. He matured as an artist and became a father; his work entered collections of public art museums and was exhibited nationally and internationally; and his artistic vocabulary influenced a whole new generation of Indigenous artists. In 1965, for example, the Glenbow Museum in Calgary purchased a significant group of works, which sparked more frequent exhibitions for the artist and also signalled a new importance for his oeuvre. An exhibition the following year in Quebec also demonstrated a growing national interest in his work.[60] Yet between living in northwestern Ontario, and travelling to Toronto, Morrisseau negotiated his career with little background in the mainstream art market, often relying on art dealers, politicians, and government employees to aid him in his efforts to promote his work. During this period, the press reported on him and his art within a confining narrative of primitivism and racism. In response to having an ethnographic lens trained upon him as an Indigenous artist, Morrisseau became an anthropologist of sorts, studying Canadians as the Other, astutely gauging press and popular cultural stereotypes as he painted. The artist found strategies to shape his career as he explored spirituality in diverse ways.

While the 1960s established Morrisseau as a contemporary Indigenous artist, the 1970s are largely acknowledged as a pivotal period for him artistically. His personal life was punctuated by a number of significant awards and distinctions, as well as a growing media awareness of his work, even as he struggled with alcohol abuse and personal problems. He suffered severe burns in a hotel fire in Vancouver in 1972 and the following year spent time in jail in Kenora, Ontario, because of alcohol-related problems. Still, art production during this period progressed as his artistic vocabulary matured. Reaching new Indigenous and mainstream audiences, Morrisseau also began to produce graphic art, disseminating prints to a much wider audience. Many of the early prints were produced at the newly formed Triple K Co-operative in Red Lake, Ontario. Founded in 1973 by three of Morrisseau's brothers-in-law—Henry, Joshim, and Goyce Kakegamic—the co-operative allowed Morrisseau to explore new artistic directions in his practice.

Morrisseau's six-month period of incarceration, ironically, was surprisingly productive because he was provided with an additional cell to use as an art studio. This focused period is recognized as a catalyst for a body of work that remains among his most noteworthy. Upon his release from prison, Morrisseau became the subject of two National Film Board of Canada documentary films, *The Colours of Pride* (1973) and *The Paradox of Norval Morrisseau* (1974).[61] While the films arguably served as a primer for colonial and racial politics in Canada with their strong assimilationist message, they also raised his profile among Canadians more generally as the public became acquainted with Morrisseau and his art. And while he focused on his career,

Morrisseau also found time to mentor emerging Indigenous artists. In his role as an advocate, Morrisseau strengthened awareness in a variety of initiatives throughout the 1970s.

A key member of the so-called Indian Group of Seven, Morrisseau joined a group of artists in Winnipeg organized by Odawa artist and gallery owner Daphne Odjig to promote and support Indigenous artists throughout Canada.[62] Morrisseau also took part in a series of educational workshops with Cree artists Carl Ray and Joshim Kakegamic at local schools and community clubs in northwestern Ontario, organized by the Ontario Department of Education. Introducing budding Indigenous artists to his visual vocabulary, Morrisseau, with fellow artists, demonstrated a form of visual storytelling that inspired an art movement.

A significant shift in his thinking that was reflected in his art practice occurred in 1976, when Morrisseau began to study Eckankar after Jack Pollock's assistant, Eva Quan, introduced him to this spiritual movement. The controversial Eckankar, a hybrid of Eastern spiritual traditions headquartered in Minneapolis, Minnesota, was founded by Paul Twitchell in 1965 as a variation of the Radha Soami Sant Mat, a religious tradition in the Punjab area of northern India (Twitchell was a former student of Sant Mat Master Kirpal Singh). In a series of writings published to promote and increase the credibility of Eckankar, self-proclaimed ECK master Twitchell explained that divine light is key to understanding, because the movement's teachings were shared with him by an ageless spiritual guide who appeared before him in light form.[63]

In 1997 Morrisseau wrote that Eckankar allowed him to make sense of the many spiritual directions he had pursued till then, saying, "It was not until I came into Eckankar that I was able to understand."[64] Eckankar's promotion of a concept of inner light and shamanistic astral travel touched Morrisseau deeply. Through an intense colour palette, Morrisseau infused his work with a combination of illuminating light and symbolic associations with astral travel and transformation. Hill argues that "through Eckankar, Morrisseau develops a vocabulary for his shamanism. His incorporation of this 'new age' religion brings his ancient knowledge of Anishinaabe traditions into the present day while at the same time allowing him to explore new imagery—the Eckist identity of soul travel."[65] Imagery in his art begins to reflect an adoption of these ideas, and his art works include a shift from mostly Anishinaabe and Christian themes to a more personal, hybrid concept of spirituality. Hill notes that "through Eckankar, Morrisseau develops a vocabulary for his shamanism."[66] At this point in his career, Morrisseau cast himself as a shaman artist outside the strict protocols of Anishinaabe culture. With Eckankar, he formulated a new syncretism that meshed with the training he had received from his grandfather. Morrisseau now began inventing and reinventing new forms of visual expression that were tied not only to Anishinaabe stories, but also, increasingly, to a more individualized spirituality.

Morrisseau's international reputation grew with group exhibitions held in Norway and Germany in 1976. The 1978 exhibition *Art of the Woodland Indian* at the recently created McMichael Canadian Art Collection in Kleinburg, Ontario, also included an artist's residency at the Tom Thomson house on the grounds, where the artist painted and met with visitors. Morrisseau's appointment to the Order of Canada also came in late 1978. By the end of the decade he was recognized as a significant force in Indigenous art.

An art exhibition curated by Tom Hill and Elizabeth McLuhan in 1984 at the Art Gallery of Ontario celebrated Morrisseau's significance as an artist and as a trailblazer who inspired the artistic movement called the "Woodland School." *Norval Morrisseau and the Emergence of the Image Makers* remains a pivotal exhibition for curating the work of Morrisseau within a larger group of artists who followed his lead stylistically, using visual and narrative conventions to create their own expressions with the larger art movement. Artists such as Daphne Odjig, Carl Ray, Josh Kakegamic, Roy Thomas, and Blake Debassige were included in the show. Saul Williams's *Homage to Morrisseau* (1979–80), the cover art for the exhibition catalogue, illustrates his importance to the group of artists as Williams combined his own artistic interpretation with Morrisseau's visual vocabulary.

What seemed like an unstoppable career largely unravelled in 1987 when Morrisseau's alcoholism took centre stage in the media. While in southern California attending a series of art events and a solo exhibition in Santa Barbara, Morrisseau, who had been sober for a number of years, returned to drinking. This resulted in a dramatic downward spiral, and in March 1987 he was discovered living on the streets of downtown Vancouver. The press pounced on this story, giving it front-page news coverage for most of a month as reporters charted the ups and downs of Morrisseau's misfortune. Although the artist recovered and began painting again, negative press images of Morrisseau haunted him, and the press largely lost interest in the artist and his art.

That said, in 1989 Morrisseau was included in an important international art exhibition in Paris that was curated to coincide with the two-hundred-year anniversary of the French Revolution. *Magiciens de la Terre* has since been scorned as one of the last gasps in the practice of framing Indigenous arts within a discourse of primitivism. Still, inclusion in the show marked another milestone in his career.

Aging and suffering from Parkinson's disease, Morrisseau was not at his most productive during the 1990s, and interest in his work waned. That changed, however, when the National Gallery of Canada chose to mount a retrospective exhibition of Morrisseau's oeuvre in 2006. Never before had so many of his key pieces been displayed at the same time. As the first retrospective exhibition for a contemporary Indigenous artist at the National Gallery, the exhibition resonated even more deeply. Having his work hung in one of Canada's bastions of culture was a renaissance of sorts for the artist, shifting understandings of Morrisseau's importance to the history of Canadian art. Although by this time he was wheelchair bound, Morrisseau revelled in the attention at the opening in Ottawa and subsequent locations as the exhibition travelled in Canada and the United States.

Morrisseau passed away the following year, in 2007. Since then his name has once again been in the press because of a number of court cases regarding the selling of forgeries. These cases threaten to obfuscate the importance of Morrisseau to Canadian art history. Given the slow speed of the courts in Canada, it may be years before the cases are resolved, but Morrisseau's legacy through his art lives on.

The following chapters add depth to this analysis of the mythology surrounding Norval Morrisseau. Chapter 1 considers the myth and its roots, paying particular attention to the framing of the discourse and its relationship to primitivism and modernism. An analysis of two National Film Board of Canada documentaries that shaped the nuances of his mythology is included. In Chapter 2, the roots of Morrisseau's myth are formulated by examining events connected to his professional career in the 1960s. Chapter 3 closely examines what was arguably the most successful decade in Morrisseau's career, the 1970s. Morrisseau began to confidently assert his own image during this period, performatively shaping his identity as shaman artist. Chapter 4 addresses an unravelling that occurred in his personal life, leaving the press to re-establish its control of the Morrisseau myth. In Chapter 5 Morrisseau's renaissance with his 2006 retrospective exhibition is examined. With renewed success came a rehashing of the mythic elements. The Conclusion considers episodes that bring the stories told in the book closer to the present and considers how colonialism has rendered the mythology surrounding the artist.

CHAPTER ONE

Mythmaking and Primitivism

Morrisseau towers over his art. Such a figure, such a character, Morrisseau the man is intimately tied to all discussion of his art. As an art historian I have struggled to separate the cult of the artist from analysis of his work because Morrisseau's identity remains intrinsically linked to his art. Contestations with Morrisseau's mythology remain varied, interwoven with issues of racial identity, primitivism, and the ways in which the artist both shaped and interrupted elements of this myth.

What does it mean to say that Morrisseau has a mythology? It is a myth that all professors are absent-minded or that all women are intuitive. It is also a myth that all Indigenous people are shamans. Described as an accepted belief unsubstantiated by fact, in English the term "myth" is derived from the Greek *mythos*, meaning word or story. Story is key. Culturally, myths are important. We all recognize that Greco-Roman myths, for example, serve as foundational stories of Western culture. It was Canadian literary theorist Northrop Frye who, with regard to stories, explained that their mythological meaning is "inside them, in the implications of their incidents."[1] British anthropologist Percy Cohen further clarified the meaning of myth when he outlined in 1969 these characteristics: "A myth is a narrative of events; the narrative has a sacred quality; the sacred communication is made in symbolic form; at least some of the events and objects which occur in the myth neither occur nor exist in the world other than that of myth itself; and the narrative refers in dramatic form to origins or transformations."[2]

The myth surrounding Morrisseau conforms in part to the characteristics Cohen describes. First, Morrisseau is understood within a narrative of events in his life, and second, that narrative has taken on a sacred quality that is communicated in a symbolic form. Finally, some of the events in the mythic narrative of Morrisseau have no basis in fact outside the myth. In this way, Morrisseau can be understood as part of a larger colonial narrative that helps explain the Canadian nation. The myth of Morrisseau has been told and retold, until it has become a series of beliefs based upon unsubstantiated facts naturalized into a compelling tale.

● ● ●

In 1982 Grace Inglis of the *Hamilton Spectator* pronounced Morrisseau's "own place in the firmament of Canadian mythmakers" as "firmly secured."[3] While Inglis does not clarify the elements of this myth, deconstructing its aspects are important to reveal the naturalized discourse that surrounds Morrisseau. When Morrisseau entered the media spotlight, he entered a milieu where his identity was already partially formed. In *The Lives of Images*, Peter Mason examines the production and transmission of visual images representing non-European peoples since contact, showing how a stock of racialized attributes helped construct Othered conceptions that say more about Europeans than they do about Indigenous peoples.[4] Notions of the primitive or savage, of exoticism, universalism, and evolutionary social Darwinism influence the construction of the Imaginary Indian. Using images of colonial encounters from the early sixteenth century as examples, Mason contends that early imagery was often produced by artists who did not leave Europe and that the "verisimilitude of such creations derives from their conformity to the implicit rules and practice of ethnographic representation," rather than from a correspondence with encountered peoples.[5] Fictions were presented as fact, a stable of signifiers was assembled, cross-pollinated, and used at will to represent the non-European Other. And while the corpus of representations changed over space and time, what remained was the link to the imaginary over the real.

In this chapter I will discuss two key cases that contributed to determining Morrisseau's myth during the 1970s. First, in the early 1970s the National Film Board of Canada made two films that powerfully shaped the Morrisseau myth. Second, at the close of the decade Morrisseau's art dealer, Jack Pollock, and Lister Sinclair published a pivotal text, *The Art of Norval Morrisseau*, that served as a critical device in the mythic Morrisseau story. In both instances the imaginary and the real interweave with colonial narratives that bring the myth to life. Primitivism and discussions of primitive art impact the myth in both overt and covert forms that expose assymetrical power relations. Still, Morrisseau's own agency clearly impacts his story.

The mythology of Morrisseau takes form in a number of ways. One aspect relates directly to colonial narratives and invests the myth with aspects of stereotypical and racialized identity. Three other main elements relate to the mythology. These include Morrisseau's shamanic identity, his relationship to Picasso and his forged image as "Picasso of the North," and the enduring notion of the artist's paradoxical identity. The Imaginary Indian construction contributes directly to this mythology by conjuring, for example, notions of the "Noble Savage." These cross-pollinating tropes combine with Morrisseau's personal life. As part of the stereotype of the Noble Savage the shaman identity emerges. This, however, is not simply an imposed identity or even one that Morrisseau capitalized upon simply to market his work. The complexities of this aspect of the myth unfold throughout this text and speak also to Morrisseau's own spiritual pursuits and his performative gestures that insert significant aspects of his being as a shaman artist into the narrative.

Picasso of the North

One aspect of Morrisseau's mythology is its enduring connection to the Spanish modern artist Pablo Picasso. In 2006, *Ottawa Citizen* reporter Connie Higginson-Murray titled her story about Morrisseau's retrospective exhibition "Picasso of the North" and suggested that "his exposure in the 1960s to the world of Pablo Picasso" was one of the main influences on Morrisseau's artistic style.[6] The Picasso reference is key to Morrisseau mythology, though it has little to do with his artistic style. The first time Morrisseau was compared to Picasso in the Canadian press was in 1962, in the nationally circulated *Weekend Magazine*. "Picasso quality is apparent in Thunderbird's idea of how an Indian will look and dress in Heaven" was how Bill Brown's article described a work by Morrisseau.[7] By the late 1960s, Pollock and Herbert Schwarz were using "Picasso of the North" to promote the artist, notably with an exhibition that opened in Montreal and travelled widely, including to the south of France.

Rumours around whether Morrisseau met Picasso have long circulated. In 1969 the stars were aligned such that an encounter between the two artists would have been possible. Anthropologist and art dabbler Herbert Schwarz had organized an exhibition of Morrisseau's work that travelled from Montreal's Galerie Cartier, where it debuted in 1966, to a number of galleries in the United States before eventually ending up in St. Paul de Vence in the south of France in 1969. The area was famous for the number of modern art giants who lived there, including Marc Chagall and Pablo Picasso. In addition, the Maeght Foundation Museum outside St. Paul de Vence, constructed in 1964, houses important works of modern art by such artists as Bonnard, Braque, Kandinsky, and Chagall; Morrisseau may have toured the museum.

A facsimile of a poster included in the Aboriginal Art Centre Archives, of a joint exhibition held in December 1966 at La Galerie Cartier in Montreal in conjunction with the Pollock gallery, connects Morrisseau directly with Picasso. Positioned immediately below the bolded text of Morrisseau's name the poster reads "Picasso of the North." An additional photograph taken in St. Paul de Vence in September 1969, in the same archival collection, shows posters—one of Morrisseau's exhibition in France next to a poster advertising an exhibition of Picasso's art on display that September in Vallauris, where he had shown his work for more than a decade. The gallery was about thirty kilometres from St. Paul de Vence, just beyond Mougins. The proximity of Picasso's and Morrisseau's exhibition posters lends credence to the story that Picasso and Morrisseau met in September 1969. However, I have found no archival evidence supporting a meeting of the two—though that does not mean it did not occur. In an attempt to track down evidence of an encounter I searched local French papers from the area from that time but found nothing about Morrisseau's exhibition. In a conversation with Fredrick Mulder, a London art dealer who specializes in Picasso linocuts from 1951 to 1965 and who has maintained a close relationship with the artist's family, Mulder rejected the idea that Morrisseau and Picasso met. Mulder is Canadian and familiar with Morrisseau's art, and believes he would have known of such a connection if it existed. He contends that the eighty-five-year-old Picasso was not physically active by 1969 because his protective wife forbade it.[8] That said, St. Paul de Vence was only twenty-five kilometres away from Picasso's home in Mougins, and Picasso may have had a compelling reason to visit Morrisseau's exhibition.

The strongest link between Picasso and Morrisseau can be traced to Dr. Joseph Weinstein, Morrisseau's earliest patron, art collector, and art mentor. The cosmopolitan doctor, who practised for a time in the Red Lake district beginning in 1957, had studied art in Paris and was well connected to the French modernists, Picasso included. Ruth Phillips explains how after Weinstein and his artist wife, Esther, met Morrisseau, they invited him to study their library of art books and collection of wide-ranging art, which included African masks, Russian icons, Inuit art, and examples of Jewish, Tibetan, South Asian, and ancient Egyptian art.[9] Weinstein explains in

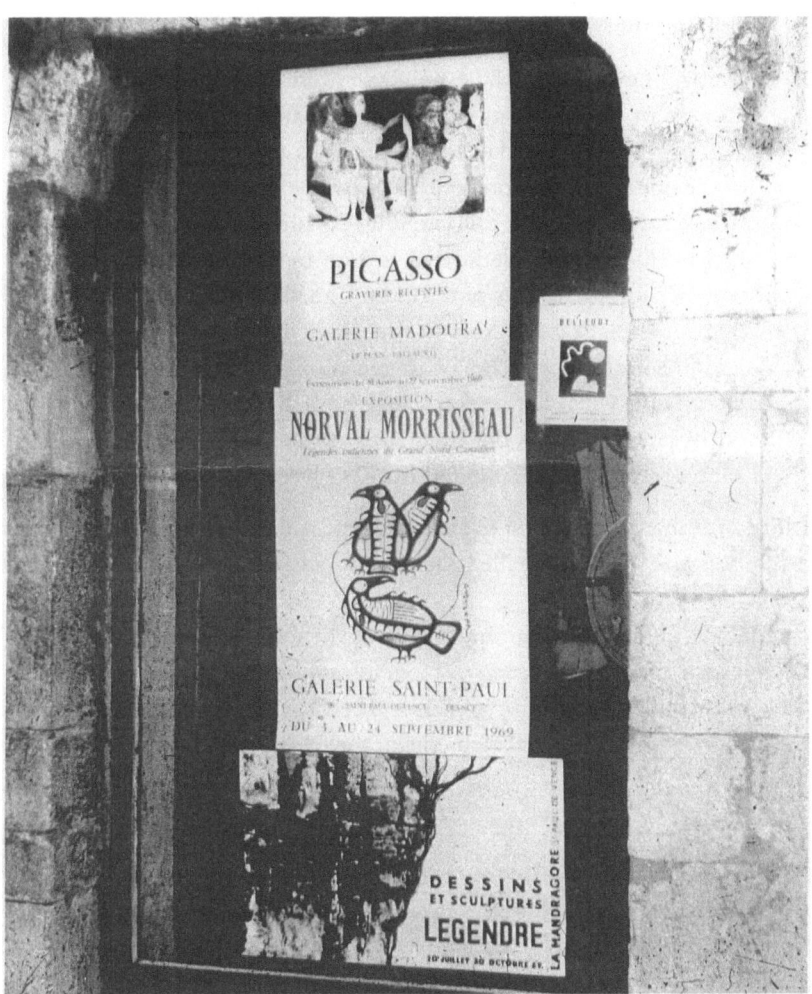

This photograph of a grouping of exhibition posters on display in
St. Paul de Vence, France, in September 1969, includes a poster advertis-
ing an exhibition of work by Picasso on display at the Galerie Madoura, in
Vallauris, France, a village close by Morrisseau's show at the Galerie St. Paul.
Reproduced with permission of the Indigenous and Northern Affairs Canada
Aboriginal Art Centre archives.

The White Ojibway Medicine Man and Other Stories that when they left Red
Lake, Morrisseau asked the doctor to pass along a small work he had cre-
ated to Picasso. Weinstein recalls offering the gift to the artist at a dinner in
France in about 1964. This means that Picasso would have been familiar with
Morrisseau's work and thus may have been interested in viewing an exhibition

he might not otherwise have visited in 1969. Weinstein tells the story:

> We will never forget the evening we were invited to dinner by
> Picasso in the company of several illustrious guests. My wife
> Esther, who was seated next to the famous artist, took advantage
> of the opportunity to present him with the drawing that Norval
> had sent him as a gift. She carefully explained that the drawing
> had been especially dedicated to him by an aboriginal artist
> who lived in the forests of northern Canada. Picasso responded
> by contemplating the fine drawing for a few moments before
> nodding his head as a sign of appreciation. His face broke into a
> broad smile when Esther translated the dedication at the bottom
> of the picture: "From one great artist to another, signed Norval
> Morrisseau, Copper Thunderbird."[10]

Morrisseau, hailed as painter of Indian legends on the poster advertising the
exhibition, may have compelled Picasso to seek out the work of this "great
artist."

Since being batted about in the 1960s, the term "Picasso of the North"
has not gone away. Most recently, a biography of Morrisseau written by James
Stevens includes the term in its title.[11] The Picasso moniker and narrative
endures with other essential elements of the Morrisseau myth.

Paradoxes

Morrisseau is paradoxical, or at least that is what we are told. A key theme
in the Morrisseau mythology, the notion of the artist as paradoxical emerged
from two documentary films made in the early 1970s: *The Colours of Pride*
(1973) and *The Paradox of Norval Morrisseau* (1974). The documentaries
were produced by the National Film Board of Canada (NFB) from footage
taken in 1973, a demonstration of Morrisseau's rising importance and his
significance to Canadian identity at the time. The NFB was instituted as (and
remains) a bastion of Canadian culture, having received Royal Assent in 1939
to "make and distribute films across the country that were designed to help
Canadians everywhere in Canada understand the problems and way of life
of Canadians in other parts of the country," under the direction of Scottish
documentarian John Grierson.[12] As part of its nation-building exercise, the
NFB produced a number of films during the 1960s and 1970s that showcased Indigenous art and artists. Beyond the many documentaries on Inuit
art, films about such artists as Arthur Shilling and Bill Reid demonstrate a

focus on Indigenous artists from southern Canada. Neither of the two films that featured Morrisseau offered Canadian viewers much sense of Morrisseau as an artist. Instead, both focus on notions of identity.

Marshall McLuhan's dictum "the medium is the message" resonates powerfully when considering the NFB's two Morrisseau films.[13] Underwritten by the Department of Indian Affairs and Northern Development, the documentaries present a construction of the artist that is arguably more powerful than press reports. Because of the stellar reputation of the NFB, viewers have readily and unquestioningly accepted the information supplied by the films, which have therefore had a long and influential effect on the mythology surrounding the artist. Both films enhanced the myth of Morrisseau, but it is *The Paradox of Norval Morrisseau*, a documentary that focuses directly on the artist, that continues to resonate today in terms of setting in play the narrative sequences of Morrisseau's life.[14]

Paradox makes good use of the language of documentary to unconsciously create a text about race and colonialism. Like the earlier *Colours of Pride*, it introduces themes that contribute to the Morrisseau myth, but its direct focus on Morrisseau delves deeper and provides more material for mythmaking. Largely fashioned in the editing suite, using evidentiary editing (cutting to bring together evidence to best support a point) from a range of footage that suited the needs of both *Paradox* and *Colours of Pride*, *Paradox* engages the spectator's ability to read the signs of colonialism. It does so by reinforcing stereotypes long displayed in mass media representations of Indigenous peoples. It also accomplishes this by using fragmenting camera angles, succinct edits, iconic images, authoritative narration, and a powerful theme song—all packaged to teach the spectator, the viewer, Canadians, about an imagined Morrisseau.

Tom Hill, then director of the Indian Art Centre at the Department of Indian Affairs, worked with the NFB to produce this film. In an article in *Tawow*, Hill explained: "For all the film's shortcomings, it is an intelligent and sensitive viewpoint developed on an artist so complex that any attempt at an analysis of his art and personality would ultimately skim the surface. *The Paradox of Norval Morrisseau* is a must for all students studying Canadian art and to the society at large who might be interested in the human condition."[15] Hill acknowledges that the editing of the film obscures the character of Morrisseau but argues that such details do not take away from the film. I cannot agree. While the documentary does offer viewers valuable information about the artist, the overwhelming colonial message brands Morrisseau detrimentally. Although the film was produced forty years ago, making many of its themes antiquated, it provides a useful overview of assimilationist messages advanced at the time, messages that continue to resonate more subtly in national discourse.

The "look" of *Paradox* can be described as a clinical gaze, though at the same time it is also a spectacularized one. Documentary film theorist Bill Nichols explains that a clinical gaze operates in a documentary under the guise of a professional code of ethics to ensure a sense of personal detachment between the filmmaker and the subject of the film. The clinical gaze, common in documentaries from that period, includes a special form of empowerment in which the filmmaker works in service of the greater good, or the viewer's "right to know."[16] Filmmakers exonerated themselves from accountability for their bodily presence in the name of the greater good. Unlike reflexive documentaries fashionable today, where the camera and the director are implicated in the film, NFB documentaries in the 1970s maintained a clear distance between filmmaker and subject, giving the illusion of unbiased reportage.

A fitting example of *Paradox*'s clinical gaze can be found in the inclusion of footage showing Morrisseau in a state of drunkenness, a sequence that also suggests spectacularization of the event.[17] Morrisseau was inebriated during one occasion during the filming of the documentary, but because the segment was edited and portions included throughout the film, viewers continually observe Morrisseau in this state, coming away with the impression of habitual drunkenness. Morrisseau thus becomes a spectacle that reinforces negative stereotypical constructions of the "drunken Indian" at play in popular culture.

The director's decision to include such footage serves a number of aims. First, Morrisseau showing up drunk for the filming offers viewers an "authentic" representation of the artist. The "truth claim" that Morrisseau is a drunk is validated—a construction that was also reinforced in news articles. Here, however, viewers see this for themselves on the screen. Second, by including factual evidence that supports a common media stereotype of Aboriginal people, the entire film is given credibility as being "real." Morrisseau's drunkenness becomes meaningful as more than an isolated incident because the director places it in this expository frame. Third, by including this uncomfortable footage, the film communicates an objectivity and impartiality by demonstrating to viewers that it has not shielded them from any aspect of the artist's life, maintaining a gaze that was part of NFB documentary practice at that time.

This factual documentation serves as evidence for viewers and the filmmaker alike, but evidence of *what*? This is a fundamental question. The fact of Morrisseau's drunkenness fits into a system of signification, a web of meanings—of stereotypical behaviour, of Morrisseau's volatile and untrust-worthy character, and of mainstream society's need to carry out colonization and assimilationist policies. Thus *Paradox* specifically presents a way of seeing that reinforces popular culture stereotypes, and in addition to its clinical gaze the camera adopts a colonizing mode of looking that objectifies and manipulates Morrisseau's position in Canadian society. News coverage of Morrisseau's drunken behaviour, together with the visual revelations in *Paradox*, contribute to his myth and the continued focus on behaviour over artistic achievement.

The director adeptly manipulates the camera to express the NFB's unconscious racial gaze. For example, throughout the film the director shoots Morrisseau in a series of fragmenting angles. The camera includes close-ups, upper-body shots of him sitting, and on a few occasions, three-quarter-length shots of the artist. However, seldom does the viewer see Morrisseau as a whole body—nor, symbolically, as a whole man. Additionally, still photographic images of Morrisseau, frozen on the screen and included throughout the film, further reinforce the artist's marginalized position in society. Conversely, when Morrisseau's so-called discoverer Jack Pollock is shown on screen, the camera presents a full-body shot, visually conveying to viewers his dominant presence. Self-assured body language further reinforces Pollock's principal role as expert and orchestrator of Morrisseau's successful career.

The interview scenes contain a treasure trove of information. To begin, Pollock is shown on screen supposedly speaking about Morrisseau to an unidentified Native man. The mystery man is Tom Hill, who plays a significant role in *Colours of Pride* as guide and interviewer and directs questions toward Pollock in that film. This information is only available to viewers who watch both films, however. In *Paradox*, Hill never speaks though Pollock addresses him throughout his interview. Seemingly fascinated by Pollock's story, he nods and listens closely, with the art dealer cast as a knowledgeable professional. The nameless, objectified Indigenous male is denied a voice in the film, symbolically reflecting his place in Canadian society.[18]

Pollock's conversation, or more correctly, his sermon, takes place along a lakeshore near Kenora, Ontario, as do most of the interview segments with Morrisseau. However, unlike in the Morrisseau scenes where the artist is framed by rugged wilderness, Pollock is situated in front of a comfortable cottage on Kenora's waterfront. Visually, this cottage reinforces Pollock's attachment to civilization—à la Rousseau.

Images of Morrisseau, in contrast, conjure up notions of his imagined life in the wilderness and his stereotypical emergence from the wild. By 1974

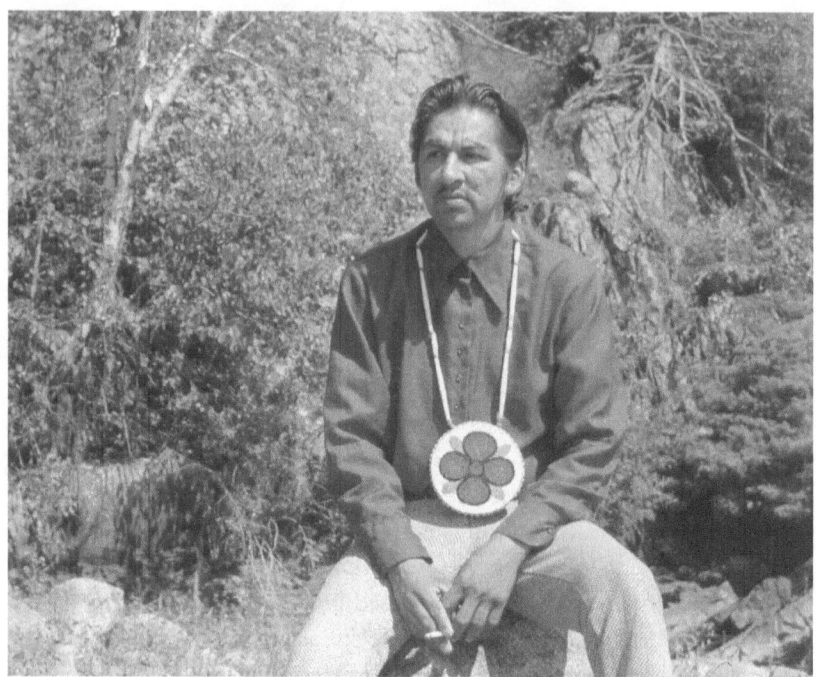

This candid photograph of Norval Morrisseau was taken during a break in filming a scene where Morrisseau discussed his pivotal vision quest for the National Film Board of Canada's *Paradox of Norval Morrisseau* in 1974. Reproduced with permission of the Indigenous and Northern Affairs Canada Aboriginal Art Centre archives.

many contemporary Anishinaabe people, Morrisseau included, were living a more urban existence in large Canadian centres such as Toronto, Winnipeg, and Vancouver. Yet throughout the film the camera finds Morrisseau in remote outdoor settings, linking his mythical narrative to uncivilized wilderness.

The artist is shown painting *en plein air*[19] on a sandy shore rather than in a studio setting. The film contains footage of Morrisseau painting a canvas on a beach—using a rock as an easel. This same footage is repeated in *Colours of Pride*. By staging the scene in this manner, the director constructs Morrisseau as the idealized essence of a spiritual descendant of a shaman communing with nature rather than as a serious artist at work. As Morrisseau paints, the off-screen narrator explains that his subject is "the last treasure of a way of life ransacked to the edge of oblivion which traditionally had been concealed from strangers, especially white men." The narrator interjects that Morrisseau "paints for a society to which he is a complete stranger ... and paints with a white man's acrylic plastics while he takes his life's directions from the great god Manitou" (*Paradox*, 1974). Both of these unquestioned hyperbolic statements communicate racist assumptions that are then relayed to Canadian viewers, who internalize such information.

Feminist film theorists Claire Pajaczkowska and Lola Young find that "the unconscious mind is evident in the meanings racism attributes to physical and visual difference."[20] This documentary exaggerates physical and visual difference throughout, as in the noted juxtapositions between Morrisseau and Jack Pollock. Similarly, in *Paradox* the NFB employs racist signifiers to subconsciously frame Morrisseau by placing the artist and his art in a symbolic semiotic network. The viewer, too, projects onto the film aspects of his or her own experiences and stereotypical assumptions, reinforcing and endowing it with additional meaning.

In *Paradox* it is not simply Morrisseau's identity or a stereotypical Indian representation that is presented. Importantly, though perhaps not surprisingly, whiteness also figures prominently in the film. Whiteness is assumed as the dominant form of identity in *Paradox*, as it is in *Colours of Pride*. Ordinary identity for the NFB when *Paradox* was produced included being white, being male, and being middle class. Therefore processes that preserve and maintain this dominant identity as the assumed cultural norm remain evident in the making of the film. This assumption contributes to the marginalized framing of Morrisseau and his art. Yet this dominant identity is, of course, illusory (like the one assigned to Morrisseau), dependent on unconscious Othering to affirm the imagined character. Evidence of the film's racist framing exists throughout. Although the film ostensibly focuses on Morrisseau and his art, white males occupy positions of power throughout, making race part of the overt filmic language. The interview segments with Pollock, coupled with the use of a white male narrator who frames the film, clearly reinforce and ensure white autonomy in the film.

The role of narrator, a common device in many NFB films from that period, clearly assumes a forceful position in *Paradox* vis-à-vis Morrisseau. The narrator demonstrates an authority to speak about Morrisseau and his art, and the viewer comes to rely on the judgemental tone of the narrator as a source of information about Morrisseau. Interestingly, the narrator's pronouncements do not often coincide with Morrisseau's own commentary.

With an acerbic tone, the narrator explains, for example, that the Ojibwe were "once a proud people" and that Morrisseau clings to this "dying culture" (*Paradox*, 1974), hinting at the effects of colonization and confirming the assumption that Ojibwe or Anishinaabe culture was a thing of the past rather than a contemporary, living culture. The emphasis that the Ojibwe are no longer proud frames Morrisseau as the "last of his breed," conjuring for audiences the romantic and fantasizing tropes of Morrisseau seemingly clinging to moribund cultural traditions.

In *Paradox* the desire for and promise of knowledge, implicit in both the documentary medium and in the NFB's educative mandate, impacts analysis of the film in formulating a mythical narrative for Morrisseau. Viewed as a master signifier, *Paradox* provides a sense of the man for Canadians. Compounding this is the illusion of realism, as viewers watching *Paradox* learn through a linear, "organic" flow of events or signifiers that lead to their understanding of the man and his art. Yet this filmic representation remains an illusion, because had the director chosen to frame the documentary another way, retroactively presenting a different series of events or signifiers to construct the organic whole, viewers would just as naturally feel they had met the artist. Floating signifiers such as the Noble Savage (innocent, childlike, spiritually connected to nature), the Ignoble Savage (drunk, violent, uneducated), the moribund Ojibwe, the dependent artist, pulled to Christianity, construct the object and the myth. Morrisseau's complicity in this objectification matters little because the object construction leaves little room for his agency. It is the authorized NFB that produces, directs, edits the product.

Philip Deloria writes about the power of the "Indian Sound" and how with just a few bars of drumming and random notes, an "array of expectation and imagery" is formed in our minds that relates to the Hollywood Indian.[21] The music in each of the NFB films often emphasizes stereotypical signifiers, similar to musical sound tracks found in movies and cartoons. Yet in *Paradox*, the theme song differs from other musical interludes. Here, an Indigenous troubadour sings to viewers about Morrisseau. The use of the Indigenous performer Shingoose helps relate Morrisseau's story and also repositions the Morrisseau narrative.[22] The song refreshingly and somewhat surprisingly offers viewers a version of Morrisseau's role as artist and spokesperson from an Indigenous perspective. In *Paradox* the ballad clearly enriches the film and provides structure both as a whole and in its individual shots by developing a sense of pace corresponding to the pace of the editing.

The lyrics written by Anishinaabe poet Duke Redbird do not correlate with images found in parts of the film. Though Redbird's lyrics are romanticized and filled with pan-Indian references common for the period, he constructs Morrisseau as an important symbolic and cultural hero to all Indigenous peoples. His lyrics tell of a man manipulated by the mainstream art world, a victim, yet a figure worthy of respect. On four occasions within the film Shingoose is dropped into incongruous locations to sing the verses of the song. As the camera follows the performer, the background images at times reveal conflicting information about the artist.

Wearing his red- and black-checked lumberjack shirt and leather cowboy hat, his long hair tucked behind his ears, Shingoose is captured by the camera silhouetted on a rocky cliff as he begins singing the hypnotic and catchy theme song he co-wrote with Redbird:

> *Norval Norval, what's driving you? Are the spirits talking, are the spirits coming through, are they talking to you?*

After the refrain, Shingoose sits in a canoe on a lake and sings:

> *You lived in the forest all your life,*
>
> *You've been hungry and you've suffered strife.*

As the camera focuses on some pictographs painted by Morrisseau's Anishinaabe ancestors, he adds:

> *You paint with the blood of a thousand years.*
>
> *You painted the legends and you paint the fears,*
>
> *And you paint the birch bark and you paint the sand.*
>
> *And you paint your sweat with an ancient hand.* (*Paradox*, 1974)

This musical interlude frames Morrisseau as an "authentic" Imaginary Indian steeped in ancient traditions. According to the lyrics and accompanying images, Morrisseau paints legends and stories that relate to an idealized and timeless past. However, as Barthes notes, "the rites, the cultural facts, are never related to a particular historical order, an explicit economic or social status, but only to the great neutral forms of cosmic commonplaces (the seasons, storms, death, etc.)."[23]

In the second verse of the song, inserted later in the film, Redbird's lyrics explain that Morrisseau was painfully exploited by mainstream culture when he exhibited his work in the city. Barthes talks of inoculation, whereby a limited number of inhumane actions are admitted by the perpetrators. This "immunizes the contents of the collective imagination by means of a small inoculation of acknowledged evil; one thus protects it against the risk of a generalized subversion."[24] In *Paradox*, by admitting that Morrisseau's culture is dying and by alluding to unpalatable effects of colonization evidenced in Morrisseau's drunkenness, the NFB disentangles itself from the evils done by mainstream society. By romanticizing Ojibwe tradition as an "ancient culture" frozen in time, dirty details such as Morrisseau's residential school experience in Thunder Bay, systemic poverty, or the roots of his alcoholism can be smoothed over in favour of moribundity. As Barthes observes, "A little 'confessed' evil saves one from acknowledging a lot of hidden evil."[25]

Throughout the performance of the ballad, the director adeptly uses the filmic device of intellectual montage (a combination of images and sound, explicitly to comment on some aspect of the story). Elements of the world required to support the text's argument are gathered together from separate sources. In the singing of the second verse, rather than canoeing in the wilderness, the performer now sits cross-legged, wearing his moccasins, sympathetically strumming his guitar on the steps of Toronto's Pollock Gallery:

They took your paintings, and they hung them in town.

And they took your body and they flung it around.

So the world could see an Indian in high society.

The camera cuts to Shingoose sitting on a stool inside the gallery among Morrisseau canvasses, singing:

You drowned their pale faces in brown whiskey,

You painted their Jesus, to expose their hypocrisy

You lived in their churches

And you've known their jails. (Paradox, 1974)

The camera edits present images featuring Shingoose strumming in a number of locations, from a manicured and well-kept churchyard to a busy street framed with the grey facade of a prison.

At times the images and the lyrics to this catchy ballad are at odds. Shingoose telling of Morrisseau, a prophet and an inspiration, while images of a church, a prison, and the wilderness flash by sends competing, confusing messages. Redbird's lyrics sometimes undermine the off-screen commentary and the visual imagery provided. Yet just as with the scenes of Morrisseau in a drunken state, the inclusion of the ballad gives viewers an impression that the NFB has achieved a balanced picture of Morrisseau and his life. The actions of the NFB, couched in the realist platform of documentary with its veiled attempt at objectivity, appear to be driven by seemingly timeless values rather than by the code through which those with power police themselves and others.

Christianity plays a central role in *Paradox* and becomes the boundary or frame that supplies its repertoire of values and the means to apply them to Morrisseau's life. Morrisseau's so-called paradoxical relationship with Christianity serves as a central theme in the film and becomes a key element of the Morrisseau myth. It is here that the referent of colonization is most clearly evident. Christianity has historically been the vehicle through which colonization has been imposed on Indigenous peoples throughout Canada. The images in *Paradox* tell a story of a man longing to assimilate, though continually pulled back because of his attachments to his "dying Ojibway culture" (*Paradox*, 1974). Morrisseau's connections to both Native spirituality and Christianity are juxtaposed and polarized throughout the film.

One of Morrisseau's paintings of himself as Christ, *Indian Jesus Christ* (1973) painted while at the Kenora jail, becomes a pivotal visual image in the film, shown several times. While Redbird's lyrics recall that Morrisseau painted this canvas to "expose" the church's hypocrisy, the narrator repositions this notion, asking rhetorically: "Could it be possible that Morrisseau sees himself on a cross, crucified for what he is and what he is not; damned by the present and tormented by the past?" (*Paradox*, 1974) Whom is the viewer to believe, a singer or the narrator? Additionally, during one of the musical segments in the film, the profiled image of the painting of the artist as Christ overlays a similarly framed shot of Morrisseau's profile, and for a time the two images commingle on screen. Reinforcing Morrisseau's paradoxical attraction to Christianity, a second painted face, this one representing an Ojibwe shaman, then fades into Morrisseau's photographed visage, visually confirming Morrisseau's polarized religious beliefs.

A forest scene with an ornate church steeple glistening above the tree line confirms by the symbolic placement of the church above the trees—above nature—Christianity's superior standing. The guiding narration constructs Morrisseau as a man struggling with the binary aspects of Christianity and Native spirituality: "A church among the trees, a bastion of Christianity in a forest of Native wild spirits and gods ... It [Christianity] is foreign to him yet he is obsessed by it, by its ideas, by its ritual, above all by a sense of guilt about its saviour who died for him" (*Paradox*, 1974). The narrator provides a moral/political overlay that doubly contributes, like the editing, camera angles, and composition, to establishing the film's representation of Morrisseau and his world. This intertextuality is what gives the text its convincing and complex dose of public education, making it apparent that colonization is clearly the better path for Morrisseau to choose. In this way, the paradox is resolved.

A collage of scenes showing Morrisseau deep in prayer, lighting a prayer candle, along with images of the cross, religious icons, a close-up shot of leather-bound Bibles, a statue of Christ, and a print of the Virgin Mary, confirm Morrisseau's urge to acculturate. Even though Morrisseau bitterly explains in the previous scene that "Jesus died for the white man not for Indians," the director frames him as someone who seeks refuge in Christianity because of his volatile nature: "As well as guilt and love, there is violence. As well as the urge to create, there is the impulse to destroy … In the past he tried to find escape in alcohol as well as in faith" (*Paradox*, 1974). Guilt and love are paired with Christianity, while violence, not surprisingly, coincides with Native spirituality. The moral superiority of Christian doctrine over Native spirituality is justified through this series of binary opposites, using evidentiary editing to corroborate the argument. All the while the documentary builds a case that favours Morrisseau's Christian leanings while framing his descriptions of vision quests as exotic. Yet the segment of Morrisseau's description of his vision quest can be read another way. This scene, like his paradoxical pull to Christianity, provides credibility for his links to shamanism and ceremony, and ensures an authenticity that strengthens the Morrisseau myth. This is one of the few scenes in the film that is well done. On the few occasions when Morrisseau is given licence to speak about his art or his culture, the film gains significance as an archival document that does provide hints of the artist's motivations.

Distributed to libraries throughout Canada and screened in classrooms as one of the few sources of information about the artist in the 1970s and 1980s, the imposing visual and documentary power of *Paradox*, reinforced by the credibility of the NFB, reached audiences across the country. In a 1983 essay, Valda Blundell and Ruth B. Phillips analyzed Canadian media responses to both Woodland School painting and the works of Morrisseau, finding they fit into what they call either a "survivalistic" discourse, with artists presented as "surviving primitives," or into a "revivalistic" discourse, where media reports note that Morrisseau, for example, records legends and folklore.[26] In an essay that utilizes the terms "paradox" and "paradoxical" twice in its conclusions, Blundell and Phillips employed constructions that framed Morrisseau throughout his life, despite their cogent argument that his art should be understood within a contemporary art discourse that some reporters had begun to adopt. The mythology is compelling and, judging from more recent reports, hard to shake. Print media underscored the film's framing in its reportage through 2010. In a *Maclean's* cover story written by Christopher Hume in 1979, for example, the laudatory article titled "The New Age of Indian Art" reinforced the notion that Ojibwe "old tribal ways were almost obsolete," and that the artist helped the new generation of Indigenous artists to "reach back to their almost forgotten heritage."[27] Media coverage of Morrisseau's 2006 retrospective exhibition in Ottawa played similar messages, recalling the *Paradox* narrator's sober characterization of Anishinaabe culture as a relic of an indeterminate past. *Paradox* was also screened in the education space that accompanied the artwork at the 2006 National Gallery retrospective. Such exposure reinforced the myth, complete with its colonial rhetoric.

The Colours of Pride,[28] a joint venture between the Department of Indian Affairs and the NFB, outlines in twenty-two minutes the work of four Indigenous artists: Morrisseau, Daphne Odjig, Alex Janvier, and Allen Sapp. The film finds Morrisseau wanting when it assesses his career in relation to those of Janvier and Odjig. A hierarchy based on modernist artistic ideals is demonstrated in *Colours of Pride*, revealing the importance of the modernist art movement at the time. Directed by Henning Jacobsen and Duke Redbird, this was the first film produced by the NFB in the 1970s about contemporary Aboriginal art, and in many ways it serves as a primer for notions of contemporary Indigenous art at that time. Though the director offers viewers less than six minutes of information on any given artist, broken up into short, edited clips, a framework emerges for understanding how to judge contemporary Indigenous art and, by extension, how to understand Indigenous identity and Canadian cultural politics. The Department of Indian Affairs supported the production of both *Paradox* and *Colours of Pride*, and both share common visions. Though credited as co-director of *Paradox*, Aboriginal filmmaker Duke Redbird receives no acknowledgement for *Colours*. And while the film introduces Canadians to four significant contemporary Aboriginal artists, it fails to advance a discourse related to art. Canadians learn more about assimilation and Canadian colonial control than they do about contemporary Aboriginal art.

"I'm going to take you on an art odyssey across Canada in search of some Canadian Indian artists whose work in recent years has stirred interest both nationally and internationally," invites Tom Hill, the documentary's Seneca host from Ontario's Six Nations Reserve. Although a white narrator introduces the artists chosen for the project as "four artists from four provinces," geographic representation seems not to have been a determining factor, as only artists from the Prairies and Ontario have been included in the film while both East and West Coast art is neglected. Except for Sapp, each artist was part of the Professional Native Indian Artists Incorporated (PNIAI) formed through Odjig's gallery in Winnipeg in 1973, the same year the film was released. The so-called Indian Group of Seven also included Jackson Beardy,

Eddie Cobiness, Carl Ray, and Joe Sanchez, but the film makes no mention of the professional organization. Instead, the documentary organizes the artists according to the level of European aesthetics displayed in their art.

In the documentary, Morrisseau is cast as the originator of a unique, self-taught approach to painting that integrates traditional Anishinaabe elements with his own creativity, while Odjig, from Ontario but living in Manitoba, incorporates Western artistic influences as well as Indigenous influences found in the work of Morrisseau and adds gender balance to the film. Saskatchewan artist Sapp represents a self-taught Western realist tradition, painting in a narrative style that relates to Plains Cree art but conforms to European aesthetics. Janvier, from northern Alberta and educated at the Alberta College of Art, provides viewers with an example of a more mainstream artist—or at least that is how the film frames his art. While Janvier infuses his art with Indigenous themes and elements, the film pitches his work within a discourse of modern abstraction conforming to mainstream sensibilities. Therefore, while the choice of painters may not seem representative of the broad base of Canadian Aboriginal artists, the four together provide a fitting opportunity to visually judge the art and the artists' standing in Canadian culture, based on their training and adherence to mainstream art movements. Even as Hill discusses the art of these Canadian Aboriginal artists, a narrative fraught with assimilationist and colonialist motivations emerges as a subtext anchored to conformist art practice and cultural assimilation.

On one level the film introduces an appealing didactic dialogue with each of the four artists as Tom Hill, dressed casually in jeans, comfortably engages each artist in conversation about their art. Such discussions provide the viewer with a cursory impression of the personality and art of each artist. Yet on closer inspection, judgements continually occur in the script and visual scenes, evaluating the work and lives of these artists and imposing Western authority over Indigenous art forms and cultures. Art historian Charlotte Townsend-Gault confirms: "[First Nations artists'] work is prone to ready valorization by sensitive description, but they are scarcely allowed to work from their own home base, as the grounds on which to be legitimated. Everything they do, including strategic essentializing, including withholding or protecting knowledge, is seen and judged through liberal tolerances."[29] The commentary provided in *Colours* does not allow the artists to provide their own understandings of their art. The film, like *Paradox*, is heavily edited, so that it is the NFB and the documentary medium that legitimate and choose the narratives worth telling. Thus the two-dimensional, painterly arts practised by each artist in this film relate most closely to Western notions of "high art." Still, within this category, a range of value judgements exists. Symbolic art remains closely connected to assumptions of primitivism.

The Colours of Pride manipulates the work of these artists, fashioning a narrative that echoes assumptions of praised mainstream art practice based on modernist sensibilities, and promotes the policies undertaken by the Canadian government, advancing identity politics evinced by popular culture stereotypes. For example, the film casts Morrisseau's unique artistic style, steeped in Anishinaabe artistic conventions, as symbolic (read primitive) and lesser than the art of Janvier, which the documentary film disseminates as abstract and expressionistic in a universal, modernist (read civilized) sense. This does two things. First, it privileges Janvier's seemingly non-representational art; and second, it adds to the myth of Morrisseau as a primitive painter of legends.

Common themes regarding colonization and assimilation intermingle with discussions of art, creating a multi-layered discourse that cleverly structures this documentary through visual signifiers. Ordering images of each artist's home and studio from reserve living to suburbia, from painting in a kitchen to creating work in a conventional studio, allows viewers to easily discern which artist conforms to mainstream cultural ideals about art production and success. The film visually praises artists with mainstream training and judges more harshly the self-taught artist, instructing viewers on the importance of conformity with mainstream ideals.

As noted, the media serves as a useful tool for discipline and the NFB uses it to good effect in *Colours of Pride*. The ordering of the four artists, the expert testimony given by white, male authorities on the art, and noted visual signifiers such as homes and studios provide a structure for an assimilationist hierarchy. Canadians have long understood the myriad of signifiers used to manipulate this message in popular culture and therefore were primed for such messages.

Homi Bhabha's concept of mimesis applies to this film: "Colonial mimicry is the desire for a reformed, recognizable Other, as a subject of a difference that is almost the same, but not quite."[30] As Odjig and Janvier, as well as Tom Hill, for that matter, more closely mime mainstream Canadians with their dress, smoking habits, and success in assimilating, the camera's gaze visually rewards such concessions. However, as Bhabha argues, no matter how much the Other appears to fit in or assimilate, she or he will never be fully accepted as equal: "Mimicry is, thus, the sign of a double articulation; a complex strategy of reform, regulation, and discipline, which 'appropriates' the Other as it visualizes power. Mimicry is also the sign of the inappropriate, however, a difference or recalcitrance which coheres the dominant strategic function of colonial power, intensifies surveillance, and poses an imminent threat to both 'normalized' knowledges and disciplinary powers."[31] By visually "normalizing" Odjig and Janvier, a change or splitting occurs. While these two artists appear in the film as most closely aligned with mainstream artists, a certain mockery continues to haunt them and their art as they are seen as almost the same, *but not quite*. Like the other noted NFB films on Indigenous art, this documentary separates and thus excludes such art from the mainstream Canadian art world. *Colours* subtly teaches its audience to value more highly Indigenous art that adopts mainstream influences and whose connections to Indigenous subject matter are abstracted and less visible over art that employs apparent Aboriginal styles and forms. By emphasizing modernist notions of universal truths, an assimilationist agenda is exerted. Art serves simply as a vehicle in this documentary to teach an even more meaningful message: Canadian society values Indigenous peoples who work to assimilate into mainstream society. *Colours of Pride*, then, reinforces both government policies and stereotypical constructions found in popular culture and media to effectively promote the benefits of assimilation.

Formulaic constructions of the romanticized but vanishing Noble Savage also abound here through the camera's gaze. *Colours of Pride* accomplishes its colonial agenda, in part, by utilizing a number of visual signifiers that often juxtapose Norval Morrisseau with Alex Janvier. The film opens with footage of a Janvier painting emerging onto the canvas. Using time-lapse photography, the abstract painting takes form as if on its own—the invisibility of the artist in effect assimilates him into mainstream society. Janvier's piece has a strong modern, abstract style, and its place at the opening of the film privileges it and proclaims it as a measure for other contemporary Aboriginal art and artists to aspire to. Erased in this assimilating gesture is overtly Indigenous content, Indigenous technique, or Indigenous cultural connections. In terms of Greenbergian modern art discourse, even the artist is absent.[32]

Moving from Janvier's privileged work of art, the next scene offers a sharp contrast. Morrisseau sits at a table in his modest home, painting on a birchbark scroll using a style of painting closely connected to the traditional Anishinaabe scroll painting. The primitive-looking image painted by Morrisseau serves as a strong counterpoint to the opening sequence just described. As Morrisseau paints what appears to be a reconstructed artefact rather than a contemporary work of art, the viewer recognizes stark differences from Janvier's art.

The film establishes a number of hierarchies. One hierarchy, connected with artistic success, stems from Morrisseau, who, as the NFB demonstrates, paints "primitive" paintings and who, in the film, distances himself from mainstream modern art movements and art theory, dismissing the importance of the colour wheel just as he dismisses abstraction. Allen Sapp, who paints realist, memory paintings from his youth about the "almost vanished" reserve life he clings to (*Colour*, 1973) is equated with Morrisseau. The camera then introduces Daphne Odjig, whose work in this documentary is deemed more mainstream, and thus more successful. After all, she uses cubism, surrealism, and other Western modernist art styles to interpret the "legends of her people" (*Colours*, 1973).

A second hierarchical structure of signification is related to assimilation. Employing the common NFB documentary method of narration, the director introduces some of the themes of the film with the help of a voice-over as the camera surveys Morrisseau painting figures from Anishinaabe legend on a piece of birchbark. In setting the mood for the film, the male narrator authoritatively communicates a racially charged commentary:

> For the Indian, daily life was a canvas and each man was an artist. He decorated his moccasins, tipis, and costumes with intricate designs and brilliant colours that vigorously expressed his love of design. But the exclusive right to paint the legends and lore was jealously guarded by powerful medicine men. The legends were the last of the great secrets and to release them beyond the bounds of the tribe was unthinkable ... They [contemporary Aboriginal artists] painted the legends and feelings of their people, drawing strength from the traditions but adapting them into a language that would be understandable to a modern world. (*Colours*, 1974)

This dramatic introduction expresses several stereotypical notions about Indigenous peoples and art. The narrator also assumes that the mythology of this nebulous group of "Indians" had all but disappeared; still, they foolishly clung to "the last of the great secrets" in the face of assimilation, of colonization, of progress. The same narrator also closes the film with the following conclusion: "Four painters from four provinces, separated by miles in distance and style, each paints independently of the other and each is a distinctively individual artist. Yet they are linked by a common source: their Indian heritage. And together they form a new and unique expression" (*Colours*, 1973). This gentle reminder reinforces the idea for viewers that even though some of these artists are moving towards mainstream art practices and all have been affected in some ways by assimilation practices and the championing of the individual, they are still Indigenous artists foremost, and in that way are enclosed in, and thus excluded from, crossing over into the mainstream art world and mainstream society.

The film structures the introduction of each segment using similar camera angles and shots. During all four introductory interviews, Hill frames the discussion around topics related to development of artistic style and colour preferences, making it easy for viewers to make aesthetic comparisons. As each artist is introduced, the director adds a visual reinforcement in which the given artist writes his or her name on the screen in white paint, as if signing a canvas as they answer questions about their work—in effect, sanctioning their portrayal in this documentary. For example, Sapp is called "a shy, gentle, sensitive man." Hill describes Janvier as "subdued, quiet spoken, cryptic." Odjig's description correlates to a different stereotypical construction—viewers learn that Daphne Odjig has a "soft, feminine nature." Morrisseau, in contradistinction, is assigned separate descriptors: "his darkly chiselled face wears the marks of an intense and passionate life" (*Colours*, 1973). As viewers learn, Morrisseau's actions more closely align him with stereotypical images of the Ignoble Savage, a theme more fully developed in *Paradox*.

One convincing way the camera visually slots each artist into their hierarchical station is by an image of each of their homes, which proffers a thick description of that person's station in life, their achievement, and their respective place in Canadian society. The house, then, serves as a metonymic sign. In *Colours of Pride*, the director exploits viewers' cultural awareness to offer "real" evidence in order to more objectively support their underlying assumptions. The residence of each artist visually expresses relative levels of assimilation into mainstream society. For example, during a Janvier segment, the camera pans the split-level stucco and brick suburban house on a street filled with similar middle-class homes in Sherwood Park, Alberta. Janvier's home thus conveys his apparent ease of living in suburbia. In his mod-'70s polyester outfit and his suburban existence, Janvier resides much closer to mainstream culture, and therefore it is not surprising that he embraces modern art tenets. Janvier is patted on the head for his efforts to distance himself from his earlier radical views on civil rights: "I quit that. I quit trying to evangelize but I still try to subtly put across ideas" (*Colours*, 1973). The NFB thus presents a constructed image of the man and his modernist abstract art as it approvingly proclaims a commensurate level of assimilation into mainstream culture.

The documentary finds Daphne Odjig living in a conservative, two-storey heritage house painted white with green shutters, in Winnipeg, Manitoba. This home clearly announces her comfortable success both as an artist and as an Indigenous person inhabiting mainstream society. While she continues to maintain connections to nature and to paint legends, as illustrated through her art and interview with Hill, the image of her home firmly declares assimilation and acceptance by mainstream society.

Morrisseau's rented house in Kenora, Ontario, is humble. The camera focuses on a Christian cross in the window and a reproduction of a Madonna and Child in the living room. His red and white abode (a curious coincidence) is nestled among the trees on the shores of a lake. Morrisseau's home illustrates a lower level of success and assimilation into Canadian culture. Sapp's house, too, a modest, government-issued reserve house on Red Pheasant First Nation near North Battleford, Saskatchewan, complete with a matching outhouse, tells a different story than do the houses of Odjig and Janvier.

Like the signifier of the home, the place each artist works is another visual device used to confirm levels of achievement. In the mainstream arts community, established artists produce art in studios. In this film, the camera shows the artists in their workplace as another cultural signifier. Both Odjig and Janvier create their art in conventional studio settings. Their studios further entrench notions of Canadian identity with art making.

In contrast, Allen Sapp paints in his bedroom, his canvas on an easel while he sits on a kitchen chair in front of his spartan single bed. Morrisseau is first shown painting at his kitchen table, where he applies paint using his finger and a brush, and second on the beach with his canvas propped up against a rock—not the *plein air* experience popularized by the impressionists who painted on proper artist easels. Neither kitchen nor beach setting conforms to acceptable art studio practice. The contrived staging of Morrisseau painting on the beach strips him of status as a serious contemporary artist and plays up the myth of the Noble Savage communing with nature.

Expert testimony from Morrisseau's discoverer and gallery owner, Jack Pollock, clarifies the differences between Morrisseau and Janvier: "Janvier, of course, is a learned painter. Janvier is very different [from Morrisseau]. He takes from the Indian background a lot of attitudes and ideas *but* basically he is a very intelligent, educated, abstract painter using the Indian legends and myths and colours to his own end to create paintings that are really almost mainstream abstract art" (*Colours*, 1973). Pollock's description of Janvier confers him credibility as an artist and appears in contradistinction to his comments concerning Morrisseau's work: "I saw a sense of purpose, direction and an inner space ... there is a sense of the unique. Obviously, he is one of the few people who has interpreted the legends and the myths but his images of those demigods, the animal world, the merman, things of this type were unique to himself. I felt I had not seen these things before" (*Colours*, 1973). As in *Paradox*, Pollock's "expert" status confers on him the credibility to judge the artists authoritatively. While Pollock assesses Morrisseau's work as "unique," an important individualistic modern art quality, he clearly favours Janvier's oeuvre. Pollock appears surprised by Janvier's talents but attributes them to his tenure in mainstream art school. In Morrisseau, Pollock recognizes a nascent sense of individualism that conjures a Eurocentric discourse on primitive modernism.

Significantly, while the film champions the embracing of mainstream ideas and identities, there is a clear sense that each of its four featured artists continues to be authentically Indigenous in ways understood by mainstream Canadians. "We are people of nature and we are involved in this sort of thing," confirms Odjig. "My roots are still nature," admits Janvier (*Colours*, 1973). Sapp explains that he prefers to paint early reserve memories from his childhood rather than life now. Both Morrisseau and Odjig speak of the importance of dreams and stories in their work as artists. While these comments display a form of agency and cultural pride among the artists, the manipulative medium can be understood as conforming to stereotypical tropes of Indigeneity found in all forms of popular culture.

Colours of Pride suggests that Indigenous art is a progression towards assimilation, yet it separates Indigenous artists from mainstream society. A glass ceiling divides mainstream and Indigenous artists. Undoubtedly, the art and the artists have been judged narrowly, yet the objective medium of the documentary and the authoritative voice of the NFB leave little space for criticism. The relative merits of Janvier, Odjig, Sapp, and Morrisseau as artists and members of Canadian society rely on their embrace of Western values and mainstream culture. Just as the Trudeau government's 1969 White Paper proposed an official campaign of assimilation, in this film the colour of pride most assuredly refers unconsciously to whiteness. With twenty-two minutes divided among four artists, this second documentary has had less influence in the making of the Morrisseau myth than *Paradox* did. Yet it manages, through careful edits, to present Morrisseau as a painter of legends, in close contact with nature—descriptions that add to and reinforce his mythological narrative.

The NFB documentaries of the 1970s were powerful shapers of the Morrisseau myth. Yet that was not the end of the mythmaking process by any means. In 1979 Lister Sinclair and Jack Pollock published a coffee table–style book titled *The Art of Norval Morrisseau* to offer credibility to the artist in an effort to promote sales of his work. Throughout the book examples of a branding of the artist can be found. A statement such as "Morrisseau does more than transmit and transmute the streams of mythology that mix in his blood and being; he is himself the hero of his legends and myths" provides readers with a romantic vision of the artist.[33] This impressive text was marketed in two formats: either as a book, or in an upscale leather case with a folio of prints by Morrisseau that sold for $1,000 at the time. It was through this text that the myth became more fully framed. Compared to the earlier NFB films, Morrisseau's voice is much stronger here and he takes a hand in managing his public persona. The first two pages of the book include a drawing of a medicine fish and a statement by Morrisseau that includes a signature—not Copper Thunderbird in syllabics, but a handwritten script in the artist's hand. It is as if this signature imparts additional veracity to the publication: this is not simply a marketing of Morrisseau's art, but also includes a window into Morrisseau the man, endorsed by the artist as visually recorded by his personal signature. In a three-paragraph statement, the artist definitively claims his role as shaman and his importance as a communicator of spiritual power (see Chapter 3 for analysis of Morrisseau's shaman identity). This is a different Morrisseau than the one who had publicly refused in 1963 to position himself as a shaman or medicine man when reporters asked for clarification.[34] Sixteen years later, Morrisseau confidently guides readers: "I am a shaman-artist. Traditionally, a shaman's role was to transmit power and the vibrating forces of the spirit through objects known as talismans. In this particular case, a talisman is something that apparently produces effects that are magical and miraculous. My paintings are also icons; that is to say, they are images which help focus on spiritual powers, generated by traditional belief and wisdom. I also regard myself as a kind of spiritual psychologist. I bring together and promote the ultimate harmony of the physical and the spiritual world."[35] Following this preface, playwright Lister Sinclair offers his sense of Morrisseau, describing him as a romantic artistic in the Eurocentric tradition of Baudelaire, Liszt, and Wagner: "Morrisseau's imagination is turned on by a story, as were the artists of the Romantic Revival."[36] Sinclair recounts the significant events in Morrisseau's life that help shape his "still developing" identity, summing him up as follows: "Blissfully self-centered, and ruthlessly eclectic, he is in the full tide of his remarkable career."[37]

Unlike Sinclair, who situates Morrisseau within a Eurocentric artistic movement, Pollock includes a personal narrative about his first encounters with the artist and places himself at the centre of the story. Pollock describes setting plans for a 1962 art exhibition, and after describing Morrisseau's squalid living conditions, recalls:

> On my way home I realized what I had almost missed by trying to avoid "the famous Indian artist." I began to be intoxicated by the magic of my discovery, but also became aware of the imbalance of the two cultures confronting me. The white man in the name of Christianity and Western civilization had replaced the logic of tribal law with a different standard of morality and justice. Sin and guilt concepts, alcohol and disease had fermented and corroded the once strong and powerful indigenous peoples of this land. Later I was to find that both sides of this conflict were embodied in Morrisseau himself.[38]

Pollock draws on stereotypical tropes present in popular culture and the press to make his claims of discovery. To convey the artist's childlike innocence, Pollock recounts how Morrisseau foolishly and naively offered him all of his paintings for five dollars each. Reinforcing the polarized forces presented in the NFB film *Paradox* as a way of describing Morrisseau authentically, Pollock also confirms that Morrisseau had, for about five years, been "trading pictures for booze, and some of his work had been stolen while he was drunk."[39] The art dealer shares his first impression of Morrisseau: "Here was a man of power, and I felt that this lean and handsome warrior of another time had the quiet majesty of someone special. Absent was the devious, the manipulative, the fractured duality of Morrisseau's personality, all of which I was to be confronted with much later."[40] Unlike Sinclair's essay, Pollock's creates a caricature of the artist that both confines him and (re)presents him mythically as he sketches Morrisseau's exploits and successes through 1978, all the while inserting himself into the centre of the narrative.

Following Pollock's essay, Morrisseau once again takes up the pen in a personal essay. Next to a full-page image of Morrisseau smudging at the 1978 tea party (described more fully in Chapter 3), Morrisseau shares that "being a shaman as well as a spiritual person, I do think I have visions."[41] He then explains how even as a child he was "playing the role of a shaman" and that he was not allowed to make a birchbark scroll "until my full initiation." Morrisseau confesses that community members felt he was acting rashly by making art, but that his grandfather told him to make up his own mind. Morrisseau responded, " 'I am going to be a shaman.' I wanted to be a shaman and an artist. I wanted to give the world these images, because I felt this could bring back the pride of the Ojibway which was once great."[42] Although the book includes a passage that states "the man who changes into a Thunderbird is Norval Morrisseau," it does not overtly promote the symbol of the thunderbird, which gains most traction in the twenty-first century.[43] That said, Copper Thunderbird, the English translation of his Anishinaabe name Miskwaabik Animiiki, was in use publicly as early as 1962 as the title of Bill Brown's feature in the *Weekend Magazine* and helps frame his development as a shaman artist during the 1970s.

In *The Art of Norval Morrisseau*, the artist anoints himself as a shaman artist, an identity that took shape throughout the 1970s and that by 1979 was emphatically claimed and performed. A brilliant marketing ploy at the time, the text today serves as an important archive and as a fulfillment of Morrisseau's shaman identity, a construction that conflated aspects of cultural knowledge from different spiritual traditions with romantic tropes to create the artist's own version of shamanism. However, in his 2011 book *A Picasso in the North Country*, armchair art historian James Stevens decries Morrisseau's claim of the "mythic theme of Norval as a 'shaman artist,'" questioning whether he was a shaman and concluding that "the so-called Urban Shaman concept as applied to Norval is simply a construction of very fragile sticks."[44] He adds that if Morrisseau were a shaman, in a traditional Anishinaabe sense, he would be the only one in 15,000 years of history "that was a practitioner of Eckankar."[45]

In a 1981 review of a gallery exhibition at the Pollock Gallery, John Bentley Mays commented on the recent publication of *The Art of Norval Morrisseau*, noting that an "engaging story has been well told."[46] Two days after Mays's review, a somewhat odd letter to the editor followed in the *Globe and Mail*, written by Lister Sinclair, co-editor of the *Art of Norval Morrisseau*. Sinclair takes exception to the review and points out that Mays did not credit him as a co-editor of the text.[47] Sinclair then launches a complaint about how it was he, not Pollock and not Morrisseau, who had written each section, contending that as a playwright he had, in fact, orchestrated the entire book that resulted in a play, of sorts, of the relationship between Pollock and Morrisseau. Sinclair's declaration amounts to an admittance of massaging Morrisseau's life story creatively to bring the myth to its fullest form.

The 1970s are significant because it was during this decade that the mythic identity of Morrisseau—an imaginary Morrisseau—came into being. In both the NFB documentaries and *The Art of Norval Morrisseau*, the mythology is reinforced. Colonialism remains a constant in this framing, as part of the larger discourses of primitivism, primitive art, and modern primitivism that evince a subtle presence in the making of the myth.

Primitive Art/Primitive People

"Primitive art rarely holds the sophistication and strength we find here," explained Jack Pollock in 1974. Pollock offered his expert opinion on Morrisseau and positioned his art within a discourse of primitivism in an essay for the Department of Indian Affairs–supported *Tawow* magazine, penned in part to promote sales of Morrisseau's work.[48] Also describing the artist as a master, Pollock had no problem conflating the primitive with excellence. He was not alone in characterizing the artist's work as primitive. Such binaries were common in discussions of Indigenous art in the 1960s and 1970s in Canada, as were discussions of primitivism and modernism, and impacted ways in which Morrisseau and his work were received.

Newspapers at the time often batted around notions of the primitive, and art critics also drew upon European and American connections between modern art and primitivism. In September of 1962, for example, an article in *Time* magazine describes the artist as a "hulking (6 ft. 2 in.) Primitivist."[49] Primitive art, primitivism, and modern primitivism are slippery terms, especially so through much of the twentieth century, and carry within them baggage. The discussion below attempts to illuminate the many discourses surrounding concepts of the primitive that impacted Morrisseau. The *Toronto Telegram* called primitive art an antidote to "our high pressure era" and contended that Morrisseau's art falls within this category. Art critic Paul Duval refers to Morrisseau's designs as "a kind of juiced up folk art based on tribal traditions," and Morrisseau as being in danger of becoming one of "our growing host of native souvenir makers."[50]

Categorizations around the term "primitive" are porous and difficult to pin down in any definitive way, and while the story of primitivism is tied closely to European modernism, its impact has resonated deeply with Indigenous arts in Canada, indicative of the strong ties between European and Canadian art histories. Leslie Dawn's discussion in *National Visions, National Blindness* of the 1927 exhibition of Canadian art (*Exposition d'art canadien*) at the Musée de Jeu de Palme in Paris, for example, clearly details the complexities around the label of primitive. French critics, for example, used the term differently than Canada's National Gallery did in the showing of works by James Wilson Morrice, Tom Thomson, and the Group of Seven, with a "small sampling" of Indigenous Northwest Coast art.[51] Dawn notes the distinction made between primitive in reference to Indigenous art as "sauvage,"[52] versus the use of primitive to refer to "a new wave" of artists considered naive.[53]

Art historian Lynda Jessup's book *On Aboriginal Representation in the*

Gallery similarly lays out an early frame-setting example of how the boundaries between ethnology and art and the primitive and the modern were blurred. In her analysis of the National Gallery of Canada's 1927 *Exhibition of Canadian West Coast Art, Native and Modern* and the accompanying essay on page two of the exhibition catalogue, she describes how art by anonymous "Kwakwaka'wakw, Nuxalk, Nuu'chah'nulth, Tlingit, Haida, Tsimshian, Gitksan, and Nisga'a" artists was combined with "pieces by prominent Euro-Canadian artists" to position a history of Canadian art that juxtaposed the "'primitive art' of the Indian," with the "'modern work of Emily Carr and the Group of Seven.'" Jessup contends, "This narrative ... relegated Native cultures to an indeterminate past" and set a precedent for subsequent exhibitions of Indigenous arts in Canada.[54] The National Gallery chose not to collect Native arts again until the 1980s, though totem poles, for example, became a sort of Canadian emblem beginning around this time.

Jessup's frozen-in-time argument builds upon art historian Marcia Crosby's provocative 1991 essay, written in response to the National Gallery of Canada's 1991 Emily Carr retrospective of that year, challenging the notion that Emily Carr had a "profound understanding" of Northwest Coast First Nations.[55] Confronting Western academic scholarship, Crosby, speaking as a Tsimshian and Haida woman, questioned whether the move to reflexively critique historical depictions of the Other "is not just another form of the West's curious interest in its other; or more specifically, the ultimate colonization of 'the Indian' into the spaces of the West's postmodern centre/margin cartography."[56] Her frank words opened a lively and important debate on the subject that included a notable essay by art historian Charlotte Townsend-Gault in the *Canadian Journal of Communication*. Townsend-Gault considered the diverse ways Native and non-Native observers engaged with contemporary First Nations art.[57] At the heart of these discussions resides the hangover of primitivism. That different cultures and world views approach "art" in different ways, or that there is no single way to understand the debate seem self-evident today. Yet especially in the 1990s, when academics began to step away from primitivist discourses, it became clear that the tentacles of colonial influence ran deep.

Since the Enlightenment, various notions had influenced cultural assumptions regarding so-called primitive art. Both social Darwinism and imperialism were pervasive concepts that were largely unquestioned until well into the twentieth century.[58] Sally Price's seminal *Primitive Art in Civilized Places* offered a needed indictment of ongoing discourses surrounding primitive art in the twentieth century. She cites H.W. Janson's definition of primitive in the revised edition of *History of Art* (1986), a popular text used in art history survey courses across the United States and Canada, as evidence of the ongoing usage of the term: "Let us continue, then, to use primitive as a convenient label for a way of life that passed through the Neolithic Revolution but shows no signs of evolving in the direction of 'historic' civilizations."[59] In an effort to broaden such criticisms, art historian Steven Mansbach adds that American art history survey texts such as Janson's also sanitized the meanings of modern art, and he stresses the ideological implications of those efforts as well.[60]

Primitive art, which took on new importance with the surrealist movement, built on a central modernist understanding of art as a "universal language." Price notes that Freudian thought, too, influenced the idea that "Primitive Art emerges directly and spontaneously from psychological drives ... Primitive artists are imagined to express their feelings from the intrusive overlay of learned behavior and conscious constraints that mold the work of the Civilized artists."[61] The innocence and naïveté associated with primitive art romantically projected non-Western artists as purified and unpolluted by Western civilization. Modernists sought to appropriate the unmediated energy of primitivist arts and situated so-called tribal work in a positive light, yet at the same time presented it as something Other—a binary to Western high arts.

The terms "primitive" and "primitive art" remain highly problematic both because of their colonial baggage and their various usages over time. In *French Primitivism and the Ends of Empire 1945–1975*, art historian Daniel J. Sherman explains that he "treats primitivism as at once a discourse, a myth, a fantasy, part of a larger colonial or neocolonial apparatus, and a metaculture, with one or more of these roles predominating at any given moment."[62] In questioning why France continues to hold on to an "unselfconscious primitivism" well into the twenty-first century while much of the rest of the world has dismissed it, Sherman's framing of the discourse as naturalized is useful in understanding how Morrisseau and his art was received prior to 1990. His argument also helps elucidate the diverse and varied modes in which primitivism was entangled with the Canadian art scene and Canadian culture.

In the discipline of art history, distinctions between primitivism and modernism were distorted early in the twentieth century, when Picasso's exploitation of African masks for *Demoiselles d'Avignon* prompted European art history to "turn a corner," as Price describes it.[63] This is a common claim, and art historian Robert Goldwater mined similar territory in his classic *Primitivism in Modern Art* and in his book specifically on Gauguin, where he posited that Gauguin had primed modern art with his trips to Tahiti.[64] That art historian Hal Foster calls Picasso's *Demoiselles d'Avignon* a "bridge between modernist and pre-modernist painting, a primal scene of modern primitivism" in his cutting review of *"Primitivism" in 20th Century Art: Affinity of the Tribal and the Modern*, the controversial 1984 exhibition at New York's Museum of Modern Art curated by Kurt Varnedoe and William Rubin,[65] demonstrates how powerful the discourse of primitive modernism's link to Picasso is, a discourse he considers to be "fetishistic" and "threatened by loss, by lack, by others."[66]

Such ideas also influenced New York School abstract artists such as Barnett Newman, Mark Rothko, and Adolph Gottlieb in the 1940s, who began to appropriate Native American sources in an effort to redirect nationalist culture in America. Art historian Bill Anthes explains, "By aligning their art with the Primitive, Gottlieb, Rothko, and Newman sought to create art that would transcend ... sentimental and blatantly nationalistic expressions [of American high culture]."[67] Clearly, many abstractionists working in the United States, Canada, and Europe understood their art as a form of universalized "spiritual kinship" with the primitives that transcended outmoded European and American colonial ideologies. Anthes notes that Newman's form of primitivism, for example, should not be viewed as cultural appropriation but as a more complex relationship that "opened up the notion of a 'third space'" and provided a "platform from which Native and non-Native artists asserted the value of cultural difference."[68] Still, because that "platform" was built on colonial notions of modernism, primitivism skewed Indigenous culture as homogeneous and ahistorical. The discourse resonated more broadly in understandings of Indigenous arts articulating Foster's earlier caution that "different orders of tribal cultures are made to conform to one Western typology."[69]

Primitive art has taken on new resonance lately in relation to scholarly directions in global modernism and Indigenous modernism. Key figures such as Ruth B. Phillips, Ian McLean, and Kobena Mercer have begun to shape new territories for fresh concepts within histories of art. McLean, in reference to Australian Aboriginal art, contextualizes this discussion when he states: "While modernity also challenged traditional cultures in other parts of the globe, modernism remains the brand name of European (and more generally western) aesthetic engagements with modernity... Modernity is blamed for the destruction of Aboriginal culture rather than the inspiration of new Aboriginality."[70] McLean argues instead that Aboriginal modernism is "a productive idea" that "re-positions contemporary Aboriginal art in its own colonial origins, and consequently challenges art history's dominant Eurocentric discourse."[71]

Ruth B. Phillips adds to this inquiry by noting that when Eurocentric notions of modernist primitivism were introduced to Indigenous artists in North America, they were taken up in different ways. In three case studies of encounters between displaced immigrants and Native artists, Phillips argues that twentieth-century European arrivals, steeped in the tenets of modernist primitivism, introduced artistic concepts that were repurposed by artists as "counter-modern" in ways that were "dialogic" and beneficial to both the immigrant and the Indigenous artist.[72] Notably, one case study focuses on the artistic relationship forged between immigrant Dr. Joseph Weinstein and Norval Morrisseau. Weinstein's encouragement, Phillips finds, "enabled Morrisseau to enter the modernist art world of southern Canada and, eventually, Europe" with a high level of success.[73] Because of Weinstein's appreciation of primitive art and his acceptance of the role of the contemporary primitive artist, Phillips concludes that Morrisseau (like the artists in her other two case studies) shifted the meaning of primitive, "so that modernist primitivism could become indigenous modernism."[74] Therefore, while the press remained complicit in maintaining rigid categories assigned to primitive arts, as did most art institutions and museums at the time, Indigenous artists such as Morrisseau pushed beyond such confines in his art practice, recasting primitivism in new and productive ways.

Primitive Art in the Media

Press coverage of Indigenous arts in the 1960s and 1970s often focused on the enduring notion of primitive art as simplistic and stuck in a prehistoric time warp, but at the same time made links and comparisons to modern art. Such stories conveniently positioned Indigenous art as moribund, like the cultures from which it emanated. Aligning the primitive with Indigenous art seemed to dispel guilt associated with colonialism and confirm possession claims and the ongoing need to manage Indigenous peoples more generally.

The *New York Times* printed a number of articles in 1962 related to primitive art that helped define the discourse for its readers. One story praised New York City's recently opened Museum of Primitive Art and offered the following definition:

> Primitive art might be defined as the art of communities that have not learned to conjugate cause and effect with any particular efficiency, and whose art is part of an attempt to facilitate or stabilize the process as they conceive it. Although the word "primitive"

is thoroughly inoffensive in its literal meanings, it does imply our superiority and to many people brings an image of bone-in-the-nose unsophistication. A circumlocution such as "art of underdeveloped countries and lost civilizations" only proves that the longest way round is the longest way round ... "Indigenous art" was tried for a time, but no one knew what indigenous meant so it was abandoned ... The British favored the label "Tribal Art" for a time. One of the best names, according to Dr. Goldwater [Director of the Museum], is "Art of Preliterate Peoples."[75]

This pseudo-academic discussion regarding primitive art occurred at the same time as U.S. Indigenous leaders were promoting greater awareness of the denial of civil rights for American Indians. To that end, the *New York Times* reported that according to Robert Burnette, executive director of the National Congress of American Indians, discrimination in the United States against Indians in the early 1960s was comparable to "that against Negroes."[76] A *New York Times* story about an Indigenous art exhibition at the Seattle World Fair in 1962 suggested links between the European moderns and non-Western art when it noted that "[University of Washington anthropologist] Dr. Gunther's show may be the most illuminating of the art exhibitions to many people especially to Europeans who have hardly begun to recognize that American Indian art is not always a matter of artsy-craftsy beaded belts and decaying war bonnets, but is as powerful an expression and can offer as acute an esthetic experience as the African sculpture that is better known because of the geographical accident of its earlier discovery by painters in Paris."[77] The article, placed next to a larger story with several photographs describing the main art exhibition in Seattle that celebrated Pablo Picasso's eightieth birthday and his sixty-year art career subtly reinforces the association of primitivism with Picasso's legacy of modern art.

Canadian newspapers also covered primitivism during this period beyond the references to Morrisseau's debut exhibition noted above. Early in 1962 the *Globe and Mail* in Toronto ran a story that connected a primitive past with the modern. The article hooks readers with a provocative and somewhat cheeky assertion: "There is no very sure way of telling whether our Indian predecessors of 500 to 1,000 years ago indulged in surrealist dream art."[78] The article, about an exhibition of copies of "Indian rock paintings" compiled by anthropologist Selwyn Dewdney (who would later write a book on rock art with Norval Morrisseau) and on display at the Royal Ontario Museum in Toronto, contended "they" practised some abstraction as well as a "primitive realism," identifying neither the Indigenous group who created the work nor its location. (However, this lack of context was most likely the fault of the newspaper and not Dewdney). The *Globe and Mail* reporter explains, "One can speculate on the mystic significance of some of the figures; but, as Mr. Dewdney himself has said … 'there is a dreamlike quality to which we do not know the answer.'"[79] The description of the mysteriously spiritual and exotically unexplainable coupled with primitiveness summed up many discussions of Indigenous arts in the past. The poke at surrealism confirmed its insignificance.

The *Winnipeg Free Press* printed three articles in 1963 related to notions of the primitive and Indigenous art. "The Totems Fall and an Art Dies," a full-page story that ran in the *Free Press* in January, documents the decline of Gitksan villages on the Skeena River in northern British Columbia while illustrating how easily art can be claimed for nation-building purposes. "Years ago rows of totem poles distinguished many of the Indian villages of the British Columbia coast but few of these unique examples of primitive art remain today in their original locations."[80] In a story that promotes a small restoration effort by the Canadian government, four photographs provide additional nuance: one photo of the local Anglican church is placed directly above a detail of a fallen and rotting pole, nicely juxtaposing the demise of Gitksan culture and spirituality with the enduring power of Christianity. Another photograph documents the restoration of a pole in an effort to spur tourism in the region, and the final photograph shows two boats, a modest traditional craft in the foreground that clashes with the modern Kitwanga ferry that shuttles tourists and locals across the river. The report states, "Although the art of totem carving is dead, the people of Kitwanga still retain some of the old skills, and you may still see very well made dug out canoes drawn up on the river bank near the village."[81] The photographs chosen to accompany the report convey to readers a moribund existence being replaced with a mainstream Canadian identity. The totem poles serve as a vehicle to highlight assimilationist policy in Canada. Worthy of a government-sponsored conservation project because of their interest for tourists and their role in defining Canada's past, they appear to have little other importance to the future of Canada.

In "All Dressed Up in Buckskin n' Beads," a news report ostensibly about crafts on display at an "Indian Conference" in Winnipeg, the *Free Press* focuses on Mrs. Earl Good, a local Native artist who, according to the story,

> has been told by children with whom she baby-sits, "You look nice when you play Indian." And she does. The reason she looks so nice is because she is an Indian … The attractive Indian woman

could have been a chieftain as she covered plain "white women's clothing" with the natural attire of her own people. There was statuesque grandeur in every line as she wore the 41-year-old deerskin jacket trimmed with delicate needlework which her mother had made for her father. With it she wore a skirt trimmed with what might have been an Indian "sporran" but was in reality a beautifully beaded "fire bag" or tobacco weed pouch, as worn by her late father.[82]

The report uses Mrs. Good as more than a model showing off her father's regalia. She also serves an example of someone who has been successfully integrated into urban life, since she left residential school to enter "domestic service." Comments on the "statuesque grandeur in every line" of the deerskin jacket and the surmise that she might have been a "chieftain" situate Mrs. Good in a liminal state where the donning of buckskin and beaded bag transports her from an assimilated condition to a primitive imaginary.

Later, when the National Indian Council of Canada (NICC) met in Winnipeg, concern over the intrusion of fake "Indian handicrafts" from Japan into the Canadian market became the subject of debate that, according the *Free Press*, led to the passage of resolution that would include a standard seal of approval for authentic Canadian goods. Rather than consider the value of such a move for Canadian arts industries generally, the news story dismisses the importance of Indigenous art production as inconsequential because of its primitiveness. Quoting William Wuttunee, chief of the NICC, who admitted that he had been fooled by the fakes—"I even bought a belt made in Japan myself," he said, "thinking it was Indian made" —the article's message seems to be that if a "real Indian" cannot tell the difference between the fake and the authentic belt, then why should readers concern themselves with protecting this industry?[83]

Inuit art, which today is often viewed as a symbol of Canadian identity, has been assiduously cultivated as such since the late 1950s. It has served as a successful narrative regarding Canada's promotion of Northern sovereignty. A debate around whether Inuit arts production was contemporary or primitive haunted many early discussions. Communications scholar Leanne Pupchek's essay on "Inuit Art and the Canadian Imagination" clearly articulates the relationship between nation and Inuit art. Pupchek goes so far as to argue that Inuit imagery has "become a synecdoche" of Canadian identity.[84] Historian Joan Sangster contends that a reciprocal construction of a "primitive north in need of guidance from a modern south masked relations of ideological power and had profound consequences for Indigenous peoples."[85] Canadian neo-liberalism embraced these concepts with gusto, making Inuit art a recognizable image of Canada. Canadian diplomats around the globe have offered Inuit art as gifts to symbolize the nation since the 1960s, reinforcing Canada's claim to the Arctic, to inclusivity, and to forging a national identity. Since those early days, however, Inuit art has grown far beyond the nation's original aims and aesthetics, forging a dynamic contemporary art movement.

In a 1971 *artscanada* magazine article, Winnipeg Art Gallery director Jacqueline Fry confirmed that Inuit art was usually analyzed as primitive.[86] Tom Hill, in an essay in the 1984 *Norval Morrisseau and the Emergence of the Image Makers* exhibition catalogue, added that if an Inuit carving did not demonstrate a "required 'primitivism'" promoted in the marketplace, it was smashed.[87] Using an example of a carving of Elvis Presley that was to be destroyed because it was not chosen by the co-operative for sale but was rescued by a public servant who felt the piece "reflected the reality of the Sugluk community with which he was so familiar,"[88] Hill draws attention to realities that have been more fully articulated recently by Inuit art historian Heather Igloliorte.[89] Also, Norman Vorano, former curator of the Inuit collection at the Canadian Museum of Civilization (now the Canadian Museum of History), found that when contemporary Inuit carvings were first displayed at the Gimpel Fils Gallery in London, England, in 1953, they were, not surprisingly, displayed as primitive art.[90] Yet while a frozen-in-time aesthetic was dictated to carvers, the work was also marketed in Canada as contemporary fine art under the direction of James Houston, separating it from the usual trappings of primitiveness.[91]

Because art narratives related to Inuit art were branded by the Canadian government and packaged for the mass media in the late 1950s and early 1960s, it was easy for newspapers to provide coverage. A script, often prompted and shepherded early on by Houston, who had successfully engendered both the sculpture and print co-operative programs in the Arctic, gave reporters ready tools to write stories.[92] And write they did. Throughout the early 1960s numerous stories related to Inuit art were printed in Canada's newspapers, providing clear evidence of links between nation building and the art co-operatives established in the North but also revealing the power of primitivist discourse.

The Toronto *Globe and Mail* printed five stories related to Inuit art in the first eight months of 1962 alone. "A critical moment in Canadian art" is how *Globe and Mail* art critic Pearl McCarthy characterized an exhibition of "Eskimo prints" at the Art Gallery of Toronto.[93] The story includes a description of a political struggle for control of the co-operative by southern arts experts. Concerned about the continuing quality of the prints in the face of outside meddling, McCarthy, who would later cover Morrisseau's premiere exhibition, appears well versed in the politics surrounding the co-operative in Cape Dorset. She mentions her travels to Baffin Island in the past year as evidence of first-hand knowledge and expertise, and questions the merits of instituting a southern Canadian group of art leaders to advise the West Baffin Co-Operative who could override the current on-site art adviser, Terrence Ryan. Casting Ryan as Houston's heir apparent in the North, and the next region's advocate for art and for the local populations, McCarthy contends that he "is not only an expert artist specializing in prints but a man who can think in an Eskimo way." "Cape Dorset has been lucky in white collaborators who could analyze every problem in the sudden meeting of cultures," acknowledges McCarthy, as she confirms that they "knew that the Eskimo artist must remain himself and could not be treated as primitive." "James Houston laid a good foundation," McCarthy asserts.[94] A *Winnipeg Free Press* story, "The Eskimo Artists of Baffin Island," ostensibly an advertisement for a *Reader's Digest* forthcoming fall feature article, "The Remarkable Eskimo Artists of Baffin Island," endorsed constructed links between assimilation and authenticity that viewed Inuit art as both a vehicle for economic viability in the North and an enduring artistic expression, maintained because of the efforts of Houston. Judging art production as superior to fur trapping, the article confirms, "Thanks to a Canadian artist [James Houston], Eskimos for the first time have a source of income, independent of the trapline," urging readers to consider further the "hauntingly original prints" and "find out how the Eskimos learned to make *paper prints* from their carving on walrus tusk, antlers and arctic soapstone," stressing the evolutionary success of Canadian intervention.[95]

The National Film Board also had a hand in creating the mythology around Inuit art in the early 1960s that exploited romantic notions of primitivism combined with colonizing efforts by the Canadian government. The 1962 NFB documentary *Kenojuak*, for example, championed the co-operative's support for artists such as a young Kenojuak Ashevak (1921–2012), who is highlighted in the film and who went on to have a formidable and award-winning career as an artist.[96] Released in both French and English, a female narrator's voice overlays Kenojuak's voice because the artist speaks Inuktutuk throughout. The popular film is problematic for a number of reasons. It borrows heavily from the pivotal ethnographic film *Nanook of the North* made by Robert Flaherty in 1922, including scenes that mirror *Nanook* to reinforce a frozen-in-time, primitive image of the Inuit.[97] The

nineteen-minute documentary offers a compelling and romantic mythology about a static North early on while later scenes promote "advances"
introduced to the North by the Canadian government. For example, scenes
filmed in an igloo—fabricated out of Styrofoam in order to accommodate
summer filming—naturalize a primitivist discourse. Images of chest x-rays
and snowmobiles that follow the igloo sequence hint at modernization and
assimilationist policies. Surprisingly little in the film focuses on the art of
Kenojuak or her motivations as an artist. As in the later NFB film concerning Morrisseau, this female artist is similarly constructed as an exotic Other
rather than an artist.

A *Winnipeg Free Press* story from Cape Dorset printed in July 1962
rhetorically questioned, "Will higher living standards among Eskimos
destroy the beauty of their art?"[98] Northwest Territories commissioner
Gordon Robertson challenged this notion, emphatically denying that a raised
standard of living could diminish artistic quality, using the opportunity to
proudly champion assimilation in the North as the cause of the successful
art movement. "One cannot make prints in a traditional snow house. It was
only after the Eskimos had suitable space and materials that they could
work in this art form." Further signalling that Inuit art served the aims of
Canadian nationalism and reinforcing Pupchek's claim that Inuit imagery is
a synecdoche of Canadian identity, a story ran in the *Free Press* in November
1962 that highlighted the first major exhibition of Canadian art in Africa
in twenty-five years. On display in Nairobi, Kenya, in a gallery endowed by
a former RCMP constable, the exhibition included, in addition to paintings
by southern Canadian contemporary artists, "11 Eskimo stone-cuts and
sealskin prints."[99] It seems Inuit art was taking Africa by storm because
the following month the *Free Press* announced that Mary Panegoosho, staff
member of Canada's only "Eskimo-language magazine, *Uunuktitut* (The
Eskimo Way)" would visit Ghana to coincide with the display of a "major
collection of Eskimo carvings and examples of graphic art ... in Accra, the
first Eskimo art to be shown in West Africa."[100] The *Free Press* confirmed
that "Eskimo Carving is now almost symbolic of Canada," quoting Winnipeg
collector Robert Williamson, who stated that soapstone carvings "express
Canada very well."[101]

The interest in Inuit art continued to dominate arts-related coverage
in the press through 1964. Terrance Ryan, the West Baffin Eskimo Co-
Operative art director at Cape Dorset, offered his take in the *Globe and Mail*
that January, saying "the fast sweep of southern influence engulfs them [Inuit
peoples]." The article proclaims that "primitivism can be kept artificially, but

he [Ryan] does feel that action now in appreciating indigenous culture will leave the people more pride."[102] The following month in the *Globe and Mail*, George Swinton, a Winnipeg artist and educator who had recently penned a book on Inuit art, redirected Ryan's assertion when he poignantly argued that "if Eskimo art is falling off in quality, it is not because the Eskimo is losing his talent; it is because civilization as we have known it is dying. The Eskimo may not theorize about it, but he is a man who lives in the present, and he feels what is happening."[103] On the one hand is the promotion of Inuit art as a Canadian venture and assimilationist strategy for the North, but on the other lies a wariness of interference that will amount to artifice. In 1970 a guest art critic in the *Globe and Mail* pronounced "Evidence beyond Dispute: Eskimo Art Still the Only Truly Canadian Art," explaining that if Canada wants to promote a unique art identity it should not support art inherited by European culture.[104] While the story does not mention contemporary Indigenous arts from southern regions of Canada, artist and art critic Anita Aarons declares that Inuit art captures this Canadian culture with its "authoritative imagery. The Indian, by his own assertion a North American, encompasses a large field of idioms." She adds, challenging the argument for celebrating landscape art, that "a culture is not captured in totemic essence by the mere recording of its natural landscape."[105]

When John Graham, art critic for the *Winnipeg Free Press*, looked back in 1972 at what he called the "paternalistic" Inuit art market, he cautiously warned southern Indigenous artists such as Alex Janvier, Daphne Odjig, and Jackson Beardy to beware of being consumed by such a setup. He argued that Inuit art was "established as a highly marketable commodity, [and] the results have come to be viewed as a specialized ethnic expression." Graham alerted the contemporary Indigenous artist in southern Canada to "guard against the trap of an imposed stereotypical imagery if he is to achieve recognition as an individual artist."[106] News discussions about Inuit art at the time mostly ignored specific Inuit artists or personalities, focusing instead on a narrow range of imagery promoted by the co-operatives as Inuit art.

Given the privileging of Inuit art, it was inevitable that Morrisseau's entry into the public art world would be compared to Inuit art. When *Time* magazine covered Morrisseau's exhibition in September 1962, for example, it reported that "Toronto critics approved unanimously," speculating that his art might spark a "vogue as chic as that of the Cape Dorset Eskimo's prints."[107] Comparing Morrisseau's debut exhibition with Inuit art ensured interest in his work but also conflated Indigenous art as a monolith for the Canadian public.

Primitivism, as understood in the news reports, represents far more than its links with modernist art. In examining shifting settler views of Indigenous arts and the agency of Indigenous peoples in promoting their cultural expressions, anthropologist Nicholas Thomas argues that within settler cultures like Canada, Australia, and New Zealand, the specific motifs of local Indigenous art understood as primitive were drawn upon in ways that are complex. He cautions that "settler primitivism is not … necessarily the project of radical formal innovation stimulated by tribal art," and can lead to visual signifiers that serve both Indigenous and national identities with no reference to modern art.[108] In his 1974 essay for *Tawow* magazine, in which Jack Pollock offered his expert opinion on Morrisseau, evidence of the complexities surrounding primitivism are clear.[109]

When *Globe and Mail* columnist William French announced his picks for the fall book season in 1979 under the suggestive headline "Items Exotic and Raunchy Spice Up Fall Publishing Menu," French's text, on its own, was mostly bland.[110] However, it was spiced up with the addition of three photographs: a candid photo of Morrisseau was framed by standard studio headshots of authors Betty Kennedy and Margaret Atwood. The text makes no overt connection to Morrisseau's exoticism or raunchiness, yet the juxta-position of his photograph with two stalwart mainstream writers below the provocative headline connects the artist to primitivist meanings seemingly absent yet present in the signifying structure of this column. Morrisseau becomes a focus of French's column even though the review says little about the recently released Sinclair and Pollock's *The Art of Norval Morrisseau* except that it was expensive, stating twice that the limited edition copies cost $1,000.

Equating Indigenous arts with primitivism reinforces the ethnographic hold exerted on objects and peoples. It was within this milieu that Morrisseau stepped onto the mainstream art stage. Often, it was his identity, more than his art, that was pronounced to be primitive in Canada's media. Yet, once Morrisseau was inserted into the established primitivist discourse, readers and viewers required little more than a mention of his name or a photo of the artist to be reminded of meanings never fully present in a given text or image.

CHAPTER TWO

1962
Morrisseau's Arrival

The *News-Chronicle* reported on Morrisseau's upcoming Toronto exhibition in August 1962, exuberantly declaring, "Out of the hidden confines of this tiny village [Beardmore], 130 miles from the Lakehead, has come one of hottest prospects in the art world today."[1]

Outside of news coverage of Inuit art, Morrisseau's arrival in the press in 1962 was combined with coverage that often acknowledged ongoing racism. A January 1962 Canadian Press (CP) news report printed in the *News-Chronicle* of Port Arthur (now Thunder Bay) in northwestern Ontario, the birthplace of Morrisseau and situated close to his home, both reinforced stereotypical tropes and characterized them as counterproductive. "Indians are willing and eager to leave their reserves but are victims of misunderstandings when they get city jobs," stated a sympathetic and charitable Helen Gough, member of the Anglican Church Information Centre and organizer of an Anglican Diocesan Council conference on racism in Toronto, the subject of the news story.[2] The report outlined three common misconceptions about Indigenous peoples Gough found in her work as an anti-racist advocate with the church: "[t]hat he is a bloodthirsty warrior, an unkempt type unable or unwilling to learn English, or a simple pious boor, who needs to be looked after and should be grateful to those who do." Revealed by the reporter, however, was the reality that this Anglican organization also had racist problems and so therefore should not be judging Canadians. The article went on to explain that a "negro secretary" living in Toronto had confessed to the reporter covering the conference that "the church was one of the few places that she met discrimination in Canada."[3] Therefore, in the course of this news report, readers learn that an institution (long associated with racism through the Indian residential school period) that appears to want to change attitudes regarding Indigenous people remains fraught with racist behaviours. The revelation that appears to acknowledge press objectivity, in effect, disciplines Helen Gough for her seemingly sanctimonious effort. Two weeks later the same paper reports on entrenched forms of social Darwinism present in adoption practices in Canada, with the following headline: "No. 1 Among Many Problems: Few Families Are Willing to Adopt Indian Children." The news story explains that "black-skinned or yellow-skinned children are easier to place than Indians ... 'Even if there are no Indian physical characteristics and the race is based only on the grandfather, the reaction is the same,' admits the director of the Children's Aid Society, who attributes this to 'judgment of Indians by the worst of their type.'"[4] Together, these stories in the Port Arthur *News-Chronicle* work to document the entrenched but complex racial biases against Aboriginals in Canada.

Such news stories in 1962 often naturalized and essentialized images of Indigenous peoples. It had only been two years since Canada had changed the Indian Act in order to enfranchise First Nations peoples. Until 1960, First Nations were considered federal wards, and with the change in the Act they found their first opportunity to vote federally in June 1962, when Prime Minister John Diefenbaker successfully defeated Liberal leader Lester Pearson. And it was during this time of momentous improvement of rights for Indigenous peoples in Canada that Morrisseau caught the eye of the press. Morrisseau's entry into the Toronto art scene helped mark a significant moment with regard to the portrayal of Indigenous peoples in the press.

In advance of Morrisseau's premiere exhibit at the Pollock Gallery in September 1962, the *Globe and Mail*'s art critic Pearl McCarthy wrote a short report headlined "Explorers Discover New Ideas" to announce Morrisseau's unanticipated entry into Toronto's art scene; the title succinctly conjures up a colonialist discourse of claiming and discovery. She offers a number of con-structions that demonstrate the unfamiliar terrain Morrisseau had entered, mixing racial stereotypes and art criticism. "Ontario's hinterland has afforded an exciting discovery in the work of a 31-year old Ojibway Indian," implying that Jack Pollock of the Pollock Gallery had, like Christopher Columbus discovering America, entered the wilds of Ontario and discovered *his* art-ist.[5] McCarthy posits that Morrisseau has done two remarkable things: "He has realized that though Ojibway ritual law demands their metaphysics be kept secret, the Indians would benefit if outsiders knew their culture. And he has devised his stylized semi-abstraction to express the mysticism of the culture."[6] While McCarthy maintains a typically racialized construction of the artist as a frozen-in-time relic in the first paragraphs of her article, she clearly recognizes in his work an artistic genius that trumps his primitiveness and strongly argues that his work overwhelms the facile identity constructions she is using. "Morriseau's [*sic*] genius for unifying or breaking space in his designs is astounding, as is his sureness of line. It cannot be classed as primitive art."[7] Racial classifications appear far more rigid than artistic ones here, as Morrisseau the man remains trapped as a primitive while his art has moved beyond. Ruth B. Phillips confirms that in McCarthy's 15 September 1962 column related to the exhibition, the reporter contradicts her headline "Ojibwa Painter No Primitive" with a range of signifiers that clearly substantiate and reinforce Morrisseau's primitivism.[8] Indeed, in the brief paragraph devoted to Morrisseau's show at the Pollock Gallery, McCarthy notes that the work is "basic," that he represents man and beast to "convey the metaphysics of his ancient race," and that one of his "native talents" is how he isolates an idea.[9]

Similarly, the arts section of Canada's *Time* magazine for the week of 28 September 1962 noted Morrisseau's exhibition under "Myth & Symbol." This came after a short news item, which announced the upcoming wedding of Governor General Georges Vanier's youngest son at Rideau Hall in Ottawa and reported that "Social Ottawa was mildly miffed" by the disappointingly understated nature of the affair.[10] Socialites might have been unhappy with the lack of ceremony around a semi-royal wedding, but they would have surely been intrigued by the exotic arts story that followed. Beginning with the caveat "It has been long popular to consider Indian daubs as less revealing artistically than ethnographically," *Time* clarifies that "there was no such confusion in the minds of gallery goers who pried themselves into Toronto's little Pollock Gallery for a one-man show by an Ojibway painter named Norval Morrisseau."[11] The article underscores the significance of this art exhibition as a pivotal one for Canadian art history: "Few exhibits in Canadian art history have touched off a greater immediate stir than Morrisseau's. The Toronto critics approved unanimously and speculated that self-taught Morrisseau may have launched a vogue as chic as that of the Cape Dorset Eskimo's prints. Said Radcliffe-educated Jean Boggs, new curator of the Toronto Art Gallery: 'It's like looking at Chinese painting—a form of art from the past that is very attractive and appealing.'"[12] While Boggs connects Morrisseau's art to viewing relics of a distant and exotic past, the article generally approves of his work. Artistic descriptions of Morrisseau's exhibition included such phrases as "brilliant imagery" and "vivid," but much of the two-column review centred on descriptions of Morrisseau, "a part-time gold miner with a fourth-grade education," that were less generous to him than his art. The magazine article, for example, easily employed the Noble Savage construction: "Hulking (6 ft. 2 in.) Primitivist Morrisseau began to paint only three years ago, after a dream in which he was told to set down the symbols and myths of his fellow Ojibways … The constantly beaming artist himself was almost a larger attraction than his work."[13] The report positions Morrisseau as uneducated but mystical, a naive innocent, an object on display, like his art. Notions of spectacle have been a stalwart in colonial discourse—the exotic Other for consumption. And that was how Morrisseau was served up for readers of *Time*.

The *London Free Press* arts reporter Lenore Crawford also penned a racially oriented story on Morrisseau in September 1962, stating that given his "overnight success," something that rarely occurs for artists (especially in Canada), he was "more firmly determined to follow a pathway trod in Indian moccasins, for Norval Morrisseau at 31 is an Ojibway who treasures legends of his tribe and derives all his inspiration and ideas from there."[14] In her interview with Morrisseau and anthropologist Selwyn Dewdney at Dewdney's home in London, Ontario, Crawford stresses Morrisseau's lack of formal education, his primitive, poverty-stricken upbringing, and the uncertainty of life as an Aboriginal in Canada. The report offers Morrisseau's take on religion: "I pray directly to the Great Manitou of the Indian … Then a wave of Christianity comes over me and I get confused about what I believe and I am unhappy. Then I go for a walk and hunt beaver and the confusion leaves." Readers can approve of Morrisseau's assimilationist pull to Christianity, all the while placated by his authenticity as an "Indian"—his enduring belief in the "Great Manitou" or the sense of peace he gets from hunting and communing with nature. The stereotypical signifiers combine to help shape the reader's sense of the man. Prophetically, Crawford concludes, "He also will seek to resolve the problem of being himself an Indian today."[15] This reporter clearly heralds Morrisseau's entrance into the Canadian art scene as a problematic one. Not because of any artistic deficiency, as most of the arts reporters clearly judged his art worthy of acceptance, but rather because of his Indigeneity that marked him as a questionable and unsuitable art star, causing Crawford to question future success given his racial identity. Like the *Globe and Mail* and *Time* magazine, the *London Times* separates Morrisseau's artistic output from his racial identity, thus problematizing his Indianness.

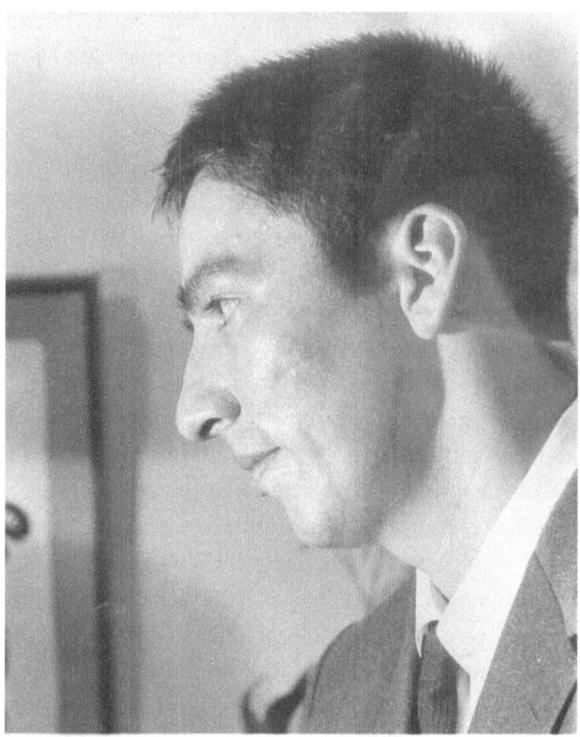

This photograph of Norval Morrisseau was taken at the opening of his Inaugural exhibition of art at the Pollock Gallery In Toronto. The photo was published alongside stories in two newspapers: David Cobb, "Indian Artist Earns High Praise" *Toronto Star*, 13 September 1962, and CP Wire "Budding Artist Discovered Twice," *Winnipeg Free Press*, 26 September 1962. Reproduced with permission of *Toronto Star* photo archives.

The *Toronto Star* took a different approach in reporting the events of the exhibition, however, a direction the paper would largely maintain throughout Morrisseau's career. In its first news story about the artist, the *Star* mostly leaves Morrisseau be and instead applauds his artwork. The paper interviews Dewdney and Pollock as experts thrilled by the art on display, stating, "Last night there was no lack of appreciation among Morrisseau's white brothers."[16] Whereas the *Globe and Mail* focused on the Torontonian art gallery owner as Morrisseau's discoverer, both the *Star* and the *Winnipeg Free Press* (CP) reports credit the politician Allister Grosart, national director of the Progressive Conservative party, and Dewdney as key mentors. The *Free Press* article, under the headline "Budding Artist Discovered Twice," further explains that Grosart, after instigating correspondence with the artist, contacted

Dewdney, "an expert on Indian paintings" who confirmed Morrisseau's artistic abilities.[17] According to the article, Grosart then provided Morrisseau with $900 in order that he could quit his job and paint full time.

The *Toronto Telegram* art critic Paul Duval "sounded a warning" in his coverage of Morrisseau's exhibition.[18] After a seven-paragraph discussion of Mogul art on display at the Isaacs Gallery in Toronto that month, Duval turns to Morrisseau's exhibition under the subheading "Primitive Art." He begins with a preface that smacks of the "white man's burden."[19] "The symbols of primitive art offer a refreshing finality to the modern mind faced as it is by a complex of decisions and concerns unknown in the aboriginal imagination," explains Duval. "Here and there pockets of authentic primitive art still remain. Though these are rapidly being emptied into commercial channels, the best of today's Eskimo, bushman, and American Indian art retains some evidence of tribal affiliation." Asserting that Morrisseau's art fits squarely within a "broad interpretation of primitive art," the report offers the most entrenched lesson on primitivism among the newspaper reviews that month. Providing little information about the work beyond its connections to a disappearing past, evidenced by designs that follow the patterns found in "early Ontario Indian rock paintings" and "brilliant" colours, Duval cynically ponders, "It will be interesting now to see how this educated Indian merges traditional Indian folklore with a growing personal expression. If he continues to repeat the designs of his tribal past he will be in danger of disappearing into our growing host of native souvenir makers."[20] Though Duval identifies Morrisseau's art as primitive and teetering on the boundaries of tourist art, he is the only reviewer to refer to Morrisseau as educated!

Closer to Morrisseau's home, the Port Arthur *News-Chronicle* and the Fort William *Daily Times-Journal* announced Morrisseau's upcoming exhibition in August and promoted the artist as a local success story and a historian of Ojibwe legends. The local papers viewed his success as an opportunity to spotlight the region surrounding Beardmore and all of northwestern Ontario. With three large photographs of Morrisseau and his art works that stretched the width of the front page and the banner headline "Ojibway Painter Recording Area's Early Legends," the paper enthusiastically promoted Morrisseau as a local who had made it in the big city.[21] The *Daily Times-Journal* reported on 5 September that his work was "decorative" and "an expression of what is still an almost totally primitive people."[22] The Fort William paper followed up with another story on 14 September to promote Morrisseau's successful debut exhibition, confirming that "their" local artist was considered "genius" by Toronto gallery owner Jack Pollock and adding that "Indian art expert" Selwyn Dewdney was "immensely impressed."[23] The report focuses on the mentorship of Weinstein and Dewdney as key to Morrisseau's success. Local readers knew of Dewdney because earlier in 1962 the rival local paper, the Port Arthur *News-Chronicle*, reported that the anthropologist had published a book about regional rock art sites and acknowledged the help of "one of our own Indian citizens," known as Ojibwe "chief" Jack Bushy.[24] In October the *Daily Press*, published in Timmins, Ontario, eight hours northeast of Port Arthur, printed an enthusiastic editorial about Morrisseau's overnight success under a headline, "The North Is Proud."[25] The editorial describes Morrisseau as "a North country Ojibway Indian gold miner" who "in the face of what would be considered to be insurmountable obstacles," has made this region proud. Explaining that Morrisseau, "completely untrained in the arts but consumed with a love for painting," has reacted modestly to recent descriptions of him as a "genius," the article quotes the artist admitting, "I never build up hopes."[26] The exuberant story adds that the artist won't need to hope because "The North country will do that for him" closing with, "The North country wishes Norval Morrisseau all the best."[27]

Boosterism was key to local news coverage—a hallmark of small market papers. No large dailies characterized Morrisseau as "one of the hottest prospects in the art world today."[28] This promotional news thread was a welcome antidote and served to satisfy local readers hoping for positive stories about their region. Another story found in the *News-Chronicle* reported on the reenactment of a "historical" scene by 240 local children, in which "hip swiveling 'medicine men' led a solemn procession" and totem poles and teepees added an "exciting and authentic flavor of Indian folklore."[29]

Each of these early media stories related to Morrisseau's entry into the mainstream art world found ways to connect Morrisseau and his art to the disappearing past. Several reporters reinforced Morrisseau's reliance on white males to manage his career. While authenticity and stereotypical tropes confine the artist to a narrowly defined racial identity, few of the reports accord his art such confining bounds. While mostly understood as primitive in some fashion, the artist's work was also understood as something unique and worth consideration beyond the usual framing of ethnographic art.

A *Weekend Magazine* insert that circulated nationally in Saturday edition newspapers across Canada included a two-page feature on Morrisseau by Bill Brown in November 1962.[30] "Copper Thunderbird: An Ojibway Who Paints His People's Past" is a lengthy story that explores Morrisseau's art and identity in greater depth than any other earlier media coverage. Brown begins to formulate what would become the basic elements of the myth of Morrisseau. Referring to the artist's signature in "hieroglyphic-like" syllabics, an alphabet designed by Protestant church minister and missionary James Evans in 1840 to teach the Bible to Cree speakers, Brown links Morrisseau's signature to an imaginary and distant past. Brown explains that Morrisseau has borrowed syllabics from his Cree wife because the Ojibwe have "no written language of their own." Morrisseau, despite his "everyday" name, according to Brown, is *authentic* because he "moves and speaks with the traditional dignity of the Indian."[31] So begins the national feature story that has less to do with Morrisseau and his work than with a reinforcement of essentialized constructions of "Indian."

Brown conveniently shapes Morrisseau's importance for the audience for the nation with this article. A large reproduction of the painting *Indian in Heaven* is printed above the text, described in the cut line, "Picasso quality is apparent in Thunderbird's idea of how an Indian will look and dress in Heaven."[32] Referring to the artist as "Thunderbird," a shortened version of the anglicized version of the Cree syllabic formulation of Morrisseau's "Indian name," Brown offers the artist high praise by comparing his work to Picasso's cubist art. As noted earlier, this appears to have been the first moment that Morrisseau and Picasso were publically aligned artistically, and since then, Morrisseau has often been referred to as the "Picasso of the North."

Well versed in stereotypical tropes, Brown also intimates that Morrisseau is better suited to the wilderness, explaining that he is uncomfortable in the city and has no plans for the future—unlike mainstream Canadians who more sensibly plan almost exclusively for the future. The reporter offers an example of Morrisseau's character by explaining that when one woman asked the artist numerous questions about his work, the artist confided to Brown, "I got confused. I wanted to say 'Woman, shut up!'"[33] This anecdote could be read in a number of ways, but including it in this feature article suggests a clinical objectivity similar to that advanced in the 1970s NFB documentaries discussed in Chapter 1. In this case, Brown subtly refers to a lack of social refinement.

Morrisseau "moves and speaks with the traditional dignity of the Indian," says Brown in an effort to reinforce the stoicism of the imaginary Noble Savage, and the reporter adds that he asked Morrisseau if he was excited about his sold-out show at the Pollock Gallery, "since no one could tell." Morrisseau belies the innocent, naive construction hailed in press reports to date by candidly responding to Brown with humour and a keen awareness of the confining frame accorded him in Canadian popular culture. Morrisseau proclaims, "I'm an Indian, I'm not supposed to show any emotion."[34] This cheeky comment dismantles the press's framing of his naïveté. Morrisseau's retort demands a rethinking of the nascent mythmaking underway in the media.

Morrisseau's Main Men

Men such as Pollock, Weinstein, Grosart, and Dewdney loom large in news reports of Morrisseau's debut. Pollock's importance, of course, is clear and necessary to the artist's exhibition, yet his characterization as a discoverer fascinates readers and critics alike, who link his role to that of saviour. Constant references to Morrisseau's male discoverers amount to ongoing examples of the "white man's burden" in popular culture and fit neatly into a colonial discourse of claiming. Albeit altruistic, the intercessions of modern-day saviours complicate Morrisseau's artistic prowess. Morrisseau's personal success is diminished as the efforts of these men are celebrated. Interestingly, one other character pivotal to the artist's early success is not mentioned in these news reports—not even in her local Port Arthur *News-Chronicle*. In his memoirs, Jack Pollock describes how he was introduced to Morrisseau through Susan Ross.[35] Ross, born in Port Arthur, was a trained artist and member of the Port Arthur art club, the wife of a Port Arthur lawyer and judge, and later an Order of Canada award winner who was keenly interested in Indigenous peoples and issues and travelled the area sketching. She knew Morrisseau well in the late 1950s and early 1960s, and Morrisseau had encouraged her to do portrait studies in the Gull Bay area on the northern shore of Lake Nipigon. She and Morrisseau had an ongoing relationship that included discussions of art, she aided him in selling work in Thunder Bay, and their correspondence clearly demonstrates a mutually respectful relationship.[36] The salutation in a September 1964 letter, for example, expresses their easy friendship, as Morrisseau writes: "Dear Sue, the second Indian Artist of the District of Thunder Bay."[37] I find it surprising that no paper, not even the local Port Arthur rags, mentioned this local woman's significance to Morrisseau's artistic success. That said, Ross signed her work S.A. Ross because she felt she was not taken seriously artistically as a female in the early 1960s; this might simply be an example of systemic sexism in Canada.

Media interest in Morrisseau's debut exhibition launched him, from the beginning, into a soup of stereotypical signifiers that were neither clear-cut nor consistent. Race first, art second. One telling example can be found in the *Montreal Gazette*. In 1963, *Gazette* reporter Dorothy Pfeiffer lumped Morrisseau together with artist Emily Carr and anthropologist Marius Barbeau as figures whose legacy would be to provide Canada with more of an understanding of the "Redman's ways." Pfeiffer describes Carr as an artist who "opened certain windows of comprehension by her magnificent paintings of West Coast Haida Indian villages," for example. Barbeau's "engrossing" books "taught us more of the marvellously imaginative rituals of our authentic 'First Canadians.'"[38] Morrisseau, according to Pfeiffer, serves as an "untutored" but important "link" and she notes that his "discoverer," Dewdney, was an authority on Stone Age art in Canada, thus emphasizing Morrisseau's seemingly close alignment with a primitive way of life rather than with contemporary Canadian culture. This description posits Morrisseau as a Canadian Ishi. Ishi, or "man" in the Yana language, was the last of the Yahi Indians found in California in 1911 by anthropologist Alfred Kroeber. Kroeber gave him the name Ishi and relocated him to the museum of natural history at the University of California, Berkeley, where he resided until he died.[39] Indeed, some of Pfeiffer's reportage reads more like an anthropology lesson than a fine arts discussion typical of the arts page of the newspaper. Terms such as "untutored," "link," and "discoverer" indicate strong ethnographic ties and draw direct connections to primitive peoples. Though the reporter agrees that Morrisseau "is an exceptionally articulate artist," despite the fact that he has "very little formal schooling," she positions Morrisseau's art as "stylized semi-abstractions" and expressions of mysticism of "the Indian's culture," creating a monolithic construction where Morrisseau's art represents the spiritual symbolism of all Indigenous peoples in Canada.[40] Once again, race first and art second.

A similar ethnographic lens was trained on Morrisseau in an essay published in *Canadian Art* in 1964, written by Joy Carroll and titled "The Strange Success—and Failure of Norval Morrisseau." The article concerns the October 1963 follow-up exhibition to the artist's successful premiere, and Carroll asks why the second show mounted by Pollock was unsuccessful, with only two works sold. Carroll posits: "When his first exhibition of paintings sold out immediately it seemed that his name did have magic qualities; an Indian had triumphed in a whiteman's domain. Like one of the complicated legends Morrisseau paints, his own story has drama, excitement and pathos. Unlike the legends, the ending is still in doubt."[41] Carroll sketches a mythical narrative in which Morrisseau, unprepared for success in 1962, spent money frivolously and then three weeks later "disappeared back to Beardmore with what was left of his money," where he remained uncommunicative. Quoting Pollock, who like Crawford in the *London Free Press* two years prior had stated that Morrisseau's racial identity would cause him grief, Carroll formulates her case: "Morrisseau, of course, has many problems." Pollock points out,

"He's a mixture of two cultures. He is a mystic. This shows in his work."[42] Carroll agrees with Pollock and claims that "the seeds of some of his deep personal problems could be detected" in the television interview he did with CBC's network show *Close-up* in 1962, during his first exhibition.[43] She never defines the so-called problems beyond the fact that Morrisseau had told the interviewer, "But I don't really practice Christian faith or Indian faith," leaving readers to assume Morrisseau suffered from either a religious or racial identity crisis.

One of the elements at issue for better understanding the artist was whether Morrisseau was or was not a shaman. This information was pertinent to a stereotypical conception of the Noble Savage. Significantly, Crawford cites once again the 1962 CBC interview in her search for answers. Carroll remembers that "he became almost inarticulate and withdrawn. He would not say he actually *was* a medicine man, only that he *might* be."[44] This is an important point, because Morrisseau would shift his perspective on being a shaman by the 1970s. His reticence to performatively declare himself a medicine man in 1962 is all the more noteworthy given what occurs in the 1970s.

Carroll's essay, although included in an art magazine rather than a general-audience newspaper, devotes little space to Morrisseau's art. The large cropped photograph of Morrisseau, his wife Harriet, their young daughter Victoria, and baby Eugene, displayed in his beautifully beaded *tikanagan*, offers little evidence that the tall man in a buckskin jacket is an artist. For a reader unfamiliar with Morrisseau's art—and in 1964 that would have included most readers of the magazine—the essay would do little to promote or position his work within a larger Canadian art discourse. Two small images of Morrisseau's work, *Loon* and *Bird with Power*, are shown on the following two pages, but they are not discussed in the article. Like other news reports, the *Canadian Art* feature finds Morrisseau's racial identity more compelling than his art.

The essay shifts in focus from a description of the success and failure of the first and second shows held at the Pollock Gallery to describing an impromptu exhibition at the gallery that was hurriedly organized when Morrisseau unexpectedly arrived in Toronto with his family at a later date. Carroll describes her encounter with Morrisseau that day: "With him were his Cree wife Harriet ('I think she is Ojibway,' Morrisseau says, 'but I read in the paper she is Cree so I guess she might as well stay Cree'), a three-year-old daughter, Victoria, and a two-month-old son strapped to his back in a *tikanagan*, or carrier. This group deposited itself for interview purposes in the somewhat sophisticated surroundings of the Pollock Gallery, looking

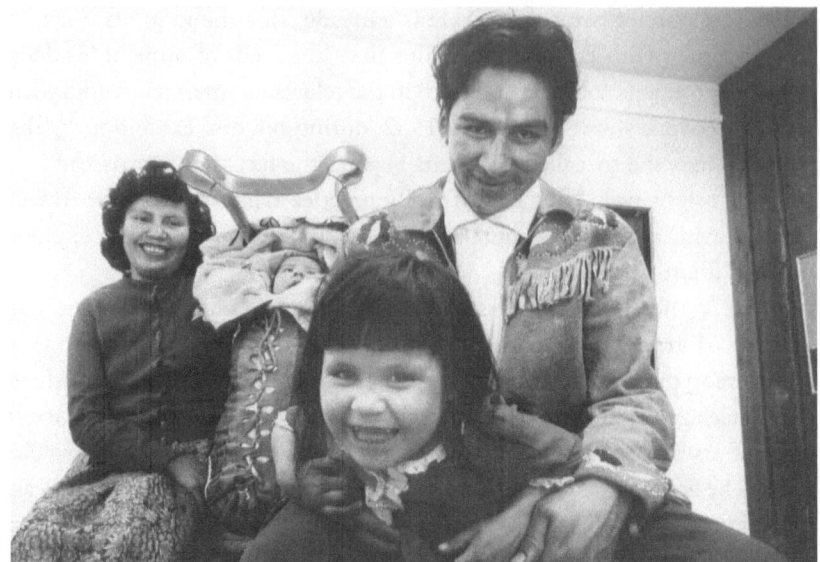

This family photograph of Norval Morrisseau, his wife Harriet, daughter Victoria, and baby son Eugene was one of a series of shots taken at the Pollock Gallery in October 1963 and printed in the *Globe and Mail* on 21 March 1964 and again on 27 January 1965. A more formal pose was chosen from this photo series to accompany Joy Carroll's *Canadian Art* feature in 1964. Reproduced with permission of CP photo archives.

much like fauna from another planet."[45] The description of Morrisseau and his family as "fauna from another planet" reinforces the ethnographic gaze of the Other conveyed by the magazine issue. The large family photograph, devoid of a background setting, underscores the notion of Morrisseau and his family as aliens. They appear on the pages of *Canadian Art* as if from another space and time, for the consumption of the Toronto art scene. Carroll notes that the crowd that Sunday in March 1964 was motivated to buy the Morrisseau paintings on display. She associates the numerous sales that day with Morrisseau's presence—the interest is more in the presence of the primitive man in the Toronto gallery than in his art. The reporter reinforces his "poignant" plan of wanting to live in the city to be closer to the art scene, leaving behind the "northland," but she is unconvinced of its success since "he will have to adjust to city life."[46]

The *Globe and Mail* printed a photograph (reprinted above) from the same photo shoot used in the *Canadian Art* feature in two separate stories, published in 1964 and 1965. In a flattering essay about his 1964 exhibition that focuses on the metaphysics of art, a clearly impressed Pearl McCarthy argues that "Indian thought can be used in fine art," explaining that Morrisseau has "high intelligence within the framework of Indian metaphysics."[47] Unlike earlier reports, this story focuses on serious ways in which Morrisseau's art fits within a larger discourse of art. The focus on shamanism that Carroll promoted was not present in this article. The following January, in a report by Kay Kritzwiser, the *Globe and Mail* used Morrisseau's family photograph again in an article that focused on Morrisseau's exhibition at Hart House Gallery at University of Toronto. Kritzwiser describes the art of the "tall, dark artist" as having received an "unequivocal seal of approval" from anthropologist Marius Barbeau. She says little about the art except to note that Morrisseau "leans heavily to the four colours sacred to the Indian" and then describes the elaborately beaded coat the artist was wearing. Already a showman, Morrisseau is quoted as saying, "I shut my eyes and think what I would wear 300 years ago and this is what came to me."[48] However, the article does describe how a group of concerned citizens, including Senator Grosart, have formed a trusteeship to benefit Morrisseau and his family.

In 1965, activist Kahn-Tineta Horn used a painting by Morrisseau to promote self-government for Indigenous peoples in a *Globe and Mail* report. Below a photograph in which she poses before one of the artist's paintings, Horn, who spoke at the Hart House Gallery at University of Toronto, explains that the United Nations modelled itself after the Iroquois confederacy and that the arts of her ancestors were "related to politics and warfare."[49]

In 1966, a *Montreal Gazette* news story reconsidered Morrisseau's opening exhibition in 1962, stating, "Some of the more cautious critics and scholars have puzzled about the art of Norval Morrisseau ever since."[50] Describing a 1965 exhibition of Morrisseau's work at Galerie Cartier in Montreal, the report, supporting earlier descriptions, views the work as a "valuable ethnological document" as it explains to readers, "It is a late gift and an unexpected privilege to be thus permitted to share in a fading culture's last secrets, to learn of a forgotten people's rites and dreams, born from fear of the unknown, and form the hope of escape from its penetrating presence." The reporter exclaims, "After seeing this exhibition, our feelings for the Red Man will never be the same."[51]

The exhibition at the Galerie Cartier consisted of pieces of Inuit art and works by Morrisseau that travelled after its Montreal showing to cities such as Newport, Rhode Island, in 1968 and St. Paul de Vence, France, in 1969. Dr. Herbert Schwarz wrote an essay to accompany the works as part of a small exhibition catalogue that otherwise consisted of a price list and images of Morrisseau's art. In his essay, Schwarz describes Morrisseau as having emerged "quite incredibly" from "amongst these wordless and defeated people," and characterizes the artist as an "extraordinary phenomenon in the history of Canadian art."[52] Schwarz, like others writing about Morrisseau's art at the time, relies on a variety of derogatory stereotypes with which to sensationalize Morrisseau's success.

Morrisseau, in an effort to make his art more accessible to audiences, had done something out of character for someone from a so-called wordless people. He wrote a book. With the aid of Selwyn Dewdney, Morrisseau published a collection of personal stories he had collected related to Anishinaabe mythology. *Legends of My People: The Great Ojibway* (1965), written in a first-person narrative and organized thematically into stories with illustrations, was edited by Dewdney to better help audiences relate to Morrisseau's work. In the preface, Dewdney explains that the book is based on two manuscripts he received from Morrisseau, the first in 1960, shortly after meeting him, and the second in 1962. Dewdney describes their first meeting in Cochenour, a gold-mining community in northwestern Ontario, calling Morrisseau a "tall spare figure," with "strong elegant hands" and a "sensitive brooding face."[53] "I have a power within me," Morrisseau told Dewdney, who writes that Morrisseau stated this "with factual dignity."[54] Morrisseau's unselfish educative ambition was to disseminate Anishinaabe stories and images more widely, in order to foster greater cultural understanding in Canada, says Dewdney. Unlike the 1960s media stories that inserted Morrisseau into a confining stereotypical frame, relegating him to a collection of descriptors such as primitive, naive, childlike, uneducated, uncivilized and at times untrustworthy, Dewdney's description is frank and honest, though somewhat romantic. In his effort to capture for readers the stark reality of Morrisseau's life as a Native man living in Canada in the 1960s, Dewdney satirically adds: "In his twenties he became an authority, by empirical research, on malnutrition and chronic unemployment, and gained some insight into pulmonary infections during a year in the tuberculosis sanitarium in Fort William. Of this decade he writes, *Lets leave it void—too much Involved.*"[55] Dewdney's characterization of Morrisseau has little connection to the mostly wooden character projected in news footage between 1962 and 1965. Representing Morrisseau as a man rather than as an imaginary construction, Dewdney seizes the opportunity to undo the racial tropes assigned to Morrisseau and Indigenous peoples in Canadian culture:

> It will be all too easy for some to bring to this book the posture of amused condescension that we of the Anglo-Saxon tradition too easily assume. Too often, I suspect, a real contempt lurks

behind the mask of our self-advertised tolerance. Such will see no more here than a collection of superstitious rubbish. At the other extreme, I am reminded of the sentimental books of Grey Owl without an inkling that the emerging image of a "noble red man" was their own wishful projections, shared and exploited by one of themselves, who as an English lad called Archie Belaney dreamed of being an "Indian."[56]

Dewdney boldly positions the racist leanings of Canadians as bifurcated between utter dismissal and erasure, or romantic blindness associated with the colonized Other. Using Grey Owl as evidence of the nation's preference for the faux Indian, trained in the British school system, over the voices and writings of actual Indigenous writers such as Morrisseau, a product of Canadian colonialism and the Indian residential school system, Dewdney admits his personal frustration over the ongoing dismissal of authentic Indigenous efforts in favour of romantic but imaginary expressions. Unlike Grey Owl's writings—internationally successful, widely read, and still in print today, sixty years later—Dewdney's pointed words, buried in the preface of *Legends of My People*, reached a limited audience and the text is difficult to acquire today. The *Ottawa Citizen* favourably reviewed Morrisseau's 1965 *Legends of My People* in August of that year under the title, "Proud Indian," prefaced by an unrelated comment that "Canada's native Indians are on the warpath these days" demanding treaty rights.[57]

Letters written between Dewdney and Morrisseau, beginning in 1960 and held in the archives of the Indian Art Centre of the Department of Indigenous Affairs and Northern Development, attest to the close relationship between the two men and further elucidate Morrisseau's aims to didactically assist viewers and Canadians interested in Anishinaabe culture. Dewdney and Morrisseau first met through Constable Ron Sheppard of the Ontario Provincial Police, who wrote to Dewdney and suggested he would like to meet Morrisseau.[58] Barry Ace, who has studied the correspondence in great detail, believes that Dewdney may have originally thought of Morrisseau as simply an informant but after meeting the artist, their relationship quickly blossomed into a friendship.[59] Joy Carroll, too, in her 1964 *Canadian Art* essay, acknowledges Morrisseau's interest in explaining the meaning of the oral stories on which his work is based. She says he "painstakingly" attempted to place his work in the context of the oral narratives he had been told.[60] In a letter sent to Dewdney from Morrisseau in January 1962, for example, nine months prior to his 1962 opening exhibition at the Pollock Gallery in Toronto, Morrisseau expresses his aims: "[I] want to built that solid foundation here at this studio. I want to break the barrier between the white worald [*sic*] and mine's [gold mine in Cochenour, ON]. I am sure and firmbly [*sic*] believe a lot of my people will take this example I will make."[61] At different points Morrisseau addressed his letters Dear Selwyn or Dear Mr. Dewdney, but in all the correspondence there is an implicit sense of trust and respect between the mentor and artist. In a January 1964 letter, Morrisseau shares the good news that he sold eleven paintings to the Glenbow Museum in Calgary, Alberta, which allowed him to move to and furnish a better house with rent paid four months in advance, and to buy art supplies. He amusingly relates that the purchase of a television "is very good for all of us here at the Copper Thunderbird's dwelling."[62] Morrisseau also outlines a new agreement that will protect his artistic business and explains that he has reinstated Pollock as his art dealer, demonstrating his concern with the business side of the art world. As Morrisseau sketched the terms of this agreement, Dewdney's valued opinion on the topic would further protect the artist. These policies included a more complete record-keeping system of all paintings shipped to Pollock, and a trust fund comprising sales profits set up for the artist. He confides that a $150.00/month allowance would ensure a steady source of funds. In the letter, Morrisseau seeks Dewdney's guidance and approval of this legal agreement: "I hope you agree with my arrangements." The artist then outlines his ongoing efforts to increase his artistic knowledge, explaining to Dewdney that he plans to purchase "all kinds of books and … records for all music that will be helpful to further my knowlegde [*sic*]."[63] In addition to discussions of his professional practice, Morrisseau shares personal family news regarding the birth of his son Eugene. Morrisseau also conveys, with pride, his family's new and more comfortable living arrangements—so as to more aptly reflect his status as a "famouse [*sic*] artist."[64] Morrisseau self-reflectively admits to personal problems regarding his alcohol consumption and writes honestly about his attempts to maintain sobriety. His correspondence with Dewdney demonstrates the artist's intentions in all aspects of his life. Unlike the news reports that imagine Morrisseau stepping naively out of Canada's wilderness and into a gallery, the artist clearly worked assiduously to improve his artistic sensibility and personal well-being, unsettling the myth that was taking form.

The personal style with which Morrisseau wrote in *Legends of My People* not only provides insights into Anishinaabe culture, but also demonstrates his character. Morrisseau shares personal reminiscences and stories about Ojibwe cultural beliefs and practices in the Lake Nipigon area. The stories, punctuated by line drawings, reveal the artist's sense of humour and level of understanding of Anishinaabe spiritual practices within the Medewiwin lodge. Most Canadians had long considered Indigenous myths as amusing stories about colourful creatures. Morrisseau understood this Eurocentric bias and attempted to reposition the narratives and also his art by publishing this book. Like his personal correspondence with Dewdney, the text demonstrates Morrisseau's wish to more effectively educate the Canadian population. *Legends of My People* offered readers an understanding of Morrisseau's visual narratives.

The press of the day preferred to fixate on race through an ethnographic discourse. Today, it does not seem surprising that such language of ethnography and primitivism was employed to situate Morrisseau in 1960s Canada. Similar language and signifiers remained commonplace in discussions about Indigenous peoples and events. In 1964 the *Globe and Mail* reported plans for a new art centre for Six Nations reserve with a focus on Tom Hill, who later becomes an important artist, curator, and advocate for the arts, including Morrisseau's art. Reporting on an art exhibit that coincided with the announcement of the planned art centre, the article notes that "many showed great surprise by the quality of the artists." Describing how most of the paintings depicted "early Indian Legends," the report notes that the "younger set" have painted "modern Indian heroes like Jim Thorpe and Richard Burton." A twenty-one-year-old Tom Hill stands out because he has begun training to be an artist at Toronto's Royal College of Art. The story praises Hill for using a Eurocentric impressionist style to present a "legend that dates back before the coming of the white man." "Prophecy of Chaos predicted by the old squaw who had visited the gods and destroyed the snakes … and then returned to her tribe."[65] The report describes Hill among artists such as Daphne Odjig and Carl Ray, whose art gained further attention during the later 1960s in news stories that employed similar tropes.

A 1968 article featuring Odjig's exhibition sponsored by the Manitoba Indian Brotherhood, for example, was the subject of *Winnipeg Free Press* art critic John Graham's first review of her work. Dismissive of a number of her pieces, in part because Odjig "lacks formal training," he found promise in her "inventive use of images, pattern and spaces."[66] Graham explains: "While the art of the Coast Indians of British Columbia is well-known and recognized, and much attention has been focused on the carvings and prints of the Eskimos of the northern settlement, there has been little significant parallel development in this region, where the traditional society was by nature nomadic … While there may be little of cultural heritage in visual terms of painting for her to build on, there is a rich and potent background of folk tales and legends from which she has built her images and style."[67] Graham acknowledges a hierarchy that had been long established by anthropologists with regard to Indigenous arts in Canada. Odjig's art, like Morrisseau's, formulates a visual narrative that offered her the opportunity to create an individual artistic vocabulary.

The *Free Press* also positioned two other of Morrisseau's artistic compatriots within a similar ethnographic frame in 1968, when J.R. Stevens wrote about the then twenty-five-year-old Carl Ray, whose work was proposed for an exhibition at Brandon University "along with paintings of primitive Indian painter Jackson Beardy."[68] Primitivist language was not limited to describing artists, of course. In coverage of the 1969 White Paper controversy, a political story closely followed by Canadian newspapers, similar tropes were employed to describe Cree lawyer and activist Harold Cardinal. Terms such as "militant" and "violent" were commonly used to describe him in news reports at the close of the decade.[69]

Shaman Yet to Come

Morrisseau remains closely aligned with shamanism for anyone today who knows his art. In 2006 Greg Hill titled Morrisseau's retrospective exhibition *Norval Morrisseau Shaman Artist*. From the 1970s onward, associations between Morrisseau and a shaman identity were forged—both in the press and by the artist himself. Performative gestures by Morrisseau that reinforced a shaman identity became increasingly common in the 1970s. This was not the case in the 1960s, however.

Since his debut in 1962, Morrisseau had been described as a translator of Indian spirituality, and the press pushed to associate him with shamanism. He clearly stood in for all Indians for the purpose of press reportage and in that way, the trope of the shaman or medicine man was often introduced by interviewers. Joy Carroll's 1964 *Canadian Art* essay illustrates such an effort to pointedly draw out from Morrisseau whether or not he was a medicine man. She intimates that in earlier media interviews in 1962, he was evasive about the subject: "He would not say he actually *was* a medicine man, only that he *might* be."[70] The emphasis placed on "was" and "might" reinforces the author's belief that Morrisseau was a shaman—he had to be, didn't he? It was part of the package.

Little interest in his particular First Nation affiliation or cultural background was pursued in press coverage in the 1960s. Morrisseau himself exerted his identity as Ojibwe, more commonly know today as Anishinaabe, but that was not always taken up. Instead, the stereotypical frame more naturally confined Morrisseau as Noble Savage. News coverage anointed him as being one with nature, stoic, naive, and mixed these signifiers continually to find ways to apply them to their referent. For the press, Morrisseau represented all Indians—Imaginary Indians—devised by popular cultural constructions. All questions, all discussion was framed around this lens.

In his book, Morrisseau describes a number of events in which medicine men and women use spiritual power for healing. He even tells a story of his encounter with a local medicine woman who challenged Morrisseau by asking why he has such a "strong name," saying, "I am powerful, too. Also I have known the thunderbirds. Let us try our sorcery to see who is the stronger." Morrisseau responds: "Look, lady, whoever you are or feel you are. Drunk, you may feel like a demi-goddess. Listen to what I have to tell you. Know that I don't fear you, for you are not God. Only God know what death or sickness will fall upon me, not you who are full of pride, yet lowly. You are an old lady who should be advanced in wisdom. Compared with you I am young, like a son who knows nothing … All you do is put fear into Indians through sorcery."[71] Morrisseau persuades the woman of his knowledge, and she responds, "Indeed, you are a man with great knowledge of the ways of our ancestors."[72] While Morrisseau uses this anecdote to demonstrate his level of understanding of Anishninaabe culture, and throughout the book describes ceremonies and events to articulate a level of knowledge commensurate with someone who had been given sacred knowledge, he does not profess to be a shaman. Yet within the next decade, Morrisseau would remake himself, claiming and performing the role of shaman.

Performing Agency

Expo 67, held in Montreal, Quebec, as part of Canada's 100th birthday celebrations, included the Indians of Canada Pavilion, which is viewed today as a pivotal moment for both Indigenous politics and Indigenous contemporary art. Morrisseau took part in planning and implementing the art project for the pavilion. Through his performative gestures he exerted an agency that demonstrates how, in just five years, he had become a leading figure in contemporary Canadian art.

In advance of Expo 67, a diverse group of contemporary Indigenous artists from across Canada were invited to Ottawa to discuss plans for creating art for the Indians of Canada Pavilion. A *Winnipeg Free Press* report situates Morrisseau at the centre of a story about the invited group brought to Ottawa as part of the planning activity.[73] While the report notes the three Winnipeg artists among the eleven invited to attend (Ross Woods, Noel Wuttunee, and

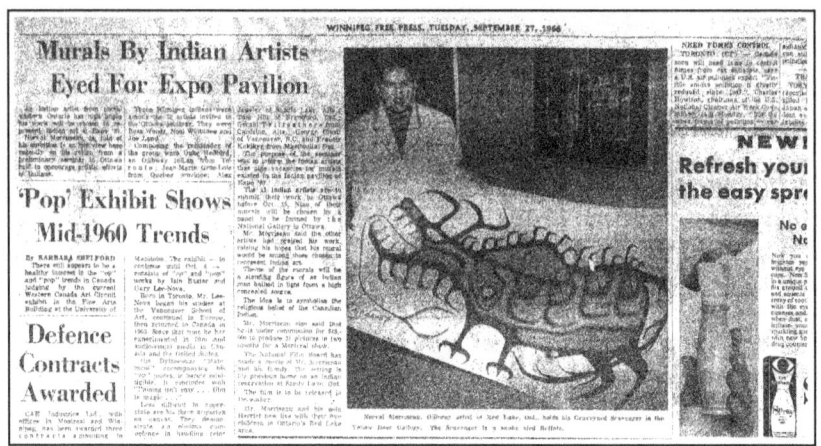

This photograph of Morrisseau with his *Graveyard Scavenger* (1966) accompanied a news story related to an upcoming preliminary meeting in Ottawa to discuss artworks for Expo 67, "Murals by Indian Artists Eyed for Expo Pavilion," *Winnipeg Free Press*, 27 September 1966. *Graveyard Scavenger* (1966) is currently part of the University of Regina Art Collection, Regina, Saskatchewan. Reproduced with permission of *Winnipeg Free Press* archives.

Joe Land), it is Morrisseau who drives the narrative. The *Free Press* includes a photograph of the artist with one of his paintings and quotes him directly, confirming that his work will be included in the art program. The report, in an effort to demonstrate Morrisseau's success, mentions a $15,000 commission for two gallery shows in Montreal. The artist assuredly steps into the spotlight afforded him by the *Free Press*.

Ruth B. Phillips and Sherry Brydon agree that the Indians of Canada Pavilion was pivotally important to the history of contemporary Canadian Indigenous art, noting that "in the years since Expo 67 many Indigenous people who worked on the pavilion have identified the experience as a formative moment in the development of an activist Indian cultural politics."[74] They explain how the political manoeuvring behind the scenes that began in the early 1960s resulted in a 1965 decision to create a discrete pavilion under the direction of an Indian Advisory Council (IAC), which the federal Department of Indian Affairs and Northern Development (DIAND) monitored closely. Given the global impact of Expo 67 and its conjunction with Canada's centennial, this new model for presenting narratives related to Canada's Indigenous past, a departure from how Indigenous peoples had been framed at prior world expositions, was a rare opportunity.

Architecturally designed to recall iconic signifiers in its tall teepee form, the six hexagonal footprints of the pavilion also included a monumental totem pole carved by Kwakwaka'wakw carvers Henry and Tony Hunt. Together with the Plains teepee form, the edifice reinforced the static and homogenous sign of the Imaginary Indian made popular in Hollywood and other popular cultural sites.[75] Still, as part of the exterior decoration of the building, contemporary Indigenous artists from across Canada were chosen to execute a series of commissioned murals, paintings, and sculptures. After the initial meetings with the eleven artists in Ottawa in 1966, three large murals were chosen for the facades. These included *West Coast* by Tseshaht artist George Clutesi, *The Land* by Anishinaabe artist Francis Kagige, and Morrisseau's *Earth Mother with Her Children*. Other artworks by Alex Janvier, Noel Wuttunee, Gerald Tailfeathers, and Ross Woods were created for the exterior. Tom Hill designed a composition that was executed by Jean-Marie Gros-Louis in ceramic. The assembled artists from Quebec westward included older artists like Clutesi, Henry Hunt, Kagige, and Tailfeathers who had long worked under the confining rules of the Indian Act.

The inclusion of this diverse group of contemporary artists from different parts of Canada illustrates a positive step forward for contemporary Indigenous arts. However, it also created tension because of the government's intent to monitor the content for the pavilion. Phillips and Brydon explain, for example, that the artists' contracts, written from a paternalistic DIAND perspective, "provided for an unusual level of surveillance."[76]

Invited to take part in the Ottawa discussions as reported in the 1966 *Free Press* article, Morrisseau submitted maquettes for two murals, one interior and one for the exterior walls of the teepee-shaped edifice. In 1979 Tom Hill recalled details of the meeting in Ottawa to discuss the pavilion: "Morrisseau entered the room, humbly taking his seat at the conference table with a faint smell of alcohol on his breath."[77] Hill recalled that Morrisseau "accused the coordinator of trying to tell him what to paint. 'When I paint,' he said to his hushed audience, 'it is as if a force inside of me starts pouring out.'"[78] Greg Hill adds that Morrisseau's exterior mural was changed because the original drawing depicted both a bear and a human child "suckling the Earth Mother" and was sanitized so that the bear and child were no longing nursing, censored to "better reflect the social attitudes of the time."[79] Morrisseau was not alone in being censored in the project. Alex Janvier's mural was relocated to the rear of the building because he added his treaty number to his signature.[80] Janvier later admitted in a 1988 *Edmonton Journal* interview that "when the government asked the artists to paint a positive, cheery picture, he and the other artists bristled. 'How come our people are dying in the jails and rotting in the mental hospitals and there we're going to tell the world we're doing great?' they asked. 'Let's tell it as it is.'"[81] The project was close to falling apart but senior artist George Clutesi kept things moving forward, according to Tom Hill, when many of the frustrated artists wanted to quit.[82]

Morrisseau's negative reaction to the government's meddling with his art and its dictated deadlines resulted in an agential decision. Leaving the project in the hands of his assistant Carl Ray to complete, Morrisseau exerted his autonomy without fully deserting the Indians of Canada Pavilion. The 1966 *Free Press* news story does not draw upon the mythological construction of the artist. However, in Tom Hill's 1979 recollection of the Expo commission he references the binary of Morrisseau's drunken behaviour and his mysticism, noting that during the lead-up to the opening of Expo, Morrisseau would "slip away for days at a time to indulge in a series of alcoholic binges." In the same passage he also describes how Morrisseau was "emerging as the spiritual mentor, totally possessed by the forces that create his art."[83] Morrisseau's decision conforms to neither representation but demonstrates his determined nature.

The Toronto *Globe and Mail* published news reports and editorials concerning the Indians of Canada Pavilion. A 1966 story explains, "Canadian Indians will have their own 100-foot-high, $1,000,000 teepee at Expo 67." Noting that the project design "evolved at a conference of Indian artists and [was] modified to accommodate the wishes of Indians across Canada," there is no mention of particular artists in the article, which does however highlight that the most important feature of the pavilion will be its landscaping: "The teepee is to rest by a small lake surrounded by rugged natural landscape."[84]

Even though Morrisseau's pavilion murals were censored so as not to offend visitors, the interior messages found in the pavilion were provocative and raised the ire of some. Three stories published by the *Globe and Mail* during Expo demonstrate the pavilion's success in largely staying on message. "Canada's Indians have used $500,000 of federal money to build an Expo 67 pavilion showing the world how poor a deal the white man has given his native brother," one article states, characterizing the pavilion as a "monument to Indian disillusionment."[85] A pointed article written by Leslie Millin makes only one reference to the art, noting the "magnificent Kwakiutl totem pole from the west coast, carved by Henry and Tony Hunt, a father and son carving team." However, Millin concludes by noting that a symbolic fire "asks the question of the future of Canada's Indians. Significantly, the question is not answered."[86] The following month the *Globe and Mail* added that the Indians of Canada Pavilion, reported to have cost $400,000, offered "a fascinating collection of ancient ceremonial masks" while confronting viewers with messages that left some "non-Indian visitors with little to be proud of. 'This is horrible. I'm not going to stay here,' one Montreal woman told fellow visitors yesterday as she came face to face with a large panel reading 'The white man's school is an alien land for the Indian child.'"[87] The *Globe and Mail* followed up with an editorial that agreed with the pavilion's presentation of reality. "Visitors in the Canadian Indian pavilion at Expo are not elated at what they see. Indeed, some of them leave … depressed, though all that the Indians have done is describe with photographs and statistics the story of their progress since Confederation."[88] Admitting that most Canadians have been "insulated by distance and disinterested from the reality of Indian life in Canada" the editorial posits that the "Indian pavilion" succeeded in delivering messages that must be confronted. The *Globe and Mail* published a second editorial that summer framed around the many ignored reports by the government on Indigenous issues, noting, "It would be more constructive and more hopeful if the thousands of white Canadians who visit the pavilion are stirred to a new appreciation of our past failures and present difficulties in meeting the needs and aspirations of our country's original inhabitants."[89] These news stories and editorials clearly speak to the significance of the Indians of Canada Pavilion and the importance of opening an honest dialogue with Canadians and the world about contemporary issues facing Indigenous peoples. Indeed, many of these same issues remain unresolved today. Morrisseau understood the significance of the Expo opportunity when he submitted his design for *Earth Mother with Her Children*, which promoted an Anishinaabe world view and a biocentrist solution for caring for our world. The censorship of the mural left him disillusioned with the entire project and taught him valuable lessons about Canadian politicians.

Having exhibited his work for only eight years, Morrisseau accomplished much in the 1960s. With a growing exhibition record, a changing artistic style, a burgeoning understanding of how to manage himself and his career in the media, Morrisseau ended the decade with an international tour mounted by Herbert Schwarz that pushed the artist into an even more public sphere.

CHAPTER THREE

1970s
The Shaman Arrives

I am tired of hearing about Norval the drunkard, Norval with the hangover, Norval in jail, Norval torn apart by his allegiance both to Christianity and to the old Indian ways ... They speak about this tortured man, Norval Morrisseau—I'm not tortured. I've had a marvelous time. When I was drinking. Now that I'm not drinking. I've had a marvelous time in my life.[1]

Norval Morrisseau, *Toronto Star,* 1975

The 1970s was a decade of change for Indigenous artists in Canada. Morrisseau had led the way into the 1960s, when only Inuit art had a presence in popular culture. Expo 67 opened doors for artists, and by the 1970s real growth and interest in Indigenous arts occurred across the nation, with Morrisseau sharing the media limelight with artists who pushed new artistic directions. The gains, however, did not mean an end to constructions of the Imaginary Indian artist in the media.

A 1970 art auction held in Toronto by Sotheby's illustrates the enduring interest in the Imaginary Indian. *Globe and Mail* art critic Kay Kritzwiser wrote in May 1970 that the top-selling piece of art was a painting by Fredrick A. Verner (1836–1928), an artist who considered Paul Kane to be his mentor. Verner's *Two Indians Hunting a Moose by Canoe,* from 1887, sold to the highest bidder for $2,500. Other canvases with images of "Indians, in camp or on the trail, proved the backbone of Canadiana offered attentive bidders," explained Kritzwiser.[2] Collectors remained eager to purchase paintings whose subjects displayed romantic attachments to an imaginary past—a time where settlers witnessed the "last of the dying breed." Today, Indigenous artists like Kent Monkman directly challenge such romantic imagery in their art, but at the time, no overt decolonizing discourse was present in the public record.

A second story found in the *Globe and Mail* in the summer of 1970 documents the public's interest in Inuit art as a romantic frozen-in-time commodity. At Expo 70 in Osaka, Japan, a purveyor of Inuit items at the "Canada Shop" had received permission from the Canadian government to reproduce an "Eskimo figure and for this he paid a small royalty." Toongak, a three-inch-high figure made of felt, was the top seller for the New Zealand shop owner. According to Zena Cherry, the reporter, an explanatory tag attached to Toongak hyped its apparent significance to buyers: "The all-sensing three-eyed interpretation of a timeless Eskimo spirit is undoubtedly a charm of immense fortune. Toongak's three eyes look to the past, the present, and the future. If treated according to his age-old status he will heap success and happiness on his owner. Toongak is a talisman of success, welfare, treasure and prosperity and will guide and protect you as long as you possess him and respect him."[3] The good-luck charm was so popular that it was selling by the thousands, claimed the report.

Rounding out coverage that summer was a story about Indigenous handicraft makers on display at Toronto's Mariposa Folk Festival. "They were silent, mostly, but soft-spoken and gentle when they did speak, this first wave of a total of 40 Indians and Eskimos who arrived in Toronto,"[4] the article states, positioning the artists as childlike and innocent, feeding established tropes. The story is organized around an interview with Alanis Obomsawin, who was performing at the festival for the third year running. A large photograph of Obomsawin with her daughter examining an "Indian headdress on display at ROM" visually speaks to the ongoing monolith of the Imaginary Indian, long portrayed in popular culture as wearing feather headdresses.

This was the climate for reporting on Morrisseau and his art at the start of the decade. Though these were artistically significant years for Morrisseau, much of the press coverage in this decade continued the uneasy juxtaposition of stereotypes with realities about his impressive creative output. Still, his artistic practice flourished as his visual language evolved. A widening range of subject matter demonstrates his sophistication. His paintings from this decade are considered some of his finest. The range of topics and the strength of his visual language reveal Morrisseau's pivotal importance as an artist. However, his behaviour, of most interest to the media, became increasingly problematic and open for discussion in newspapers and documentaries. These were volatile years for Morrisseau as he struggled with alcoholism, which whetted the media's appetite for more.

A number of themes arise in relation Morrisseau's representation in press reports and the two NFB documentary films in this pivotal decade.

Two central narratives that will be more fully explored in this chapter include Morrisseau in relation to other Indigenous artists, and Morrisseau's blossoming as a shaman artist. The media promoted an overt assimilationist discourse during the 1970s by pitting Indigenous artists against one another during the 1970s—positioning Morrisseau in relation to artists like Alex Janvier and Robert Houle, both still actively producing art today. How each fit in with Canadian culture and how closely their artwork could be interpreted within a lens of modern abstraction formed a clear narrative in the 1970s. Aesthetic judgements were linked directly to primitivism, modernism, and above all, assimilation.

The second theme that is formulated in the 1970s relates to Morrisseau's shaman persona—a key element of his mythology and his identity. Unlike in the 1960s, when the artist purposely deflected such discussions in the press, in the 1970s he deliberately shifted his tactics. Rather than dissuading interest in his personal spirituality, the promoting of his own unique brand of shamanism became a central narrative. As such, Morrisseau performatively announced himself as a shaman. A direct engagement with shamanism illustrates Morrisseau's intention to both confront and concede stereotypical constructions. By branding himself in this way, the artist took control of his public, mythical identity. Morrisseau's turn to Eckankar in 1976 further channelled his shamanistic performative gestures, creating, as with his art, a unique brand of shamanism all his own—untrammelled by Anishinaabek cultural imperatives and protocols that might be questioned within his home community.

Morrisseau's efforts to confront and reimagine his identity in the face of a media more interested in promoting an imaginary construction had limited success, as the press maintained representations of him within the confines of stereotypes. This did not stop Morrisseau from continuing to find new ways in which to assert his agency in the press. Over the course of the decade the artist exerted that agency in increasingly forceful ways in order to redirect the confining ways the press presented him and his work.

In June 1972 the *Winnipeg Free Press* summed up Morrisseau as "a 40 year old Ojibway [who] has earned acclaim throughout Canada for his paintings of Indian folklore."[5] There was nothing new about calling Morrisseau an artist who painted folklore, yet it was this one-dimensional description that Morrisseau sought to change—unconsciously and consciously. Such a trite description maintained a link between him and the frozen-in-time past, and reinforced for readers the impression that Morrisseau knew little beyond these cultural stories. A news story that outlines Morrisseau's commission

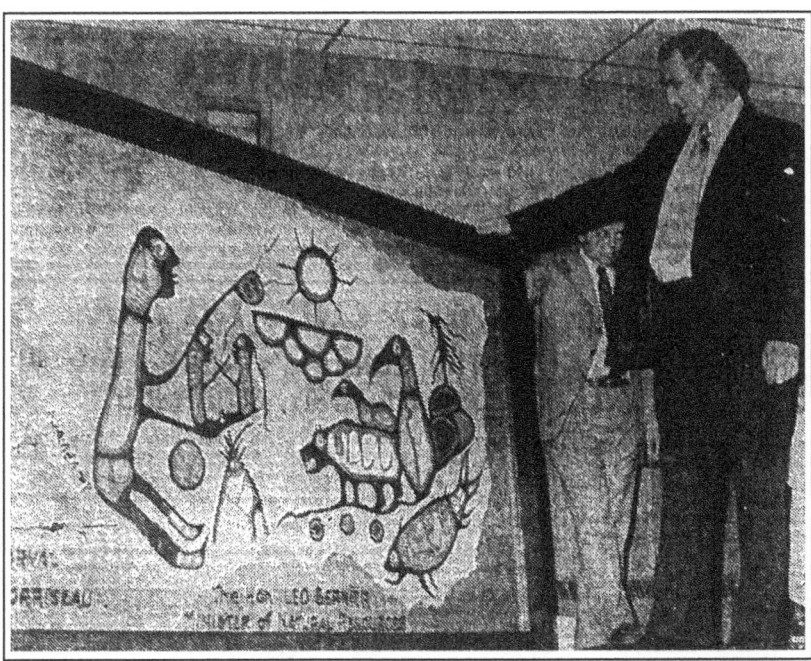

This photograph shows Ontario Resources Minister Leo Bernier accepting a painting by Norval Morrisseau that was commissioned by the Kenora, Ontario, Chamber of Commerce. The item was printed in the *Winnipeg Free Press*, 10 June 1972, though no news story accompanied the photo/description. Permission from *Winnipeg Free Press* archives.

to paint Ontario Resources Minister Leo Bernier on behalf of the Kenora, Ontario, District Chamber of Commerce offers insight into a more subversive attempt to shift romantic notions.

Morrisseau's moose hide painting does more than simply capture "Indian folklore." This work, represented in the *Free Press* in a quarter-page photograph of Bernier with the painting, reveals a veiled political pronouncement, undetected by the recipient, who appears pleased with the painting. The description below the photo explains that the minister, with "a rattle in hand," demonstrates his "power over the birds, fish, animals, rocks and trees," a gesture that parallels his political portfolio.[6] Yet a close reading of Morrisseau's visual vocabulary confirms that the artist has done more than simply venerate this public official. The visual signifiers challenge the *Free Press*'s assessment of a harmonious cultural love-in. Morrisseau manipulates this message by positioning Bernier in confrontation, separated from the animals and land, distanced and out of touch rather than connected to his political purview.

And while the paper also notes that in Bernier's palm sit "a whiteman and an Indian living in harmony," the arrogance of such a notion was not lost on Morrisseau. Satisfying the patron's wishes, Morrisseau also pushes beyond such pap in subtle ways, utilizing his visual vocabulary to offer clues that all was not as it seems. He paints dark clouds obscuring the sun from this cozy scene. Are dark clouds ever a good sign in a painting? Both the cloudy sky and a disconnection between the two sides of the composition visually and symbolically tell a story quite different from that which accompanies the photograph in the *Free Press*. The subtleties of this painting confounded the press's labelling of Morrisseau as simply a painter of legends and folklore. The Chamber of Commerce, Leo Bernier, the press, and most likely readers of the paper that day unquestioningly responded favourably to the colonial narratives imparted by the text. Yet Morrisseau visually encoded the work symbolically and compositionally to tell a different tale—one about colonialism, a Canadian brand of folklore.

Some news reports began to do more than present Morrisseau as a naive chronicler of Native legends, however. When the *Globe and Mail*'s Kay Kritzwiser reported on the "daring" curatorial decision by Jack Pollock to hang Morrisseau's "formal composition with bold colors in his new work, *Mother and Child*, opposite compositions on the square by [abstractionist] Josef Albers" she refreshingly framed Morrisseau within a mainstream art discourse, adding no racial signifiers to her description.[7] Yet, for the most part, the sorts of constructions found in media reports in the 1960s remained present, even as his art gained international attention. Some reporters seemed stuck on telling a simple tale that had little to do with art, preferring to tell and retell titillating aspects of Morrisseau's personal life while others were ready to cover Morrisseau's art.

"Proud Native Heritage" was the headline used to introduce an exhibition of Indigenous art curated from Dr. Bernard Cinader's collection at the Oakville Centennial Library. Curator Esther Demeny was motivated to create this exhibition after attending a government-sponsored Heritage seminar, where she sensed "bitterness" and "resentment" of the "Indian artists." "Of the painters," Kritzwiser explains, "Norval Morrisseau the Ojibway Indian who lives at Red Lake, has had by far the most exposure in Canada. Certainly paintings like his Warrior with Thunderbird, his Self Concept and Fish-Tailed Woman measure his inspired colour sense and identification with his heritage." The reporter leaves the last word to Dr. Cinader, who owns the work on display: "We are allowed into a world in which dream, nightmare, observation, collective memory all make their contribution to a statement which represents the rediscovery of the value of a traditional myth-enshrined view of the world and proud cry to self-identification."[8]

Toronto Star staff writer Wayne Edmonstone, under the headline "Indian Artist Clings to Legend," reported in 1972 on a ten-year retrospective exhibition of Morrisseau's work mounted at the Pollock Gallery in Toronto. Morrisseau "survived a decade of recognition by a non-Indian public from whom he is almost wholly alienated, by clinging to the mythic-mystical subjects of Indian legends, interpreting and at times involving his own persona in them," posits Edmonstone.[9] Terms such as "survived," "alienated," and "clinging" signify moribundity. Explaining that "he is almost wholly alienated" from Canadians alerts readers to Morrisseau's difference, his otherness, and his separation from mainstream Canadian society. Positioned next to a reproduction of Morrisseau's *Self-Portrait of the Artist as Christ* from 1972, where he paints himself dressed as a Medewiwin shaman but with a cross on his chest and a halo around his shaman hood, the article explains that while his artistic themes remain focused on interconnectedness, Morrisseau does not exhibit such balance. Edmonstone claims: "The confusion, mistrust and instinctive pride of an intelligent and talented man torn between two cultures (in Morrisseau's case not a cliché, but a fact) can be seen in his portraits of haughty pre-Columbian ancestors and relatives."[10] Not mentioned by the reporter but made clear to readers by the image and painting's title is Morrisseau's audacity to represent himself as Christ.

The same year, Joan Sutton, in the *Toronto Sun*, noted in her column that after recovering from a recent fire in a hotel in Vancouver, Morrisseau's life "is a triumph of talent and courage over every possible obstacle."[11] It seems the main obstacle, however, remained Morrisseau's Indigeneity. Just as London *Free Press* reporter Lenore Crawford in 1962 contended that Morrisseau's biggest task would be "to resolve the problem of being himself an Indian today,"[12] twelve years later Sutton agrees that Morrisseau's biggest hurdle remains his race. Sutton explains that much of Morrisseau's art "was inspired by his need for alcohol," though she adds that Morrisseau's current sobriety has not lessened his talents.[13] Intimating that Morrisseau's creative force was somehow connected to alcohol abuse crosses the boundaries of what should be printable. No letters to the editor followed, however, to challenge Sutton's characterization.

By August 1975, Gary Michael Dault mused in the *Toronto Star* that Morrisseau was turning into a living legend. "He's the perfect candidate for folkloredom." Morrisseau, it seems, was moving from a painter of folklore to becoming a folk hero. Dault describes the artist as a "hot property," attaining legendary status: "He's as big as Paul Bunyan, as moody as Clint Eastwood, as funny as Will Rogers, and as gentle as Uncle Remus. He also looks as potentially dangerous as Charles Bronson. He is a visionary, a mystic, a hard-headed businessman. He talks with his Shaman and he talks with Jesus. He talks with *Time* magazine and with the National Film Board."[14] After amusingly connecting the artist to a variety of popular cultural images that do little more than denigrate him, Dault explains that Morrisseau wants his art to be discussed as art—like the work of other Canadian artists. The report then includes a powerful and honest quote by Morrisseau: "I am tired of hearing about Norval the drunkard, Norval with the hangover, Norval in jail, Norval torn apart by his allegiance both to Christianity and to the old Indian ways ... They speak about this tortured man, Norval Morrisseau—I'm not tortured. I've had a marvelous time. When I was drinking. Now that I'm not drinking. I've had a marvelous time in my life."[15] Directly challenging press reports and the documentary construction of the artist in *Paradox* (and without knowing it, Dault's own list of cultural comparisons), Morrisseau demands the same treatment as other artists in Canada. Dault, who admits to Morrisseau's brilliance as an artist, cannot help but reinforce stereotypes even as he prints Morrisseau's honest plea to be taken seriously. Morrisseau demonstrates both his keen awareness of the negative constructions and also his aim to reposition his image in the press. He reiterates his position in a 1979 *Maclean's* interview with Christopher Hume, when Morrisseau muses "They speak about this tortured man, me, but I'm not. I've had a marvellous time when I was drinking and now that I'm not, a marvellous time in my life."[16] Still, most media ignored the artist's complaints.

In 1977, for example, in the *Toronto Star*, Arnie Hakala maintains a negative frame, reporting that Morrisseau "has stopped running, but as he shuffles down the dusty streets of his old hometown you can see that he'll never be able to escape his past or the sorrows of the Ojibwa nation." A frank discussion of Morrisseau's struggle with alcohol, where the reporter describes the artists as a "lanky 6-foot-3 painter with long stringy hair," ensues. The reporter notes that Morrisseau has joined a "cult that he believes is a form of soul travel." During the course of the interview, the reporter explains, Morrisseau slips into "a trance-like voice" and describes his visions: "he says he has met with Lucifer and Jesus Christ."[17] Judging by this report, the *Toronto Star* was not heeding Morrisseau's request to reporters to resist reporting on his behaviour and instead focus on discussions of his art. Happily, Morrisseau was being taken seriously as an artist in other news stories.

Morrisseau's art was promoted in a 1975 *Globe and Mail* story about a move to collect Indigenous art at the McMichael gallery in Kleinburg, Ontario. Reporter James Purdie explains that "from an invitation to a handful of these [Indigenous] artists to show their paintings at Expo '67, a whole movement has emerged. It has continued to flourish, attracting a second generation of accomplished painters like [James] Simon." Purdie offers an amusing anecdote passed on to him by Robert McMichael. When the gallery owner mentioned to the nineteen-year-old Simon that he and his wife were surprised by Morrisseau's seeming use of surrealism, McMichael asked if Salvador Dali's work had influenced Morrisseau's style. "I don't think so," Simon replied. "What reserve is he on?"[18] It is innocent enough to poke fun at Simon for not knowing his art history, but no one challenged Purdie when he conflated Alex Janvier with Morrisseau, Francis Kagige, and Carl Ray as artists who "defy the taboos of their elders and tell the old legends in a new way—through pictures."[19]

Unlike most news articles that continually rehashed the same information, correct or not, discussing the defiance of taboo, a reliance on legends, and a lack of formal education, *Time* magazine instead shifted Morrisseau's importance into a larger frame, acknowledging him as he wished to be considered—as both a successful artist and a mentor. In August 1975 *Time* presented a fresh view of Morrisseau in a review of his fifth show at the Pollock Gallery. Deeming it Morrisseau's best show yet, reporter Jon Anderson affirms that after being tormented by a host of personal doubts and "a serious problem with liquor," Morrisseau in his latest work demonstrates his "new inner strengths, both as a painter and as a man."[20] The story broadly sketches Morrisseau's career for readers and includes three images, one a photograph of Morrisseau standing before his *Artist with His Four Wives*, and reproductions of *Self-Portrait Devoured by His Own Passions* and *Nature's Balance*. As an overview of his success, the laudatory report notes that works by Morrisseau are included in thirty-two public collections in Canada, and that the twenty-nine paintings on display at the Pollock are expected to sell for $46,000—ten times the amount of sales from his first exhibition in 1962. *Time* also includes another important statistic, which is that "more than 40 young Indian artists, inspired by Morrisseau's work, have followed his path away from traditional Indian artefact decoration to formal painting."[21]

Charting Morrisseau's evolution as an artist, the *Time* magazine article explains in awkward evolutionary terms how Morrisseau first drew in the sand on the beach, then used birchbark and hide, but that now he "uses the accoutrements of the conventional painter—best quality artists' board, stretched canvas and acrylic paints—as he discovers and explores different

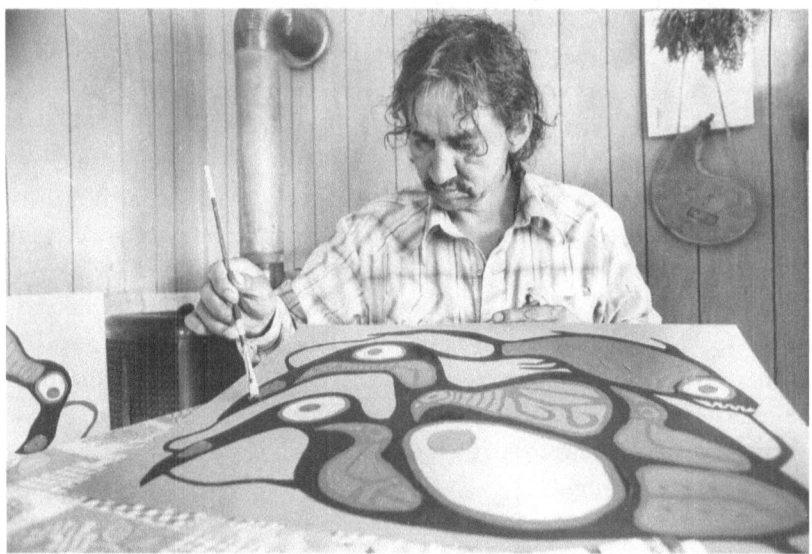

This staged photograph of Morrisseau painting was included with the 24 September 1977 *Toronto Star* report, "Norval Morriseau [*sic*] Isn't Afraid Now He's Back in Tune With Nature," by Arnie Hakala. The description below the photograph notes that Morrisseau used to sell a canvas for five-dollar bottle of wine in his "bad days." The reporter also draws attention to Morrisseau's personal hygiene in the story. Photo by Graham Bezant. Reproduced with permission of *Toronto Star* photo archives.

ways in which he is able to set out his personal visions."[22] Yet as Morrisseau's artistic growth is referenced, it is not stylistic growth that is lauded but instead an assimilationist one. The author notes Morrisseau's shift in materials, and how he has influenced larger changes in the Indigenous arts movement in its embrace of "formal painting." Neither of these points has much to do with Morrisseau's art practice but illustrate, instead, a move towards conformity with mainstream notions of art. His evolution as an artist—normalizing his practice to become more like mainstream artists—feeds a discourse that positions Morrisseau in relation to other artists whose practices are characterized in assimilationist terms.

Morrisseau was now a mentor and had come into his own as a painter. He was admitted to the Royal Canadian Academy of Art (RCA) in 1970 and presented with the Order of Canada in 1978. The Royal Ontario Museum of Art acquired eleven Morrisseau paintings for its collection in 1972, described by the *Globe and Mail* as "decisive interpretations of the folklore the Ojibway artist knows so well."[23] The following year he became part of the

Professional Native Indian Artists Incorporated (PNIAI), a group organized by Daphne Odjig in Winnipeg, sometimes referred to as the Indian Group of Seven by the media.

During this period the mythical construction of Morrisseau was also fully cast as the media framed him, by contrasting him with other Indigenous artists and forging a relationship between modern art and assimilation. Abstraction was valued in the art world as a more sophisticated and thus more civilized form of art. Emerging from this notion was a hierarchy that pitted arts concerned with legends and specific subject matter against formal abstractions, which the art world valued as higher forms of artistic expression. The noted 1974 documentary *Colours of Pride* privileged modern abstraction, too.

Colonial Hangover: Modernism and Morrisseau

Linkages between assimilation and art criticism were nothing new, as press reports of Morrisseau's first exhibition at the Pollock Gallery demonstrate. Ten years later, however, the art/colonial discourse had become more entrenched, and with a growing pool of Indigenous artists exhibiting in Canada, comparisons became prevalent in press reports, offering a clear sense of how criticism was steeped in modernist and primitivist discourse. Countless European artists had demonstrated their interest in primitive art since Picasso's celebrated visits to the Trocadero museum in Paris, where he reinterpreted African mask motifs into his cubist aesthetic. With American artist Jackson Pollock's shamanistic interests in Navajo sand paintings in the 1950s and the 1970s performance art connections to shamanism in the work of German Fluxus artist Joseph Beuys, who placed himself in a room with a coyote in *I Like America and America Likes Me* (1974), a discourse that adeptly melded colonialism and modern art ideas remained prevalent in the media and in art criticism.

Art critic for the *Winnipeg Free Press*, John Graham reflected these concepts in his review of the pivotal *Treaty Numbers 23, 287, 1171* exhibition mounted at the Winnipeg Art Gallery in 1972 by curator Jacqueline Fry, featuring art by Jackson Beardy, Daphne Odjig, and Alex Janvier.[24] Graham stresses the importance of individuality over group characteristics—a theme prevalent in modern art discourse: "To rely solely upon one's cultural heritage however is to say nothing, while to deny or sublimate it is an exercise in futility. That these three painters do neither commands our attention." Arguing that their paintings "move on" from a common ground, Graham argues that the paintings in the exhibition "reveal them to be three graphically articulate

individuals, meriting the same consideration as that afforded any professional artist"[25]—high praise from a mainstream art critic. Graham stresses
the artists' separateness as a way to insulate their work from the monolithic
notion of primitivist Native art considered a tribal, pan-Indian expression.

By describing Beardy's work as a bridge between the art of Odjig and
Janvier, Graham makes clear that he critically judges the three artists differently and in an evolutionary manner. Halfway through the review Graham
makes clear his preferences. "Of the three, Alex Janvier has produced the most
elegantly sophisticated expression," says the reporter. "The way in which the
paintings expand beyond the edges focuses one's attention upon the sense
of space and the attendant freedom of movement and delight in the effect
of color set against the whiteness of the ground." While Graham does not
evoke the term abstraction, he speaks of Janvier's art in ways that recall
Greenbergian tenets of modern art. Graham ends his review by conjuring the
words of Picasso to lend further credibility to Janvier's accomplishments: "In
the words of Picasso, if you want to draw, you must shut your eyes and sing,
and so Alex Janvier has done ... Inextricably part of a multi-layered and
multi-cultural society, such creative statements give promise of greater appreciation of the contribution to be made by this part of the whole mosaic."[26]

The *Globe and Mail*'s Kay Kritzwiser similarly positions Janvier in
ways that distinguish him from Morrisseau. She judges Janvier as "a proud
Indian, with a responsible sense of his worth to Canada." Though she does
not explain what this might mean, she does clarify that he is "no self-taught
primitive." This direct allusion to Morrisseau is unmistakable, given that
Janvier's exhibition is at the Pollock Gallery. Pollock is quoted as saying, " 'I
waited 12 years to exhibit another Indian,' referring," clarifies Kritzwiser, "to
his first, the painter Norval Morrisseau."[27] Kritzwiser otherwise discusses
Janvier's work by referring to his "abstract interpretations," and his "line
surprisingly Art Nouveau at times, in the way it carves up negative space."
Although she described a Morrisseau painting as a "formal composition"
in 1972, here she favours Janvier by situating his art within a discussion of
abstraction that makes clear references to European modernism.

In 1974 Pollock attempted to move Morrisseau into an elite art milieu
of abstraction when in *Tawow* magazine he argued, "Growth and maturity
from the early bird-fish forms, through ancestral portraits, to a newly-realized
abstract structure indicate the probing and continuing intellect of the artist."[28] This effort to align Morrisseau with other artists working in abstraction
might have been more effective if Pollock had not prefaced his remark by
referring to Morrisseau's art as "primitive" in the same article.

In 1975 the *Globe and Mail*'s art critic James Purdie assessed Morrisseau against the art of Janvier in ways also found in the noted documentary *Colours of Pride*. Under the headline "New Assurance, Maturity in Native Art," Purdie acknowledges that improvement had occurred in contemporary Aboriginal art. Referring specifically to a multi-artist exhibition at the Pollock Gallery that included work by Morrisseau, Janvier, and Inuit artist Akitaq, Purdie finds "the best artists of both communities [Eskimo and Indian] are continuing their forward development as confidently as any other group or movement in North America." "The most interesting comparisons for experts and amateurs both," he notes, "are of the works of Morrisseau, an Ojibway whose art extends the figurative legends and myths traditionally depicted by his people, with those of Janvier, a Chippewa whose university education in art has led him to extract from the same sources abstractions and dreams for filtering through the inner eye of a modern intellect."[29] Purdie points to Janvier's post-secondary training as a key component in his value as an artist. The association of education with assimilation runs deeply in colonial Canada. No mention of Morrisseau's or Janvier's training in residential schools is included in this equation. And abstraction beats out figurative art.

Roger Bainbridge of the *Kingston Whig-Standard*, reporting in 1975 on an exhibition curated by Tom Hill at the Royal Ontario Museum called *Canadian Indian Art '74*, with art by Morrisseau, Janvier, Beardy, Cobiness, Sam Ash, and Benjamin Chee Chee, drew sharp attention to Janvier as the only artist among the group who "had a complete formal art training. He studied for four years at the Southern Alberta College of Art in Calgary." The reporter quotes Thelma Edge, proprietor of the Canadian Shop, as an expert on Indigenous art: "The Ojibway nation does not have a tradition of fine art as did the Indians in British Columbia where art was part of their ceremonies … The only historic Ojibway work was in decoration."[30] Such pronouncements illustrate a prevalent assumption, found in art and anthropological circles that since the nineteenth century had privileged Northwest coast art over other pre-contact, contact, and contemporary arts. The monumentality of Northwest coast arts fed a Eurocentric bias for large-scale sculpture and architecture as indicators of civilization. Yet, in a *Globe and Mail* report of this same exhibition, Seneca curator Tom Hill describes things differently. He refers to the art pieces assembled as "products of 'extremely intelligent working artists'" and explains how "Indians never distinguished between craftwork and art." In an effort to situate the exhibition in a broader, contemporary context, Hill adds, "the techniques and the traditions are coming to be influenced by currents and styles from around the world."[31] In this report a painting by Joseph

Sanchez, a member of the PNIAI, is compared to "the surrealistic vision of a Miro or a Dali." [32]

A *Globe and Mail* story on Rama, Ontario–based Anishinaabe artist Arthur Shilling, who painted expressionistic portraits, quickly separated him from Morrisseau. The report, titled "Shilling Takes Indian Art beyond the Old Images," begins by describing Morrisseau as the "current guru" who "recreates his heritage by plumbing its traditions in a very graphic way. Around him is a cast of Indian artists painting as individuals certainly, but also in much the same way." Reporter Peter White notes that it is important to disengage Shilling from this movement and that his "fat brush strokes are reminiscent of Van Gogh's." White argues that Shilling is "making an attempt to bring [Indian artists] to their senses." What Shilling has done, according to White, is "reorder what we expect of Indian Art. Before he can be an Indian he must be a man. In his art he has brought to being a man what it is to be also an Indian. It is this beginning with what is most fundamental that makes these paintings startling … they speak to universal experience and consequently carry him to a higher plane." [33] Shilling's expressionistic paintings, in other words, are preferable because they conform to Eurocentric modern styles. Morrisseau, however, rather than connecting with the moderns, remains a revivalist, stuck in the past.

In 1977 James Purdie signalled a renaissance of sorts in Indigenous art that he argued was embodied in Morrisseau's *Unity of Man and Animals*. The work was on display at Hart House Gallery at the University of Toronto, part of Dr. Bernhard Cinader's collection shown as a survey exhibition *Native Canadian Art: Tradition and Aspiration*. "It has helped a whole generation of Indian artists to make the transition from tribal narrative painting to themes of universal interest," Purdie argued. [34] Acknowledging Morrisseau as a leader in the arts community, Purdie here recognizes Morrisseau's art as transcending assimilationist markers. Pollock, too, describes *Unity of Man and Animals* as "an abstract composition" in the *The Art of Norval Morrisseau*. [35] Yet Purdie continues to acknowledge a disconnection between Woodland art and mainstream Canadian art discourse that he ascribes to a lack of training. "Part of the fascination of this entire art movement is the rapidity of its development and the sometimes astonishing directional changes that parallel the emergence of major art movements within this century," explains Purdie. "Since few of the artists involved have had any formal training outside the reserves, historians are faced with the problem of figuring where the knowledge is coming from. (When one of the newest young artists was asked, a few years ago, if he had been influenced by Michelangelo, he replied, 'NO. What reserve is he working in?') "[36] Purdie had used a similar anecdote in November 1975. [37]

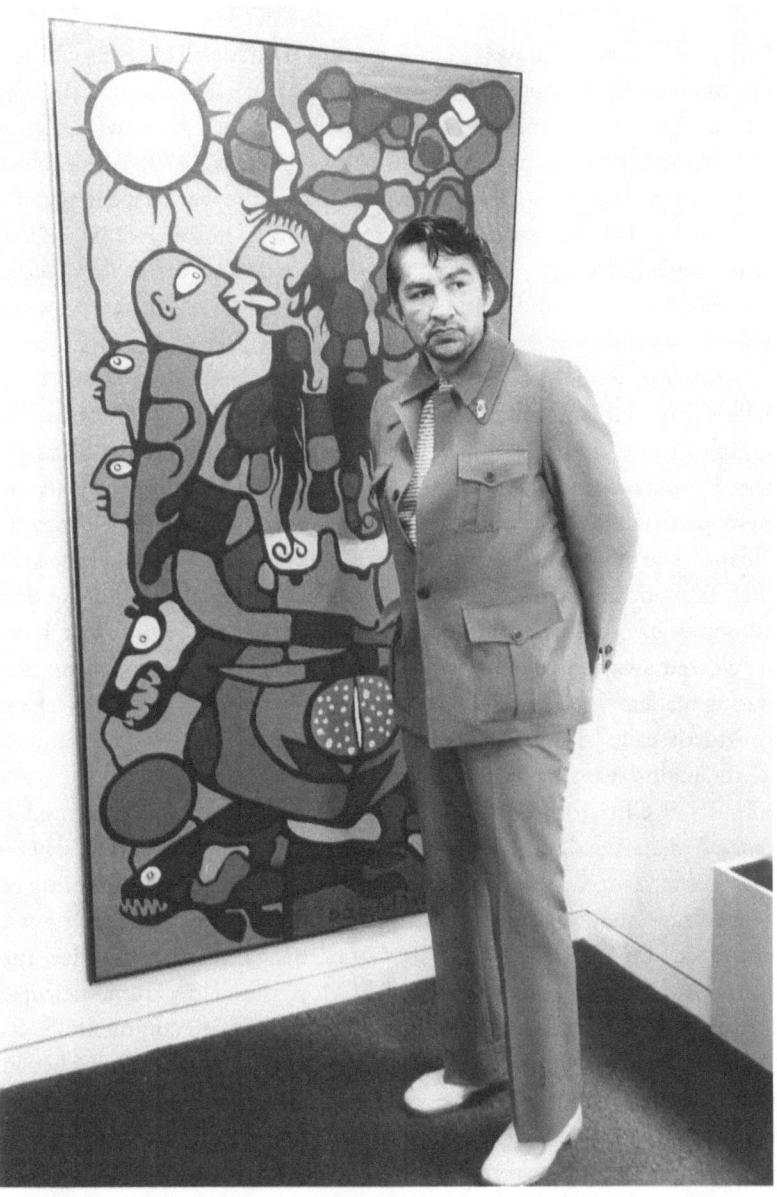

A nattily dressed Norval Morrisseau stands before his painting *Mother Earth* (1976) displayed at the Pollock Gallery on 18 August 1977 as part of an exhibition titled "Changing into Thunderbird." A cropped version of this photograph was reproduced above a letter to the editor by Jeanne Pattison of the McMichael Gallery regarding the accessibility of viewing works by the artist at their gallery, "Canadians Keen on Morrisseau," *Globe and Mail*, 19 October, 1977. Photo by James Lewcun, *Globe and Mail*, reproduced with permission of CP photo archives.

The fickleness of arts reporters at the time is evident when *Globe and Mail*'s Kay Kritzwiser moved from favouring Janvier to Robert Houle as an Indigenous artist who embodied everything Morrisseau did not. This was evident when she crafted a review of Houle's art on display with a group of Morrisseau's drawings at the Pollock Gallery in 1978. While Houle admitted a great debt to Morrisseau, who "paved the way to recognition" of Aboriginal artists, Kritzwiser opines that "there is nothing of Morrisseau in the Houle drawings" and likens his work instead to the Dutch modern artist Piet Mondrian and American modernists such as Barnett Newman, Kenneth Nowlan, and Frank Stella.[38] Associating Houle with European and American modern artists—no higher praise from an art critic in the 1970s—shifts Houle's work into a different space from that of Morrisseau's, aligning Houle instead with the art of Janvier and Odjig, who had also elicited comparisons to mainstream modern artists by critics in Canadian newspapers. While Kritzwiser had in the past acknowledged Morrisseau's brilliance, she maintained a primitivist discourse when discussing the artist, which framed him as lesser than Houle. Celebrating that "the Mondrian philosophy has infiltrated Houle," Kritzwiser gleefully argues that Houle has "cleared away all references to legend, to tradition, to representation," assuring readers that Houle is more than simply a painter of Indian legends like Morrisseau.[39] He had, in Kritzwiser's estimation, instead assimilated into the mainstream art world.

In 1979 Christopher Hume pondered, in a cover story penned for *Maclean's* magazine significantly titled "The New Age of Indian Art," whether it was a renaissance, or "as some would have it, the last great outpouring of a dying culture" that was currently attracting the attention of art collectors.[40] Hume, like Purdie in the *Globe and Mail*, heaps unbridled praise upon Morrisseau. After a biographical sketch of Morrisseau's life, Hume articulates his pivotal importance to the *new age* of Indian art with comments such as "He made Indian art possible not by ignoring the shamans, but by becoming one himself," and "Once the student, [he] is now the teacher." Hume explains that by 1979, "Indian art" has moved beyond a limited audience and has "expanded into a concern to communicate with everyone."[41] Following up on the current of modern art comparison, Hume acknowledges: "Critics have become fond of saying that the grande dame of the native art scene, 53-year-old Daphne Odjig, owes more to Pablo Picasso than to any Indian painter," yet he resists this art discourse in his feature magazine article.[42]

Indeed, two gallery owners, Jack Pollock and Walter Moos, had explained to the *Globe and Mail*'s Purdie the summer before that with regard to

Canadian art generally, "the pronouncements of critics are not as important as they once were, perhaps because a knowledgeable public is beginning to form at last."[43] Yet that didn't stop Purdie from continuing to make his own declarations. In February 1979, writing about a number of exhibitions in Toronto galleries that season, the art critic explains that Morrisseau, whose achievements "have long since assured him of an honored place in Canadian art history, also continues to invent."[44] Yet Purdie, unimpressed by Morrisseau's latest work on display at the Pollock Gallery, places him in a passé art category of surrealism while favouring Janvier's modern abstractions. Describing Morrisseau's *The Light Is the Way* as the major work in the exhibit, he finds that "the natural surrealism that unified and made a single interdependent world out of the elements, man, beast and environment, seems to me to be replaced by a tainted version. It is planned, intellectual surrealism: painting with a preconceived message that interferes with intuitive expression." Announcing that Morrisseau "has lost his innocence" and that his new work "remains, for me, awkward and untried," he prefers Janvier's arts practice: "A maturing process of an entirely different order, unclassifiable but harmonious and united, is what I found in the paintings of Alex Janvier at Gallery Moos on Yorkville Avenue. Janvier, one of the few Indian artists in Canada with four years of formal art training at the Alberta College of Art, has effected a synthesis between Indian symbolism and modern abstraction."[45]

Two years earlier, when Purdie had reviewed a show of Janvier's new work at Gallery Moos in Toronto, he noted disparagingly, "Much of the new work comes dangerously close to being merely decorative, some of the formal balances are out of tune."[46] In this review, Purdie hails Janvier as "one of the few Ontario Indian artists with formal art training at university level." This was incorrect on two counts: Janvier was not from Ontario, nor did he attend university but rather the Alberta College of Art and Design. Yet none of those details really mattered; what did matter was that Janvier was formally trained, which translated into sophistication. Purdie was impressed with Janvier's 1976 gouache *Cultural Beggar* and declares: "The painting is one of the most dignified profiles of an Indian by an Indian that I've seen."[47] Purdie calls attention to the Alberta artist's fomer habit of signing his work with his treaty number, "287," a convention Kritzwiser had dismissed in 1973 by stating, "That's his treaty Indian number, lest we forget."[48] Purdie describes Janvier as an activist in the Indian Rights movement and as such, "found the number useful."[49] He contends that Janvier "seems to have transcended through his own creative ability (with the help and encouragement of perceptive teachers in the majority culture) the 287 cipher. All the newest paintings," to Purdie's relief, "are signed but not numbered."[50]

Purdie explains, "Although Janvier's work has been described as a bridge between traditional Indian art and the modern abstract tradition, he no longer finds it necessary for his survival as an artist to turn his back on the culture in which his father was a hereditary chief."[51] Janvier's latest paintings, done while the artist was in Sweden, according to Purdie, possess "a strange and unclassifiable synthesis of traditional North American Indian imagery and the abstracted rhythms pioneered by Klee and Kandinsky." From his mention that Janvier's wife is of Irish-Ukrainian descent, to his stressing that Janvier had been painting in Sweden, to the importance he places on formal art training, for Purdie, Janvier possesses the attributes to pass easily into the mainstream art world.

Purdie viewed Morrisseau as a primitivist, a term that was retrograde. Janvier and Houle escaped such limits because of their formal training and a perceived allegiance to Eurocentric art traditions. Morrisseau's art, like his behaviour, did not quite measure up. Such artistic judgement remains inseparable from a larger framing of Morrisseau within the confining context of racial signifiers. Primitive art means primitive behaviour.

A *Winnipeg Free Press* feature article offers an extreme example. Printed in March 1979, it demonstrates that for the press Morrisseau had, as Purdie predicted, lost his innocence, a trait of the Imaginary Indian that was endearing to Canadian colonialism. "Morrisseau Meets Press but the Vibes Are Bad," by Ted Allan, offers a demeaning view of the artist, referred to throughout as "Big Fella." The reporter, personally affronted by Morrisseau, wrote a feature article about the artist that allowed him to save face while disciplining Morrisseau for his disinterest in sanctioning yet another account of his life.

The reporter, writing in the third person to deflect the experience away from himself, introduces Morrisseau as "Big Fella, Norval Morrisseau, known reverentially as Thunderbird Spirit, patriarch of Canadian native artists, reputed Ojibway shaman, mystic darling of the *haute* hip salons of the nation, top buck in the $2 million annual Indian art market and the hottest thing on canvas since Harold Town was considered outrageous."[52] Readers learn from this description that Morrisseau is famous, rich, and a Noble Savage, an unusual combination. Meeting the artist at the Cardigan-Milne Gallery in downtown Winnipeg, the reporter explains how their meeting had been postponed three times prior to the encounter and when Morrisseau finally arrived an hour late, he was clearly uninterested in speaking to the reporter after asking him what he wanted to know and hearing the response: "Well, a bit of everything. Your early life, your painting, your…" When the gallery director "called out to Big Fella: 'Oh come on, Norval, stop fooling around and come and sit down and talk,'" Morrisseau, according to the report, responded by saying that the Bauhaus sofas were "white man's furniture. I don't sit on white man's furniture."[53] Morrisseau had, according to the reporter, acted childishly and with reverse racism.

The reporter complains about the artist not wanting another story written about his personal life. As he had stated before, Morrisseau clearly had no interest in continually drawing attention to his private life. He understood the sorts of tropes that would be included in such a story. Yet when Morrisseau pointed out that reporters wrote their stories ahead of time, so that it did not matter if the artist talked to him, the reporter's bruised ego viewed the comments as personal. Incensed by the artist's disinterest, the reporter wrote the kind of story Morrisseau had tried to avoid. The *Free Press* reporter ultimately undermined the artist's credibility in order to save his own, casting Morrisseau's comments as follows:

> "Crap … you can learn more about me by my silences, Do you understand? You can learn by what I don't say. You don't need to talk about anything." Silence descended like a cloud of methane. Then Big Fella intoned gravely: "You are violating my psychic space."

> "You see," Big Fella boomed, jumping to his feet. "You see. I could tell by your vibes. You don't care about me. I would have told you anything you wanted to know. You had it all figured out. You guys are all the same. You don't know anything about me."[54]

The reporter demeans Morrisseau as he describes him as an *enfant terrible*. He retaliates against Morrisseau for not performing obediently at the interview by turning his article into a smug personal triumph, using the public forum of the *Free Press* to discipline Morrisseau by positioning him as unruly and impossible to deal with. And by his tongue-in-cheek delivery, the reporter persuades readers that Morrisseau was a childish, petulant art star undeserving of the reporter's time and attention. The reporter accuses Morrisseau of behaving as the reporter behaves, childishly and disrespectfully. As if this were not enough, the following day in a review of Morrisseau's work at the Cardigan-Milne Gallery, his art was judged no better. "For this viewer," declared Leonard Marcoe for the *Free Press*, "this collection lent nothing as a positive and uplifting viewing experience. No doubt it will elicit a more favorable response from those less concerned about art directions." This failure, according to the reviewer, is the result of "apologists of native paintings," who, in an attempt to atone for "white society's mishandling" of "native people" now are using the "goose to lay the golden egg of 'art.'"[55] The short review packs a wallop as it denounces art dealers, media "who lend themselves as publicists," and Morrisseau for a lack of artistic merit.

Morrisseau as Shaman Artist

Morrisseau's attempt to seize control of his mythical identity found more success once he began to overtly characterize himself as a shaman. Through his paintings and his performative gestures he exerted his own agency and in the process found a way to also satisfy press constructions. After all, the shaman is a key part of the Noble Savage construction, and by redirecting his image as shaman artist Morrisseau skirted the less palatable and negative aspects of the imaginary, the noted examples notwithstanding. This shift can be identified in articles written by the *Globe and Mail*'s James Purdie between 1975 and 1976.

In an August 1975 story Purdie argued that a transition was underway but the requisite history of Morrisseau's pain and trauma was still fully outlined in his arts report. "Morrisseau himself has begun to rely increasingly on his direct visionary experience," explains the reporter after two columns of outlining his lack of formal training, difficulties with jobs, a bout of tuberculosis, and problems with alcohol.[56] The following summer, however, Morrisseau's forged shaman identity became the central focus in a report by Purdie. In an article about an exhibition at the Pollock Gallery, the arts reporter described Morrisseau as someone who "sometimes believes he would have been a shaman if he was born 200 years earlier," emphasizing a shamanistic framing instead of more negative primitive signifiers that had come to define the artist.[57] This recasting of Morrisseau is a result of efforts by the artist and his dealer, and the NFB's emphasis on shamanic elements. Disassembling and reassembling his visual autobiography, Morrisseau actively presented himself as a shaman in works such as a series of two paintings he completed for the McMichael art collection in 1975, where he portrayed himself as a shaman on one canvas and presented his wife and daughter as shamans in the second. Morrisseau's efforts to create his own shaman identity were noted in Purdie's March 1978 column: "When Norval Morrisseau was in town this week to work with author Jack Pollock on his biography [*The Art of Norval Morrisseau*, 1979], he mentioned in conversation that he is free at last from the influences of his early Christian education (he called it brainwashing) and he is no longer concerned if the white culture understands his painting."

Purdie explains that Morrisseau has come to see himself as painting for an Indigenous audience, "people who recognize the unity of man, nature, and all its creatures."[58] This significant shift reported by Purdie reveals for the first time in a news story Morrisseau's reaction to Canadian colonialism and his experience with residential schools and Christianity. Morrisseau asserts himself as a shaman artist—free from the paradoxical "pull" of Christianity. In so doing he demonstrates both agency and a decolonizing effort to reposition himself in popular culture.

In 1976, Morrisseau became an adherent of the spiritual movement of Eckankar, characterized by some as a cult but offering the artist a real opportunity to embrace his role as shaman. Morrisseau understood and respected the protocols of Anishinaabe cultural tradition, yet Eckankar provided him with a new pathway to explore visionary ideas. A conflation of different brands of Eastern mysticism, Eckankar acknowledges astral travel and the importance of spiritual light. Not only did this syncretic bond created by fusing Medewiwin teaching with Eckankar concepts shift the way Morrisseau painted his subjects, it also changed the way he performed as a shaman. By the end of the decade the artist had given the press something it wanted—a brand of shamanism that was in alignment with an established set of stereotypical tropes that reference the Imaginary Indian. In promoting his brand of shaman identity, Morrisseau also fed the art market's interest in an authentic shaman. This notion of authenticity, however, is paradoxical because it is a mediated form fed by a misconstrued understanding of a modernist shamanic identity. For Morrisseau it meant something quite different than it did for most art collectors. Still, he and Pollock understood the value and cachet in promoting him as shaman, no matter how it might be understood.

A watershed moment in his public shift to recast his identity from a negative to a more positive reading came about in 1978 when Morrisseau, who had pondered the idea for some time, decided to throw a party. A tea party with fine English bone china and a silver tea service—this sounds like an everyday occurrence at Buckingham Palace, or at least that was what Morrisseau imagined. But on a reserve in northern Ontario with twenty-some guests flown in for the afternoon to have tea with an Anishinaabe artist—that had the makings of spectacle and gave the artist a venue to direct his public identity. The tea party also presented an opportunity to consider in detail racial identity in Canada at the time.

The tea party thrown by Morrisseau on 25 June 1978, at his home reserve community of Beardmore, conflates two seemingly disparate traditions—a fascination with royal traditions and his shamanism. The tea party served as a unique spectacle, one where Morrisseau invites guests to a tea party and then recasts the event as an opportunity to perform the role of shaman by serving Indigenous medicine tea, drumming and singing Anishinaabe songs, and smudging guests in a ceremony that repositioned him not as host but as shaman. Morrisseau's performative gestures secure this aspect of his mythology. This event serves as a pivotal moment in Morrisseau's public unveiling as shaman artist.

Based on recollections, media coverage, and published photographs of the event, a more nuanced understanding of performance and racial identity emerges. Having recently purchased a set of Royal Crown Derby china cups and saucers and a complete sterling silver tea set, Morrisseau had approached his Toronto art dealer, Jack Pollock, about his wish to host a garden party, "just as the Queen does in the grounds of Buckingham Palace."[59] Pollock, eager to capitalize on potential marketing ploys, supported his efforts, offering to charter a plane and invite admirers to attend the event. The group assembled included Anishinaabe curator Robert Houle from Ottawa's Museum of Man (now the Canadian Museum of History), media—including art critics from the Toronto *Globe and Mail* (Kay Kritzwiser) and the Canadian Broadcasting Corporation (CBC)—Morrisseau's lawyer, Richard Baker, and a number of art collectors assembled by Pollock. Houle took on a role of helper in organizing the smudging ceremony.

Twenty-four people were shuttled to Beardmore from Toronto in a wartime DC-3 that Baker recalls as "loud and uncomfortable."[60] Approaching a remote airstrip that appeared suddenly as a small clearing in an otherwise densely forested wilderness, Baker wondered at the time if they would survive the landing. Then, as they travelled by school bus to Morrisseau's home, Pollock recalls in *The Art of Norval Morrisseau*, "something spiritual happened."[61] Pollock offers his account of the event both textually and in a two-page spread of black and white photographs. The text and photographs together exaggerate spiritual elements of Morrisseau's behaviour in order to essentialize Morrisseau as a Noble Savage and confirm stereotypical associations promoted in Canadian culture. Passages such as "Morrisseau, artist, shaman and mystic, moved among us with quiet dignity … meticulously observing the rituals of his glorious tribal past and left us all with a feeling of awe and wonder" further confirm Pollock's construction of Morrisseau as authentic and frozen in time.[62] Quoted in the *Globe and Mail* the following day, Pollock describes the event as more dream-like than even Fellini could have "dreamed up."[63]

Morrisseau had long had a fascination with royalty. He named his first-born daughter Victoria, after Queen Victoria, and his first-born son Albert, after the Prince Consort, as he told Pollock, "or Alfred, after Alfred the Great as he told the press."[64] Houle, too, was interested in the royals, or so he told Kay Kritzwiser in an interview published in the *Globe and Mail* where he shared, "'I am also a Royalist and a Victorian like you wouldn't believe!'"[65]

Associations between the British Crown and Canada's First Nations date back to the eighteenth- and nineteenth-century colonial period. Since the War of 1812, when First Nations sided with the British, a more solid relationship with British royalty was established. The British acknowledged that they could not have defended the colony against the Americans without Aboriginal allies. Silver medals were given out to Indigenous fighters after King George signed the Treaty of Ghent in 1814. Despite a parent/child rhetoric espoused in such expressions as "Great White Father" or "our children," many Indigenous peoples viewed the Crown as a friend and the Canadian state as foe.

Performing the role as a sage shaman at this event, to the delight of guests, Morrisseau included ceremony and Indigenous practices to shift the British tradition into something wholly unique. Beginning with the smudging of all participants through a purification ceremony, the artist-as-shaman reassured guests of the authenticity promised by Pollock and Canada's colonial imaginary. The performative aspects of this spectacle serve as a particularly useful moment for a discussion of racial identity.

As noted above, Pollock viewed Morrisseau's idea for the tea party as an opportunity to sell paintings, and Pollock shaped the event in ways that corresponded to a promotion of Morrisseau as not just an artist, but a shaman artist. As Greg Hill advanced in Morrisseau's 2006 retrospective exhibition and accompanying catalogue, *Norval Morrisseau: Shaman Artist*, Morrisseau also viewed himself as a shaman artist.[66] His early appreciation of ceremony and ritual and his efforts to perform a role as a shaman conveniently meshed with racial constructions of one of the attributes of the Noble Savage—that of a wise spiritual force. Whether Morrisseau's conception of shaman and mainstream Canada's notion of the shaman aligned meant little to the media. It fed their fascination. From Pollock's perspective, the promotion of this event as "something spiritual" would confirm for some art purchasers that Morrisseau was the real thing—an authentic Noble Savage. It sold art and it made for an interesting day. Pollock added to the spectacle by serving vodka-filled oranges to the passengers on board the 750-mile chartered flight to Beardmore.

Beyond the china, the silver tea set, and the fancy dress of invited guests, little of what took place at that afternoon's garden party corresponded to sitting down to tea in a British garden. From the setting of Morrisseau's yard in northwestern Ontario to commencing the event with a smudging ceremony, Morrisseau's tea party remained entirely unique. The fifteen black and white photographs published the following year in Sinclair and Pollock's *The Art of Norval Morrisseau* offer a visual record of the day's happenings.[67] Edited and assembled by Pollock to serve his aims of promoting and selling Morrisseau's image and art, the photos differ somewhat from the textual record. Except for one close-up shot that documents the silver tea service and soiled china after the event, to signify that this had indeed been a tea party, the remaining photographs document Morrisseau and guests throughout the day involved in actions that have little accordance to a tea party.

From the photographic evidence, most guests were dressed in suits, dresses, some with fancy hats, confirming their efforts to conform to notions of a fancy tea party dress code. Morrisseau's attire, however, is juxtaposed with that of his mainstream Canadian guests. It provides evidence of how he performed a role that remained dramatically different from that of his guests. Morrisseau, his brother Wolf, and his young Cree assistant Brian Marion separated themselves racially from the mainstream by their dress. Morrisseau wore a floral Métis ribbon shirt, a buckskin beaded vest, and jeans. His braided hair conformed to Anishinaabe traditions. In a number of the photographs an eagle staff is present and in one photo Morrisseau dons a feather headdress, laughing as if sensing the irony. Two photos show him before his unfurled medicine bundle with pipe and medicines present. In addition to images of Morrisseau smudging his guests with an eagle feather fan, two of the photographs show him pouring tea from an ornate silver teapot.

In one photograph Morrisseau leans over medicines with Robert Houle, preparing the smudge for the opening ceremony. It is noteworthy that Houle, an Anishinaabe man and artist like Morrisseau, wears a Western-style pinstriped suit with vest, tie, and a carnation boutonniere. Even though Houle aids Morrisseau in preparing for the opening ceremony, his dress and short hairstyle do not signify Nativeness, whereas both Wolf Morrisseau and Marion wear buckskin and braids, signifiers that visually articulate their Indigeneity. The image troubles racial identities at play here.

As noted, newspaper reports also commented on the party. Robin Green wrote for the *Globe and Mail* the following day under the headline "FYI: This Party Would Put a Dream to Shame," explaining that the chartered DC-3 cost $3,300, flew 750 miles to an awaiting Morrisseau, who gave each of the guests a gift of "rare American buffalo nickels" and a drawing to take home. Relying mostly on quotes from Jack Pollock, the reporter tells how Pollock "arranged for one of the guests to … inject oranges with vodka for the passengers to suck on during the flight."[68] Since details regarding Morrisseau's alcohol consumption were commonplace in press reports, readers would assume, given the headline, that the event was steeped in alcohol. While this passage applies to Pollock and his guests, it creates an illusion that the party was more booze-filled than it in fact was. Richard Baker clarified that while guests imbibed oranges and vodka on the flight, alcohol was not part of Morrisseau's tea party. Characterizing Morrisseau as an odd, shaman figure, the reporter describes how the artist had ensured good weather for the event by "baring his loins to the sun goddess," and "blessed his guests … with smoke from a dish filled with burning herbs and cedar boughs … to the sounds of tom-toms and Ojibway songs." The story ends with a quote from Pollock, "And when we said goodbye, there wasn't a dry eye in sight. I'll never, ever forget it. Even Fellini couldn't have dreamed up anything quite so dream-like."[69] The following week, a letter to the editor by Gilbert Oskaboose, the assistant editor of *Indian News* in Ottawa, appeared in the *Globe and Mail*, responding to Green's article with the challenge that there is "something rotten in Indian country."[70] In a sarcastic tone, Oskaboose exclaims, "Indians have arrived in the wacky world of the avant garde art scene." Describing passages from Green's article in tandem with an Ottawa art event, the letter expresses dismay at how Morrisseau and Houle, who had spoken at the unveiling of a Daphne Odjig mural, *Indian in Transition*, had allowed themselves to be taken over by mainstream interests. Referring to Morrisseau's party as "H-Y-P-E" and to Houle as a "fascinating Indian exhibit," Oskaboose describes how Houle, "nattily dressed in a lightweight summer suit … was brought out by senior white officials who stood back and beamed … while Houle rattled off a welcome in three languages." Intimating that Houle was engaged in a form of colonial mimicry, he declares that Houle's Eurocentric analysis of Odjig's work was nothing more than "verbal flatulence."

A rebuttal, in the form of yet another letter to the editor, penned by Pollock, was published in the *Globe and Mail* on 8 July. He begins by saying, "The letter by Mr. Gilbert Oskaboose cannot go unanswered." Pollock explains that since he attended both events Oskaboose criticized, he would set the record straight. "During the purification ceremony performed by Norval Morrisseau in Beardmore, and again at the unveiling of the monumental canvas by Daphne Odjig in Ottawa, I was humbled by the greatness of a heritage steeped in pride and tradition."[71] Comparing Odjig's *Indian in Transition* to Picasso's *Guernica*, both concerned with social injustice, he notes that Odjig's mural "stands as a permanent record of the white man's early gifts of oppression and deprivation." He therefore views Oskaboose's remarks as "silly" and "fatuous." Pollock concludes by giving thanks that his attitudes are "in the minority and trust that the future will hold many more meaningful exchanges, such as those given us by both Norval Morrisseau and Daphne Odjig."[72] Comparing Morrisseau's tea party with Odjig's pivotal mural may have been hyperbolic, but after all, Pollock was defending more than honour—he was protecting future art sales.

A year later Christopher Hume wrote about the tea party in a feature article for *Maclean's* magazine, demonstrating the importance of this event to Morrisseau's mythology.[73] The details of the party are greatly exaggerated, as he refers to the tea party as "now famous," and exaggeratedly describes the attire as "white gloves and long dresses all the way."[74] Hume writes that participants "passed a delightful afternoon quaffing exotic Ojibway herbal teas and oranges injected with vodka." By now the event has become a part of Morrisseau's constructed identity. He sophisticatedly conflates the tea party with his emerging shaman identity, using the event to communicate to the art world, the media, and to himself, his power to mould himself into a shamanic force.

Media reports and the letter to the editor reveal a form of disciplining at play. Assimilationist discourse advanced by Green and critiqued by Oskaboose remains entrenched in the tea party narrative. In his magazine article, Hume finds Morrisseau's behaviour captivating and celebrates his character for readers rather than moralizing directly, as is most common in newspaper coverage. Yet by mentioning Morrisseau's disregard for the value of money, by quoting Pollock's statement "his wealth enabled the entire community of Beardmore to booze for nothing," and by admitting "nobody enjoys Morrisseau more than Morrisseau. He is a great artist and he knows it," Hume offers readers cause to judge, thus exercising a form of disciplining.[75]

However, while the performative actions of Morrisseau and Houle appear to support the seemingly naturalized constructions advanced in the media and by Pollock in his text, another reading can be discerned. The photograph of Morrisseau and Houle hovering over Morrisseau's medicine bundle brings together abstract concepts introduced earlier: Morrisseau's conformity to the Noble Savage construction, and Houle's conformity to colonial mimicry, dressing like and representing the national ethnographic museum's interest in authentic "Indian" art; each referencing Foucauldian aspects of discipline. Each also performs roles that correspond to dominant racial constructions.

Yet to argue that these artists are simply agents of colonial discourse dismisses their own performative gestures that add nuance to understandings of race in Canada.

Conventional signification is reworked in the tea party; rather than pointing to something directly through the use of a signifier, Morrisseau's performance signifies *upon* the tea party. It is a doing, and its meaning is thus conveyed indirectly and subtly. By disassembling the signifiers typically at play in this equation, Morrisseau enables both a critique and a revision within the party. With his dress and performance of ceremony and ritual, Morrisseau calls forth racial norms by invoking the "essence" of Indigeneity. At the same time, he reveals that this "essence" is a construction, the performative acts of "Indian." Morrisseau satirizes and disassembles the naturalness of the relation between signifier and the signified, disrupting the fixity of the construction by combining the notion of the tea party with Indigenous ways. Morrisseau resists the disciplinary force that insists on a racial "truth" and the belief that this truth can be ratified by the performance of identity. He does this by holding his tea party in Beardmore. By "baring his loins to the sun goddess" and singing "happy Indian songs," Morrisseau manipulates and confuses the roles assigned by essentialized tropes. Morrisseau performs a shaman role, but does so on his own terms as he demonstrates the ambiguity and arbitrariness of the sign "Indian."

Finally and importantly, the wholehearted adoption of a shaman identity by Morrisseau fed his soul. It directed him in his art in ways that did not tread upon Anishinaabe protocols but allowed him to remain actively and spiritually connected to all living things. Morrisseau expanded his repertoire of paintings, adding a greater range of subjects that assert his personal visual narratives around spirituality, combining elements from Anishinaabe, Christian, and Eckankar to more clearly express his artistic vision. In addition, the artist assuredly tackled other topics, political and erotic, demonstrating a range and engagement with contemporary concerns and passions not limited to spiritual pursuit. Morrisseau as an artist displayed a spectrum of works on a range of subjects, and the media became more interested in reporting on his oeuvre as art rather than as ethnography. Still, the press continued to print column inches about his unruly behaviour.

The 1970s changed the Morrisseau myth. While press constructions maintained adherence to the Imaginary Indian, the shift to shamanism offered Morrisseau, as it did the press, space to direct his identity. Shamanism allowed for a shift in discussion away from notions of childlike and violent signifiers to settle upon a more positive, if not romantic, dialogue. To be wise, at one with nature, visionary—these are signifiers associated with the Noble Savage but also signifiers of Morrisseau's personal brand of shamanism. Morrisseau's exertion of his shaman artist identity played much better than did his direct admonishments. The artist's disputes with reporters were mostly unsuccessful, as evidenced by his challenge to Gary Dault in August 1975 in the *Toronto Star* or in the 1979 *Winnipeg Free Press* interview that backfired when the reporter lashed back at Morrisseau with an acerbic story. It was his performative moves that found traction in the media and also supported Morrisseau's own passionate energies.

Painted in 1977, *Man Changing into Thunderbird* visually renders Morrisseau's performative evolution as a shaman artist. Conceived of in six panels, it visually documents Morrisseau's transformation into Copper Thunderbird, beginning with his apprenticeship with his grandfather in the first panel.[76] As the subsequent canvasses demonstrate, he slowly evolves into the mature shaman artist he had fashioned, recognizing his connections to Eckankar, symbolically becoming Thunderbird by the final panel. In an interview with the *Toronto Star*'s Dault while this new work was on display at the Pollock Gallery, Morrisseau admitted: "I've wanted to paint this picture for fifteen years but I couldn't do it in those days. This is the ultimate picture for me and I'm sharing it. Sharing it is wonderful."[77] Dault agreed that *Man Changing into Thunderbird* was "the best work of his career." Morrisseau's mature arts practice, and his more vocal efforts to present himself as shaman, changed how the press and how popular culture thought about the artist at the end of the 1970s.

CHAPTER FOUR

1980s
An Unruly International Art Star

[Morrisseau] lived life in epic proportions … great drunks, long absences from work, dramatic trances and probably recurring fits of suspicion of the giant he had unleashed and the giant powers of the art market … he had become a star of the fickle, fast-moving popular art market which set life at a pace and made demands that he could not temperamentally cope with.[1]

Grace Inglis, *Hamilton Spectator*, 1982

The 1980s was a time when Morrisseau was continually linked to the terms magic, magician, and shaman. Beginning in 1981 with a headline that stated that Morrisseau was exploring "Magic Forests of the Mind," reporters began to use the term "magic" in both laudatory (as in this case) and derisive ways. After a series of negative stories in May 1987, a *Globe and Mail* piece began with a quote by Morrisseau, who also uses "magical" to describe his art: " 'Now Is the Magical Moment. I Start Again.' No Regrets, No Booze for Norval Morrisseau."[2] Whether noting that Morrisseau's magic was drained or labelling Morrisseau a magician, art critics, reporters, and curators used the term to either reinforce his shamanic powers or belittle him as little more than a flim-flam artist—all smoke and mirrors. At the end of the decade he appeared in an important international art exhibition in Paris, France, to celebrate the two-hundredth anniversary of the French Revolution. The exhibition, titled *Magiciens de la Terre*, framed him and other artists from around the globe as magicians. Firmly established as a shaman artist, Morrisseau's mythical identity gels as a magician, though this part of his myth did not endure beyond the 1990s.

The main events that cropped up in papers during this decade highlight the ongoing bifurcation of the artist and the Imaginary Indian, except that in the 1980s the highs reached much higher and the lows found depths much lower than had otherwise been publicly reported. Morrisseau was both feted and dismissed in competing narratives. One example of dismissal of Morrisseau's significance occurred in an art review in 1980. Art Perry, writing in the *Vancouver Province* about an exhibition of Morrisseau's art at the Vancouver Art Gallery, lamented that the art had not remained authentically aligned with pre-contact Woodland traditions, which he characterized as a "once sincere art form."[3] The provocative headline, "It's Sham Rather than Shamanism," inspired the title of Blundell and Phillips's 1983 essay on media analysis and Morrisseau's art.[4] Perry finds fault with Morrisseau's art and image as a shaman because the artist refused to maintain a frozen-in-time image the reviewer valued.[5]

As in the 1970s, Morrisseau was compared to other Indigenous artists and for the most part, he lost out to educated artists like Janvier and Houle. Carl Beam now took the place of Alex Janvier as an artistic comparison for Morrisseau in the press, perhaps because he was also Anishinaabe and from northwestern Ontario. Beam's art practice was radically different from Morrisseau's and prompted stark judgements. Described in a 1981 news story as an artist who "reaches far beyond his Ojibway origins," Beam's contemporary and personally politicized art found favour among art critics whose commentary reinforced the modernist/primitivist divide that surrounded Morrisseau and his art in the 1970s.[6] In a 1985 story about a new gallery in Toronto exhibiting the art of Beam and Houle, the reporter boasted that it was a "far cry from the 'sentimental' Indian art many collectors demanded. Also, visitors won't find a Norval Morrisseau clone anywhere," referring to the Indigenous art movement inspired by Morrisseau's visual storytelling style.[7]

Still, Morrisseau's spirituality continued to grow in importance, and shamanism had now become an established part of the mythology surrounding the artist. A pivotal exhibition in 1984 at the Art Gallery of Ontario (AGO) afforded Morrisseau new credibility as a serious artist, and it appeared as if some of the old constructions had disappeared with the exhibition at the AGO. While the 1970s news coverage had established a mythical identity for Morrisseau driven by his behaviour, the 1980s completed the picture—an unshakable mythic narrative that defines him even after death.

Both the press and the National Film Board charted his struggles with alcoholism and his six months in jail in Kenora, Ontario, for public drunkenness in the 1970s, priming readers for Morrisseau's transgressions. His art, exotic and compelling, was often less newsworthy than his behaviour. When Morrisseau began to characterize himself as a shaman, the focus on poor behaviour favoured by the media dissipated somewhat and carried him into the 1980s. Now viewed as a senior artist, the media often embraced his considerable artistic successes through much of the decade.

Early in the 1980s, a growing interest in Woodland art—this was the name being given to the movement Morrisseau had fostered—found its way into art-related news stories. A 1980 report about art from Manitoulin Island in northwestern Ontario provides some context for a shifting interest in Woodland art. In "Manitoulin Islanders Find Roots in Art," *Globe and Mail* reporter Gary Waddell outlines ways the Ojibway Cultural Foundation had begun to promote arts from the region using a "three-pronged" approach that included travelling exhibitions to Europe, smaller art shows throughout Ontario, and another important exhibition mounted in Vancouver that was "presided over by Haida artist Bill Reid." Reid was quoted as saying that unlike Northwest Coast art, "Ojibway art is a 'totally new form.'"[8] However, Manitoulin artist Leland Bell challenged Reid's characterization by clarifying the traditional roots of his art that linked to the Anishinaabe cultural past. The report explains that the noted exhibitions focus on a new generation of artists inspired by Morrisseau. Yet while the Ojibway Cultural Foundation was promoting Woodland art, other artists were distancing themselves from it.

The opinions of Robert Houle, for example—an important player in the Indigenous art scene who had held a key position at the Museum of Civilization, played a role in Morrisseau's tea party, and whose art was judged as superior to Morrisseau's throughout the 1970s because of his formal training and connections to European modernist art movements—carried weight among newspaper art critics. Houle called the generation of artists that followed Morrisseau "imitators." Arguing that they had done more harm than good, in 1986 Houle tagged the movement the Woodpecker School: "The Woodpeckers lacked experience ... lacked knowledge about the legends, lacked sincerity, and ended up painting for the little white man with the dollar. There's a certain Andy Warholish phenomenon here, of mass production of banality. I think that Morrisseau's early art will stand. He never bothered to admonish his imitators because that's not the Indian way. The Indian way is to let children do what they want."[9] Houle's characterization of the younger generation of painters as "children" falls into a stereotypical trap of signification that haunted Indigenous peoples and also assumes the artists were blindly following, without talent. Reporter Carole Corbeil attributes a change in viewing Indigenous art beyond an anthropological frame in part to the work of artists like Houle, who, she argues, "has lucidly articulated the dilemmas and frustrations that serious contemporary native artists have faced."[10] She notes the work of Carl Beam as another Indigenous artist who has created serious contemporary work. As she, Kritzwiser and others maintained in the 1980s, Morrisseau's art, while compelling, should not be viewed as part of the contemporary art movement in Canada. Such criticism limits Morrisseau's artistic significance.

Correspondingly, a 1981 report about the BC Union of Indian Chiefs' plan to pay for elders and lobbyists to go to London to petition the British parliament to oppose the Canadian federal government's constitutional package by selling "artefacts" at an auction that lumped 100-year-old baskets, masks, and jewellery together with paintings by Norval Morrisseau and Daphne Odjig. Morrisseau and Odjig had donated their work to the political cause but the headline did not distinguish the old from the new.[11] Yet what was made clear by association was that their art, while contemporary, belonged within the same ethnographic frame as baskets and masks from earlier periods.

The *Globe and Mail*'s art critic John Bentley Mays challenged such confining understandings of Morrisseau's art when he glowingly reviewed the latest exhibition at the Pollock Gallery. Describing how the work "transports us into a shadowy archetypal realm where ordinary things are wonderful," Mays writes: "In his visionary lakes swim mighty fish, armed with bolts of spiritual lightening [*sic*]." Clearly recognizing Morrisseau's artistic genius, especially in comparison to what he refers to as "the hedonistic, pointless New York abstract painting so popular with the Yorkville carriage trade, as well as most of the sumptuous, nihilistic post-modern art being shown around town," Mays slams the art world's love-in with abstraction.[12] Mays's derision of New York abstraction is something new—different from other art critics that privileged abstraction as a superior movement that Canadian artists should emulate. The critic cogently explains that because Morrisseau has been framed racially, he had been categorized "condescendingly as a 'folk' or 'native' artist, quite beyond the pale of serious art discourse," which has limited the seriousness with which the art world has understood his work. Carefully distinguishing Morrisseau's dream-like imagery from surrealism, characterized as "magic forests of the mind," Mays clarifies: "Although rendered in contemporary material such as acrylic paint, the strong iconography of these pieces goes back to the sacred scroll-drawings and rock-paintings of the artist's people. This strongly formalized visual tradition underpins all Morrisseau's work, and gives it an impersonal authority that transcends the individual artist's whims."[13] With this, Mays's challenge to art criticism is somewhat undone. With the mention of scroll drawings and rock paintings, he re-situates Morrisseau within what appears to be the familiar primitivist discourse found in most reviews of Morrisseau's work. Yet in noting that, as one might expect from a self-taught artist, little attention is afforded to "figurative modeling," and that the work avoids "delving into the problems of perspective or pictorial depth," instead featuring a "simple system of beautifully rhyming colors and shapes, [that] are rarely adventurous," Mays has avoided stereotypical tropes. He recognizes that Morrisseau "has never been merely a tool of that tradition," citing Morrisseau's "many young native imitators" as evidence of Morrisseau's superior artistic genius.[14] Mays's review falls outside the usual media descriptions of Morrisseau's behaviour as a disciplining way to contain this artist's difference from mainstream Canadian art, preferring serious artisitic engagement.

While this story appears to signal a shift in how the artist was positioned by newspaper art critics, not all were ready to abandon the established frame accorded Morrisseau. Grace Inglis, art critic for the *Hamilton Spectator*, did not share Mays's enthusiasm when she reviewed an exhibition of Morrisseau's work at Hamilton's Moore Gallery in 1982. After sketching out Morrisseau's rocky start as an artist in an article titled "Morrisseau Magic Has Been Drained," she stingingly contends, "That was the romantic beginning of what has turned out to be a strident story of over-exposure of both artist and art and ultimately the complete absorption of this art into a very public domain through aggressive marketing and wholesale copying." Acknowledging that *Globe and Mail* art critic Pearl McCarthy was indeed correct back in 1962 to have been excited about his art, Inglis writes, "There was something hypnotic about the wild staring eyes of the figures in his large, dark-outlined and dark-hued paintings of the early years, something expressive of elemental power, which Canadians were ready for, and took to at once." However, Inglis dismissively explains that for years Morrisseau "lived life in epic proportions … great drunks, long absences from work, dramatic trances and probably recurring fits of suspicion of the giant he had unleashed and the giant powers of the art market … he had become a star of the fickle, fast-moving popular art market which set life at a pace and made demands that he could not temperamentally cope with." Contending that the "shaman has lost his magic," Inglis agrees that Morrisseau's "own place in the firmament of Canadian mythmakers" is "firmly secured."[15] She argues that Morrisseau's adoption by the art market and his pandering to it has moved his art outside the "religious-mythological symbolic art" arena and he therefore must provide a "freshness of vision" or return to his early beginnings as a Native artist.

Inglis dismisses Morrisseau as a serious contemporary artist because he has, in her opinion, not developed stylistically, yet John Bentley Mays believes that Morrisseau's greatness has been underappreciated, hindered by the label assigned to him of Native artist. Kay Kritzwiser of the *Globe and Mail*, in a review of a new CBC-TV series called *Spirit Speaking Through,* described Morrisseau as an "Ojibway shaman painter [who] hacked a warpath into the legends of his forefathers and cleared the way for the Canadian Woodland artists to follow."[16] Throughout the 1970s, she had maintained a measured enthusiasm for his art. However, in her 1982 review she admits, "Lionized, publicized, his work sought, Morrisseau today is an aging legend himself … his tiresome insistence on his powers makes him perilously close to a boring legend." She views other Woodland artists such as Blake Debassige and Daphne Odjig as "crowding his heels." In her description of the show, which focuses on seven Native artists, Morrisseau comes up short. "There is Morrisseau slashing at his canvas with a paint-laden thumb to transfer his spiritual powers. 'I don't know no color alphabet. I don't need a school. I don't prethink or plan the canvas. I don't think about these things. I know about them.'"[17] Clearly Kritzwiser does not share Mays's opinion of Morrisseau.

To better contextualize Mays's view that Morrisseau had been erroneously positioned as simply a "Native" artist, it is worth mining other news stories from this period to see how Native art was being used. In the early 1980s a small number of stories regarding Native arts were published in the *Winnipeg Free Press.* Because Winnipeg had a long history of promoting Indigenous arts in its newspapers with links to Morrisseau and Daphne Odjig, and had a developed appreciation around Inuit art at the Winnipeg Art Gallery, I focus on *Free Press* Native art news stories from the 1980s. They educe two primary themes: first, while they discuss projects and programs as Native art, the stories remain ostensibly about economic work programs funded by the federal government; second, reports also highlight the preservation of Native arts from the distant past, whether it be by artists attempting to hold on to the past or by museums preserving that past.

Carving initiatives taking place in northern Manitoba demonstrate an established connection between economics and Native art. One story explains how the Saulteaux at Fort Alexander Indian Reserve in northern Manitoba could "re-create their tribal past" through a new carving program funded in combination with the departments of Indian Affairs and Manpower:[18] "Although the program was originally intended as an employment project, he [program director Max Bossi] says, the organizers soon saw that the Native people had a natural talent for wood carving and needed only encouragement and inspiration." The paper notes that Bossi believes the carvings serve a dual purpose, "since, in addition to being works of art, they also tell stories or are based on Indian legends." Bossi says, according to the story, that "by sharing their culture with others, the artists are helping improve race relations."[19] A similar story, "Carvers Notching Up Successes," celebrates another venture at Leaf Rapids in northern Manitoba, where "a team of artists [are] producing pieces that are starting to gain international recognition because of a federal grant."[20] Even Inuit carving, long marketed as high art and a common art news thread in the *Free Press* since the late 1950s, was viewed as a vehicle for employment, as evidenced by a 1984 report about carvers in Sanikiluaq, Northwest Territories. Statements such as "We can sell everything we send," and "Carving is important to the economy of Sanikiluaq, where unemployment is around 80 per cent and half the population is under 18 years old" trumpet the economic benefits of carving to an otherwise poor community. "Carvings from the ... soapstone mined in the area can put as much as $1,000 a week into the pocket of a carver," though the story also cautions, "The money is good if a man or woman can stay at it," suggesting that the carvers lack a work ethic.[21] Attempting to market carving as both an economically viable work program and as artwork, the programs are described by the *Free Press* as a primitive art expression. The carvings have little connection to the art that is covered in the arts section of the paper, except in the case of Inuit art, where the boundaries appear to have been more fluid. A neo-liberal bent can be recognized in each of these reports. With the aid of a concerned government and citizenry, Natives (and their art) can be helped to assimilate into Canadian society, so say the three news items about the carvers.

The effort to link Native arts to an imaginary past was well established in press reports, and 1980s news stories in Winnipeg naturally reinforced this theme. Native art is thematically cast as a primitive tradition in a story about the birchbark bitings of northern Saskatchewan Cree artist Angelique Merasty (misspelled as Merasety in the paper). "Native Art Form Kept Alive" reports that 56-year-old Merasty is the last of the biters, and because she only has six teeth left in her mouth, she will soon have to stop her artistic practice.[22] The story offers readers a combination of amusement and ethnographic interest. The image of a woman creating art by biting birchbark with so few teeth left in her mouth seems far away (a long plane ride) from the cosmopolitan ways of Winnipeggers. Her work, according to the report, was on display at the Museum of Man and Nature in Winnipeg and had a wide appeal. One of her works was recently appraised at $1,000, states the paper, to convey to readers her seriousness as an artist. Two years later, the *Free Press* printed a second story about Merasty. "Artist's Plight Gnaws at McGonigal" follows up on the earlier report, using much of the same information regarding the quality of bark and number of layers needed for her practice. However, the focus of this story is that Lieutenant-Governor Pearl

McGonigal, who has a number of Merasty's bitings hanging at Government House in Winnipeg, has "promised to help Indian artist Angelique Merasty repair the tools of her craft. She's going to help Merasty find a dentist."[23] Neither the carvers nor the birchbark biter are taken seriously as artists, in a mainstream sense; in each instance the discourse of Native art is mixed up with economic viability and assimilation—colonial discourse.

A small story highlighting the efforts of Bill Moncur at the Moncur Gallery of Prehistory in Boissevain, Manitoba, who had collected hundreds (though the article also states thousands) of points and arrowheads dating from as far back as 7,000 years, describes a distant past through the eyes of a local farmer who has collected artefacts from his land:

> He can recite the movement of the Indian people from 10,000 B.C., the time nomadic hunters tracked the woolly mammoth to this region ... He can tell you that some Indians who populated the Turtle Mountains descended from warriors who fought in the Battle of Little Bighorn in Montana in 1876 ... Finally he can describe the demise of the local tribes, driven to the brink of extinction by smallpox and the disappearance of the buffalo. When the first train passenger arrived at the Boissevain railway station on Christmas Eve in 1885, the days of the Turtle Mountain Bands were all but over.[24]

The reporter who interviewed Moncur also includes a quote from the archeology curator from the Museum of Man and Nature in Winnipeg regarding the importance of this collection as a teaching tool. However, the report relies on Moncur's cloudy and romantic memory for information. The local farmer remembers an encounter with an "Indian family" almost 70 years ago that left him in awe: "I remember watching them as they went into the sunset and I was struck by how free and happy they were."[25] The symbolic association of the setting sun, the last of the dying breed, and other similar tropes clearly articulate a distant past. Since Treaty Three (governing that area) was signed in 1871, the Indigenous family he observed may have been both free and happy, but they were not living nomadically off the land as he implies. Natve art in these instances shares little common ground with Morrisseau's art practice.

"Woodland Indians Keep Past Alive," found in the travel section of the *Free Press* under "Great Getaways," suggests a visit to the Woodland Indian Cultural Centre in Brantford, Ontario, where "Indian life, from the art of Norval Morrisseau to the heated sport of a snowsnake tournament will be highlighted" and highlights the success of artist Morrisseau and his contemporaries while connecting it to efforts to "keep the past alive."[26] Travel columnist Betty Zyvatkauskas references Morrisseau's art as a bridge to a nostalgic and imaginary past by inserting it into a longer description of prehistoric arts, wampum belts, religious symbols and examples of tourist trade crafts. In describing the exhibition at the cultural centre, the columnist assuredly explains Morrisseau's art: "Anyone familiar with the vivid works of Norval Morrisseau may by [*sic*] surprised to see some of his earlier paintings: crudely rendered on birch bark, they show little evidence of the fluid style he developed during the 60s and 70s. The later works show the development of Morrisseau's pictographic style—characterized by power lines and the internal views he expressed after studying petroglyphs and bark scrolls."[27] Zyvatkauskas also comments on a work by Blake Debassige, a Manitoulin Island artist: "One of the most controversial paintings is also one of the most humorous. Blake Debassige's *Tree of Life* shows a white pine whimsically covered with colorful birds. Embedded in the trunk is the image of the crucified Christ, genitals and all, with the faces of the Apostles emerging from the branches." Her suggestion that Debassige's painting is humorous might be based on the fact that the artist shows Christ's genitalia, or it may be that conflating Christian iconography with Indigenous spirituality is joke-worthy. After her art critique, the travel writer turns her attention to a two-column description of a "traditional native sport," the snowsnake tournament, describing the event as a pan-Indian pastime that should surely send Winnipeggers flocking to the festival almost 2,000 kilometres away.

In 1983, the *Regina Leader-Post* printed a story related to a group exhibition of Aboriginal artists called *New Growth from Ancestral Roots*, on display at the Koffler Gallery in Toronto, curated by Rya Levitt. The exhibition featured, in addition to Morrisseau, such artists as Robert Houle, Carl Beam, Angus Trudeau, Joe Jacobs, and Arthur Shilling. Morrisseau, though, serves as the focal point of the story, and a large reproduction of his painting *Portrait of His Son as the Christ Child* accompanies the article. The story notes that "Norval Morrisseau, 52, and largely self-taught, was a pioneer in the field who broke tribal laws against the making of images with his paintings based on the legends and myths of his Ojibway people. He was banned for breaking the sacred taboo but the elders later relented, accepting him as a modern-day messenger recording their story."[28] A familiar description by 1983, Morrisseau's lack of formal education and his breaking of taboos continued to remain requisite elements of press stories related to Morrisseau as they had in the 1960s and 1970s. The article also pits Morrisseau against

Robert Houle, in terms of levels of education recalling art critics from the 1970s who similarly positioned the two artists against each other: "the most formally trained of the group who studied in Salzburg, Austria, and graduated from McGill University." However, the article notes that it is Morrisseau's work that commands the highest prices, citing *The Light is the Way*, a two-panel painting that was selling for $35,000.[29] Pitting education against art pricing is a competition Morrisseau wins. The public is swayed by the price of art as an arbiter of status. Twenty-one years after Morrisseau's debut at the Pollock Gallery, little has changed, except the price commanded for his work and at times a new characterization of him as a senior artist.

1984: A Year of Exhibitions

A number of large art exhibitions of Indigenous art were curated and discussed in the press in the 1980s, beginning with the Art Amerindian '81 at the National Arts Centre in Ottawa. Kay Kritzwiser reviewed the exhibition for the *Globe and Mail*. According to her, the exhibition was a "joyous splash of individuality. Not an X-rayed legendary spirit animal on any wall." She explained that the "tactful mandate behind Art Amerindian '81 was to encourage native artists across Canada to celebrate their rich heritage, but at the same time to break away from the stereotype rut into which so much native art has tended to fall."[30] Morrisseau's art was absent from this exhibition. Robert Houle organized the juried exhibition of sixteen artists that included Bob Boyer, Angus Trudeau, Glenna Matoush, and Alex Janvier. Houle is quoted as saying that the works in this juried show were purchased for the art collection of the Department of Indian Affairs and Northern Development, because "this fits in with the department's increasing role as a promoter of contemporary native art."[31]

A bicentennial exhibition of "Indian treasures" held at the Art Gallery of Ontario was the subject of a news report in the *Free Press* in April 1984. *From the Four Quarters* was touted as one of the largest exhibitions ever organized by the gallery and would include "Ontario Indian art rounded up from more than 50 European and North American galleries, museums and collections ... covering nearly 7,000 years from 5000 BC to 1867, the year of Confederation, and rang[ing] from an ancient Human Effigy Head—really a flat pebble with a smiling face etched on it—to Indian souvenir art for tourists of the Victorian era."[32] After stating the intended premise to display the objects as art rather than as artefact, the story points out that "a wide array of European art, particularly paintings and sketches, which complements and enhances the Indian works" is included in the exhibition that honours the province's 200th birthday. Anthropologist Joan Vastokas, of Trent University in Peterborough, Ontario, explains, "We know so little and have not taken Indian art seriously," and the report confirms that the introductory essay to the exhibition acknowledges that the "old categorization of native North American art as primitive; static and without documented history 'has unfortunately persisted into the 20th century.'"[33] Vastokas might have been dismayed by the *Free Press*'s interpretation and characterization of the effigy head as a pebble carved with a happy face, demonstrating the ongoing dismissal of Indigenous arts even in a news story about art exhibitions meant to undo past indifference.

The bicentennial exhibition followed another pivotal exhibition held at the AGO, this one related to Morrisseau and the contemporary art movement he inspired. *Norval Morrisseau and the Emergence of the Image Makers* was a watershed exhibition curated by Elizabeth McLuhan and Tom Hill that opened at the AGO in February 1984 and ran until April, when it then toured a number of galleries including in Thunder Bay, Sault Ste. Marie, Sudbury, and the Woodland Indian Cultural Centre in Brantford. At the time Elizabeth McLuhan was director of the Thunder Bay National Exhibition Centre and Centre for Indian Art. Tom Hill, from Six Nations, had worked for the Indian Art Centre, Department of Indian Affairs in Ottawa, and was currently director of the Woodland Indian Cultural Centre in Brantford. Building an exhibition around Morrisseau's twenty-some-year career and the work of six contemporaries, including Daphne Odjig, the exhibition continues to be recognized as an important art historical moment in Canadian art history. The press, too, seized upon this as an important exhibition that changed the way they reported on Morrisseau.

Serious press reports followed the opening, beginning with Kay Kritzwiser of the *Globe and Mail*'s review. "'They Are Not Doing Beaded Moccasins,'" leads with a pronouncement by Hill and McLuhan that demands new ways to consider Indigenous arts: "It's about time to separate Indian craft—the beaded birchbark canoe—from Indian art—the serious, painterly expressions of artists such as Morrisseau, Daphne Odjig, and their younger contemporaries."[34] The review positions Morrisseau as a bridge in two senses—first in the move from craft to "serious" art, and second, according to Kritzwiser, within his own practice, as viewed in the gallery space of the AGO: "His work becomes a bridge between two Morrisseaus. There is the tentative, almost primitive work of a young man trying to sort out on cardboard, on wood, even on bark, the conflict between his need to express old Indian teachings and his respect for the tribal rules which forbade it … In the six large panels which cover an entire wall, *Man Changing into Thunderbird*, 1977, continues that inner search, but now here is the assured painter, with a brilliance to his colors, known not sensed and a confident, clean technique."[35] Kritzwiser significantly assesses Morrisseau's art as the strongest in the show, shifting from the more negative position she had maintained throughout the 1970s. She calls Odjig "her own woman, in search of her own roots." The paintings of Carl Ray, Saul Williams, Blake Debassige, Joshim Kakegamic, and Roy Thomas are also included in the exhibition. The *Globe and Mail* review includes two images: Morrisseau's provocative *The Gift* (1975), and a reproduction of a painting by Saul Williams, *Homage to Morrisseau* (1979–80), also used on the catalogue cover. Kritzwiser describes Williams as having "created his own imagery in the quieted serpents and the halo which transforms Morrisseau into a new Old Master."[36] Heaping such praise upon Morrisseau was unheard of from this senior art critic with the *Globe and Mail*. The reproduction of Morrisseau's painting *The Gift* with the review is also noteworthy. This work, though nine years old, demonstrated to readers that Morrisseau had painted more than just the legends of "his people." This political painting, a key part of Morrisseau's oeuvre, was seldom discussed in the media and had not been reproduced in newspapers until now.

In her review for the *Ottawa Citizen*, Nancy Baele deemed the *Image Makers* exhibition "controversial" and a "knock-out." Unlike Kritzwiser, who mostly focuses on Morrisseau, Baele acknowledges that "the point the exhibition makes well is that there can be infinite variety and equally valid sensibilities at work within any style, be it impressionism or woodland art."[37] Where many art critics had refused to view Morrisseau's younger contemporaries as anything but derivative copyists, the so-called Woodpeckers, to use the label ascribed by Houle, Baele finds instead that Morrisseau "pointed the way to a structure that suited the content of the art but he didn't stifle further invention." Both reviewers agree that McLuhan's and Hill's efforts to cast the work in the show within an art historical discourse, where the works are refreshingly engaged beyond a racialized, primitivist frame, signals a change in how art critics will discuss Morrisseau's art. Like the positive review by John Bentley Mays, these accolades for Morrisseau's art mark a change.

Arts West reviewed the *Image Makers* exhibition at the AGO in April that year and was impressed with the exhibition. Outlining Morrisseau's contributions to the group, explaining that he threw in "his lot with white society," the reviewer notes that the artist's "determination to break free from the old customs that shackled his people brought him face to face with an alien way of thought. 'Art for art's sake' is a notion that is foreign to traditional Indian culture."[38] The reviewer, like so many arts reporters, separates Morrisseau from Eurocentric art. Yet arguing that he had "thrown in his lot" with mainstream culture means that Morrisseau was stuck in a sort of limbo, because he did not fully embrace modernism but at the same time had turned his back on frozen-in-time Indigenous ways of making art.

One example articulating how Morrisseau and Native art more generally had achieved a new level of acceptance was a report that sanctioned Indigenous contemporary art and politics. Mays, who sang Morrisseau's praise in 1981, reviewed the Indian Affairs exhibition when it opened at Rideau Hall in Ottawa in 1983 before touring the country. Touting it as the "first exhibition of native Canadian art ever held at Ottawa's historical Rideau Hall," Mays offers little information beyond the fact that Governor General Edward Schreyer officially opened the show.[39] No political angle was suggested beyond the headline, which read: "Native Art at Rideau Hall Capital Idea for a Showing." When the exhibition opened in Regina the following year it was a different matter. Political sparks flew, and the *Regina Leader-Post* seized the opportunity to turn the attention to politics, satirically scolding Indian Senator Edwin Pelletier for *spoiling* an otherwise harmonious celebration of arts and culture by having the audacity to bring up land claims and cultural realities in a politically charged speech. Explaining that during an otherwise seamless showcase of pow-wow dancers and an art display that included works by Morrisseau, Sapp, Janvier, Beardy, and Odjig from the permanent collection of the Department of Indian Affairs, Pelletier disrupted the government-orchestrated and whitewashed event. "Viewers whispered their displeasure over Pelletier's comments as they did the traditional gallery two-step around the east foyer where the exhibition was installed. It wasn't what he had said that bothered them. It was that overtly political comments are considered bad form at this kind of event."[40] The article acknowledges that the art exhibition was little more than a "superficial glance at the state of native art in Canada," and that curatorial decisions that brought together this impressive group of work had more to do with bureaucratic representation than aesthetics. "About twenty years ago when people like Morrisseau began to be recognized as outstanding individual artists that started to change," says the reporter. "The commercial value of work increased. Collecting Indian art became chic." Still, the report notes that while individual artists have made gains and pushed for change, the Indian Affairs touring exhibition reinforces past colonial practices, "old ways" of looking at art as ethnography, as evidenced by how incensed officials were when contemporary realities were mentioned in an otherwise sanitized and romantic view of colonial Canada.

In addition to a tide of stories that reconsidered the elder artist as a significant figure in the art world, an equal number of stories dismissing his importance continued to surface. In a story that reasserted Morrisseau's shaman construction, "Artist Seeks Strength in Indian Spiritualism," reporter Gwen Dambrofsky interviewed Morrisseau on the eve of his "first major exhibition in three years" and an upcoming tour of Europe.[41] Described as looking "haggard and weak," Morrisseau answered questions "with hodge-podge comments on Indian spiritualism, astral projection and astrology." Poking fun at Morrisseau's comments on his spirituality and status as a shaman, this reporter, like Grace Inglis in the *Hamilton Spectator*, views the discussion as little more than a farce. The 55-year-old Morrisseau had quit painting three years earlier, explains Dambrofsky, to "become the grand shaman of his Ojibwa tribe … disgusted by 'the assembly line' of the Canadian art industry" and the "psychic leeches." When Morrisseau says, "People say I'm very eccentric because I walked away from $280,000," the reporter questions the artist's odd comments. Characterized as an eccentric and an oddball, Morrisseau gets painted in an unflattering picture:

> When I got sick from hangovers, He took me up to all those different planes I've talked about and let the body get sick, because that's what it deserves. The Big Guy, the Cosmic Guy, says: "C'mon, I'll take care of all your needs. I will allow you to do all the dos and don'ts that you want. I will cure you, re-chemicalize you, transmute you, make you better."
>
> He said, "Go in that corner, take your clothes off and say, hi, handsome." I did that a few times. I was embarrassed at first but, by God, it felt good after because you put your own confidence back on yourself.[42]

Morrisseau, Dambrofsky reports, adds "a dissertation about this theory that many people think he is already dead" and claims, "I tried to be what society wants me to be." The mythic Morrisseau, not the one who speaks frankly, is of most interest in this feature. "He wore his Order of Canada medal, its metal gleaming but its ribbon ragged and dirty, on the breast of his striped pullover," a statement that says much. The allusion to the Order of Canada medal asks readers to question whether Morrisseau is worthy of the honour. The metal, like the nation, remains strong and gleaming, but Morrisseau's medal is in need of upkeep. The "ragged and dirty" ribbon might reference Morrisseau's lack of effort to assimilate into Canadian society—he has not lived up to his part of the bargain. Characterized as a "national institution," the reporter appears dismayed by Morrisseau who "sat wearily in his chair."

A Mythic Meltdown

A search of Morrisseau in the Canadian Business Current Affairs database (CBCA) shows sixteen news stories about him in 1987, the highest spike in reporting found in this database for Morrisseau. It was not until 2008 that more news stories about Morrisseau are recorded in the database. Interestingly, these news items were not related to his 2006 retrospective or to his death in 2007, but described the skirmishes that occurred after his passing surrounding his family and his estate. Newspapers like a sensational story; that much goes without saying. In 1987, the Canadian media served up Morrisseau on a silver platter.

A media frenzy in 1987 regarding Morrisseau's drinking and hitting the bottom on skid row seemed to wipe out all the positive coverage that had occurred earlier in the 1980s and left Canadians once again focusing on his behaviour rather than his art. Morrisseau's personal life remained squarely confined within a racialized discourse, made especially obvious by the media in 1987. His struggles with alcoholism became front-page news in ways his art exhibitions or his art accolades never had. A flashpoint, the media relentlessly followed this story, and the commentary reveals more about the press, its biases, and its efforts to reposition Morrisseau's scorned behaviour than it does about his art. An event held in February 1987 in Los Angeles re-established this media frame. Canadian actor John Vernon, in an effort to promote Canadian Indigenous arts more widely, had organized a group exhibition in Los Angeles and a solo show of Morrisseau's work in Santa Barbara. Headlines from across the nation captured the attention of readers in May 1987. A roller-coaster ride of news stories charts Morrisseau's extreme ups and downs. Such pronouncements as "Drink of Tequila Started Painter on Road to Despair,"[43] "Artist Sells Quickies for Price of Booze,"[44] "Native Artist Roaming City Trading His Art for a Bottle,"[45] and "Morrisseau Hits the Bottle, Wanders the Streets"[46] filled the papers on 11 May 1987. On 12 May, papers followed up with "Street Life Suits Morrisseau,"[47] "Artist 'Dry Again,'"[48] "Morrisseau Says He's Quit Drinking,"[49] and "Native Artist Leaves Street Scene: Morrisseau Says He'll Sober Up, Return to Work."[50] One day later the *Vancouver Sun* announced, "Artist Taken to Hospital,"[51] and the *Windsor Star* exclaimed, "Morrisseau Tottering on Brink."[52] On the streets, off the streets, and off to hospital in the course of three days, these sensational events captured the attention of readers across Canada. The

Ottawa Citizen announced, "Norval Morrisseau, a well-known Canadian artist, is today wandering the downtown streets, sleeping in parks and alleys and selling his sketches for the price of a bottle of liquor."[53] A Vancouver art dealer, Marion Scott, confesses, "I think he's one of the saddest people you could ever wish to meet ... Sometimes he looks God awful. He's quite bedraggled and thin and gaunt. I feel like I want to help him but any money you give him goes strictly for liquor." Most reports include a similar narrative and information, taken from the Canadian Press wire.

The CBC's *National* covered Morrisseau's plight as the lead story on the news that night. In a transcript of the news report by Karen Webb, who interviewed Morrisseau and two gallery dealers in Vancouver, a glib Webb announces: "A hot-air grid on Georgia Street is where one of Canada's most famous artists slept last night." Morrisseau clarifies, "Don't say I just crashed out there and everything was dirty and all this. I had a beautiful sleeping bed. I got a pillow and a couple of nice blankets. It's nice."[54] Clear from Morrisseau's comments is Morrisseau's ongoing awareness of how the press was framing him. He exerts his own version of the events, even though few accept his take. The reporter continues: "This is the art that made Norval Morrisseau famous—old and colorful. He was the first native artist to be taken seriously in this country. But these are sketches produced within the last two months. The signature is right, but the art is not. He has been selling these to Vancouver dealers just to buy food and booze ... He is still painting, and he says eventually his binges on booze will make him a better artist because it will clean his mind."[55] Such news must have shocked viewers of the late-night televised news program. It was an accepted practice by Canadians to purchase Native art for next to nothing; even Morrisseau had sold his work for a pittance in the 1970s. However, this was twenty-five years after the artist had made it big, and his art now sold for large sums. It did not make sense.

The *Vancouver Sun*'s Sunday columnist, Denny Boyd, conjures the symbolic characterization of alcoholism as the "Black Dog," a term used by notorious drinker and Irish actor Peter O'Toole, in his encapsulation of Morrisseau's life as a "fast four-act tragedy." Canadians were left shaking their heads and wagging fingers at the behaviour exhibited by Morrisseau, who, according to Boyd, "is the only Order of Canada winner who has been sleeping on steam grates and in shrubs around a provincial courthouse."[56]

Yet in the press, as negative as the reports were, also appeared editorials and letters to the editor that demonstrated Morrisseau's importance as an artist. A *Windsor Star* editorial noted, for example:

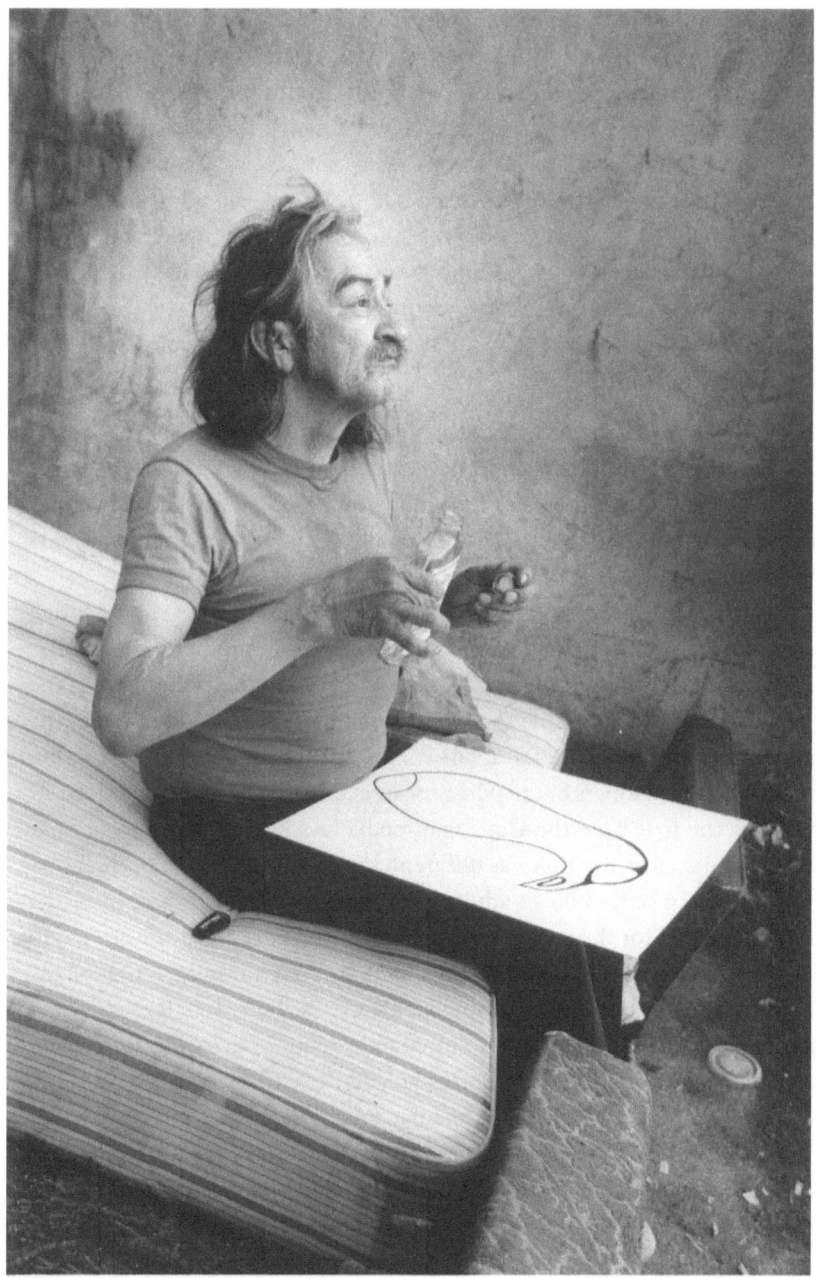

This staged photograph captures for readers visual evidence of Morrisseau's decline, taken by the *Edmonton Journal's* Brian Giebelhau in a Vancouver hotel on 10 May 1987. The CP photo was printed in the *Ottawa Citizen*, *Globe and Mail*, and the *Montreal Gazette* on 11 May 1987. Reproduced with permission of CP photo archives.

> It would be a terrible loss if Morrisseau were to become Cana-
> da's own Amadeo Modigliani, the Italian painter who enjoyed
> enormous popularity in Paris early this century, but ended up
> giving away sketches in bistros in exchange for drinks. Yet,
> Morrisseau is well on his way to being that. Unless of course, he
> is taken off the streets and detoxified … Morrisseau is fortunate
> in that he has many friends and admirers who want to help him
> … we are dealing with a unique artist, the man who has given
> us a new art, entirely Canadian in its conception and style and
> for that, as well as a humanitarian act, he deserves to be saved
> in spite of himself.[57]

No doubt all would agree that these events in Morrisseau's life were tragic. And it was clearly his behaviour that was at issue in many of these news reports. The zeal with which reporters followed the story and the disciplining commentary that surrounded it are equally disquieting accompaniments to Morrisseau's own downward spiral.

With this episode, Morrisseau performatively fulfills the negative stereotypical trope of the "drunken Indian" so often promoted in popular culture. He also undoes the goodwill he had built in the earlier part of the 1980s. Under the normalizing gaze of the press, Morrisseau embodies the attributes of the Imaginary Indian—in this case the Ignoble Savage rather than the sage shaman figure Morrisseau exhibited on other occasions. It was not the first time the Canadian media had judged Morrisseau's behaviour, of course, but this was different. It called attention to his inability to control himself, to be an adult, and it demonstrated, at least in media reports, a need for the nation to take charge. The flurry of stories found in dailies from across the country in such a compressed time period trained the public's attention on Morrisseau's behaviour. Readers were left assuming Morrisseau's life and career amounted to little more than a roller-coaster ride of alcoholic episodes. The press judged the chronicle of Morrisseau's behaviour as unbecoming of a Canadian and lamented his actions. Stories began to point to the need for level-headed Canadians to intercede on his behalf—after all, it is mainstream Canada's duty to parent Aboriginals—in keeping with the colonial pattern established with the 1881 Indian Act.

Beyond the text accounts that varied little from each other, a visual record accompanied and supported written press claims in almost every story published in May 1987. The photographs lend objective verification to the textual accounts of Morrisseau's downfall. Images of the artist sitting on a bare mattress in a run-down hotel provide evidence of the downward spiral charted by the headlines. The photos prove the veracity of the news coverage and reinforce the textual accounts.

The 11 May *Vancouver Sun* included a photograph of Morrisseau sketching. The caption reads "ARTIST NORVAL MORRISSEAU: Sketches in His Skid Road Vancouver room," and the photo shows the artist outlining a not-yet-fully articulated form.[58] Together the caption and the photograph confirm for tsk-tsk-ing Canadians the artist's inability to act properly. With his talent and recognition as an artist in Canada and beyond, with sales of his work reportedly high, there is only one reason why Morrisseau could be in such a predicament: it must be his Aboriginality. Unlike other artists who work in studios and create works of art on easels, Morrisseau's makeshift situation, in a "skid road" hotel, undermines his significance as a serious artist. Similar to the images of him creating art at the kitchen table or on a beach in the NFB's *Paradox of Norval Morrisseau*, these images reinforce a sense of incongruity around the artist.

The article's headline, "Native Artist Roaming City Trading His Art for a Bottle," combined with the caption that confirms his location on skid row and mention in the text that the photograph was taken by "Vancouver freelance photographer Brian Giebelhaus," demonstrating the photograph's authenticity, at a downtown eastside hotel room where Morrisseau was staying a few days before the story broke—all this offers clear proof of the artist's decline. Although in the photo he is neither on the street nor selling art for alcohol, a visual veracity is promoted by this image, implying that he is both drunk and planning to sell his art in exchange for more drink. Working in tandem, the text and photograph serve as signs for a stereotype that had long been reported and promoted in press reports. Morrisseau's plight as captured in the photograph, paired with textual accounts of his "roaming," his drunkenness, and his willingness to sell his art for alcohol, stands in for a whole, the stereotype of the "drunken Indian," fulfilling and reinforcing long-held mainstream constructions of the Indian imaginary.

It was not just Vancouver papers interested in a local story, however. The *Ottawa Citizen* included a photograph of Morrisseau with a similar story (noted above) on 11 May. Here Morrisseau, seated on a skewed bare mattress, stares off into the distance while a rudimentary drawing of a bird sits on his lap. The description of his personal hygiene adds to the visual record: "Morrisseau dresses in tattered clothes. He smells acrid."[59] Squalor and tragedy combined. A second photo, taken at the same time, accompanied the report in the *Montreal Gazette* that day. A glowing halo of light surrounding Morrisseau's head, juxtaposed with the tipped bare mattress, provides visual evidence of the confused ways in which Morrisseau is constructed, and adds a Christian layer that was also promoted in *Paradox*. The helpless plea projected here challenges so-called bleeding heart liberal Canadians to intercede.

A photo the following day in the *Vancouver Sun* under the headline "Native Artist Leaves Street Scene: Morrisseau Says He'll Sober Up, Return to Work" puts Morrisseau in a more active position, leaning over a more complete art work and wearing a sports jacket. Although it ran just one day after the alarming report of Morrisseau's drunkenness, this follow-up article reads more positively and places Morrisseau in control of his actions, stating, "I've made up my mind, I'm sobering up, I'm detoxifying myself."[60] The photograph captures an engaged artist at work at the Marion Scott Gallery as opposed to in a shabby hotel room. Marion Scott Gallery director Judy Kardosh clarifies that Morrisseau had "been visiting the gallery regularly during the past six weeks, and it wasn't true, as reported, that he had disappeared."[61] As is typical in the media, no attempt is made to reconcile the divergent narratives, seemingly objectively reported yet undermined by the gallery director. Similar photographs taken from this same location on the same day surfaced later in other news stories. For example, the *Globe and Mail* used a photograph from this series on 6 June in a story that attempted to encapsulate the events of the past month: " 'Now Is the Magical Moment I Start Again:' No Regrets, No Booze for Norval Morrisseau."[62] In this photograph, Morrisseau's puffy eyes and ill-fitting blazer offer proof to readers of his supposed attempt to pull himself together. Yet readers, trained by the multiple discourses and constructions that bombard them in the media and other forms of popular culture, would find little reassurance in the words and photographs that reinforce the tropes they expect of the Imaginary Indian. "Street Life Suits Morrisseau" was the headline of a CP wire story printed in the *Globe and Mail* that pokes fun at Morrisseau, using quotes by the artist to reveal that he is ill-equipped for modern life, undermining his credibility as the reporter questions Morrisseau's statements: "His current income comes from selling art on the street. He says he sells pieces for $150, but the proprietor says privately that some sketches go for $25. He denies another report that his lack of success has driven him to alcohol. 'Baloney, my paintings are selling. Still thousands and thousands of dollars.'"[63] The reporter confirms that Morrisseau requested, as he had numerous times in the past to reporters, "not to 'start asking those same kind of questions or else we're wasting our time.'" Reporters seldom like to be told what they can and can't ask and so the disciplining continues, as the reporter confides in readers that even though Morrisseau says he has stopped drinking, he has been told by the gallery proprietor where the interview took place that "she believed he had been drinking prior to the interview." The report provides additional evidence of Morrisseau's problematic behaviour with the inclusion of the quote, "I don't drink anymore" followed by a sentence that challenges his claim. "Moments later he said he needs drink 'to inspire my head.'"[64]

The plethora of stories in May 1987 related to Morrisseau's questionable actions should not be considered surprising. Readers, long fed a steady diet of what constitutes proper Canadian etiquette, have found Indigenous behaviours wanting. Morrisseau's case, charted by the press since 1962, had been established early on, as noted in Chapter 1. Clearly, Morrisseau represents not himself but all Indigenous peoples in this discourse. His body and his behaviour serve as signifiers of colonialism. The artist's performative acts as captured in May 1987 reflect a primer for racial performance, making Morrisseau's personal plight applicable to all Canada's Aboriginals.

Newspaper coverage in the 1960s and '70s, as outlined previously, shaped readers' understandings of Morrisseau in ways that primed them for the maelstrom that occurred in May 1987. *Vancouver Sun* columnist Denny Boyd's rapid-fire succession of stories over a two-week period charted a roller-coaster ride relating to a sad turn of events in Morrisseau's life. These reports, while ostensibly related to Morrisseau's behaviour specifically, confirmed media constructions of Indigenous peoples more generally.

The *Vancouver Sun* positioned one report as an alarm from friends who had helped Morrisseau in the past but who now found his alcoholism had driven the artist to such depths that he was living on the streets in downtown Vancouver. The report explains how "alcohol now has a value greater than his own art for Morrisseau."[65] Morrisseau responded to reports of his drunkenness by asking "what all the fuss was about" in an interview that took place at a downtown Vancouver art gallery, where he claimed to have rectified the unfortunate turn of events.[66] However, the report questions Morrisseau's integrity by refuting his assertion that he had stopped drinking with a caution from the "gallery proprietor" that states "she believed he had been drinking prior to Monday's interview."[67] Her opinion carries more weight than Morrisseau's words, and perhaps rightly so, as he was admitted to hospital in Vancouver later that day, where he spent more than ten days recovering from his destructive experience.

Not everyone agreed with the attention the press afforded this story. A letter to the editor by Regina resident Catherine Hopwood in the 20 May *Globe and Mail* challenged the paper's editorial decision to run the front-page story "Drink of Tequila Started Painter on Road to Despair" (May 11).

"Indeed, the story of a drinking problem is hardly newsworthy, and I am hard pressed to describe the running of this story on the front page of a national paper as anything but hostile. It feeds into the old stereotype of the drinking Indian," writes an "outraged" Hopwood.[68] Donald Clement's letter to the editor on 27 May questioned the paper's willingness to blame Morrisseau's recent problems on a "simplistic" assumption that his problems "started" with a "single drink of tequila" while attending his art opening in Santa Barbara, California. Hinting at deeper systemic and colonial issues at play, Clement challenged the paper to dig deeper into why Morrisseau struggled to integrate into Canadian culture: "This is cause for concern, not only for those interested in Ojibway art, but for all Canadians who want to see the culture of native peoples not only survive, but become the rightful centerpiece of our multicultural mosaic."[69] Clement's well-founded concerns illustrate, however, the enduring aim of assimilation at play in his wishes. More importantly, Clement's comments articulate how Morrisseau and his behaviour have been conflated with a monolithic discourse related to Indigenous peoples generally. The ongoing reportage, with references to celebrity, has less to do, however, with an individual artist, and is instead directly related to a larger discourse of race. Morrisseau, according to Clement, acts as he does not because he is an alcoholic, but because he is the product of colonialism. Morrisseau deviates from the performative demands of Canadian white society in terms of his behaviour. Press reports demonstrate that Morrisseau's lack of control with regard to alcohol lead to his inability to embody the attributes of a white citizen-subject. Clement's concern for Morrisseau then references all Aboriginal peoples in Canada, in his plea that "the" monolithic culture of "native peoples not only survives" but should be co-opted by Canadian nationalist propaganda related to Canadian diversity.

Surely all of this negative coverage must have been devastating to Morrisseau's artistic reputation, but then again, as Oscar Wilde posited, the only thing worse than being talked about is not being talked about. The *Toronto Star*'s 22 May story confirmed that Morrisseau's press attention had in fact sparked renewed interest in Indian art. "Publicity surrounding Morrisseau's battle with liquor" was good for business, according to Vancouver gallery owner Marion Scott, who nevertheless found the number of calls she was receiving for appraisals "distasteful."[70] Still, the business of selling Morrisseau art was different than that of selling mainstream Canadian art. While the press followed Morrisseau's alcohol-induced implosion feverishly, an art auction at Sotheby's in Toronto covered by *Globe and Mail* arts reporter John Bentley Mays noted that "a large 1953 abstraction by [Jean-Paul]

Riopelle sold for $150,000, the highest price ever paid at auction for a work by a living Canadian painter."[71]

Morrisseau discussed his recent roller-coaster ride with reporter Stephen Godfrey in Vancouver in June. The story was printed in the *Globe and Mail* and sketches the events after the exhibitions in Los Angeles and Santa Barbara, and offers Morrisseau's thoughts on what happened. Now sober, the artist demonstrates candour as he looks forward to productive days ahead. Admitting he enjoyed his days on the streets ("I met a lot of nice people. I might even do it again—without the booze—so I can remember them all more clearly"), Morrisseau says that alcohol allowed him to be "free to forget." He frankly discusses how he was exploited by coercive art dealers who, when he suffered his setback, did not came to his aid, although they benefited financially from Morrisseau's art. "I know I'm eccentric and difficult," says Morrisseau, astutely admitting, "I've got to get away from those guys that call themselves agents."[72] It seems that the press wasn't as ready to move on from the story as Morrisseau was. In September the *Globe and Mail* printed another story to update Canadians on Morrisseau's resumption of painting. In "Morrisseau Returns, Ready to Paint," there is little to report beyond the continual rehashing of the events of February through May. With a new exhibition opening in Edmonton in November, where prices "will command thousands of dollars," Morrisseau warns potential buyers that the bargains for his art are part of the past: "You should have come to Robson Square (in Vancouver) because $50 is the price that was going there."[73] As Morrisseau looked forward to financial and artistic stability, news stories about him slowed to a trickle.

A Magician of the Earth: An End to the 1980s, an End for Morrisseau?

In May 1989 in Paris, France, an exhibition opened at the Centre Georges Pompidou and the Villette to celebrate the two-hundredth anniversary of the French Revolution. Titled *Magiciens de la Terre*, it consisted of two massive galleries of art works culled from diverse cultural traditions. Morrisseau was chosen as one of the one hundred artists to be featured in the show, with fifty artists of European genealogy, such as Canada's Jeff Wall, and fifty others considered to be ethnic or Third World—the category into which Morrisseau was fitted along with Inuit artist Paulosee Kuniliusee. The exhibition was considered France's response to the controversial 1984 Museum of Modern Art (MOMA) exhibition *Primitivism in 20th Century Art: Affinity of the Tribal and the Modern*, in which MOMA's curator William

Rubin, according to Ivan Karp, had simply integrated "the aesthetics of other cultural traditions into a particular moment within his own tradition."[74] Karp concludes that the curators of *Magiciens* did no better than the curator of *Primitivism*. By asserting that all artists are equally conscious of the sources and meanings of the art they create, the result was "an elimination of cultural context, motives, and resources from the record."[75] In a more recent analysis of the exhibition of 1989, Norman Kleeblatt confirms that the "denuncia-tion of *Magiciens* was extensive, almost universal."[76] Jean-Hubert Martin, lead curator for *Magiciens*, failed, according to Benjamin Buchloh and Hans Belting, to negate the colonial perspectives of power because of the use of the centre-periphery model in organizing the exhibition.[77]

Three works by Morrisseau were included in the controversial exhibi-tion: *Sacred Bear* (1972); *The Gift* (1975); and *Artist with Thunderbird Vision* (1977). In the slick catalogue produced for the exhibition he was situated first by geographic location (each of the artists was pinpointed on a map of the world). Morrisseau was described in a short biography as having been brought up by his shaman grandfather, "homme des mythes et chaman."[78] Explaining that he grew up caught between two worlds, the description notes that he was forbidden to speak his own language and made to feel guilty and traumatized. Morrisseau is credited with being the first contemporary Indigenous artist in Canada and the founder of the Woodland school of painting that depicts traditional and mythological images of the Ojibwe. He uses a colour palette, explains the text, that is both symbolic and precise; white, for example, is used for spirituality. When coupled with the overall tenor of the catalogue, Morrisseau is framed once again as Other.

While the exhibition was widely covered by the French press, I have not found it mentioned in Canadian papers. An exhibition of Indigenous art mounted at the Vancouver Art Gallery in summer 1989 called *Beyond History*, characterized by Liam Lacey in the *Globe and Mail* as "angry," illustrates a shift in fashionable contemporary Indigenous art. *Beyond History* included such artists as Carl Beam, Bob Boyer, Joane Cardinal-Schubert, Robert Houle, and Edward Poitras. Notably absent in this provocative exhibition was art by Morrisseau. Lacey clearly separates the artists included in this exhibition who reference "political and social life in current artistic language" from Morrisseau by explaining, "When you think of native art, you probably think of a typical late-sixties painting: multi-colored, stylized and entitled something like Bear and Eagle, with both animals' shapes joined together like a cluster of what looks faintly like one-celled creatures."[79] Lacey contends that "The native art Canadians came to know in the sixties had the charm of exotica: vibrant, colourful, and powerful in a totemistic way...Native art was domesticated, of continuing interest only to the tourists and professional collectors."[80] It appears as though Morrisseau's inclusion in the *Magiciens* exhibition in Paris would have further discounted his significance as exotica to Lacey and Tom Hill and Karen Duffek, the curators who mounted *Beyond History*.

One of Morrisseau's exhibited paintings in *Magiciens*, *Sacred Bear*, was included in an essay that summer in *Le Point*, an art magazine published in Paris, but the text did not engage with Morrisseau's work and instead focused on art by African artists.[81] Interestingly, *Parachute* magazine, a quarterly Canadian journal, did cover *Magiciens de la Terre* in its July 1989 issue. It was written in the form of an interview between reporter René Viau, lead curator Jean-Hubert Martin, and his assistant André Magnin, who had been charged with coming to Canada to secure art for the exhibition. Magnin explains that he set out with an interest in the work of Norval Morrisseau but found that he had disappeared from circulation and could not find him.[82] Finally, while visiting the West Coast to view Haida art, he encountered Morrisseau and visited his studio, inviting him to participate. Magnin also explained his interest in Inuit artist Paulosee Kuniliusee, whose work was included in the exhibition. While the Inuit Co-operative art can be viewed as "airport art," according to Magnin, he considers Paulosee's work to be profound. This *Parachute* interview makes clear that while Morrisseau's work was known to the French curatorial team, finding the artist was not easy.

Characterized yet again as a magician, Morrisseau's inclusion in the Paris exhibition is noteworthy for a number of reasons. First, by being in an exhibition with such international art stars as Marina and Ulay Abromovic, Christian Boltanski, Claes Oldenburg, Nam June Paik, and Jeff Wall, Morrisseau's international reputation increased. However, unlike the global art stars named above, his art was not associated with the "big names" in art. Morrisseau was instead situated in a game of identity politics writ large. The huge exhibition of historical significance had a clear message, and difference was key. The contemporary white artists did art that was different from the Othered artists, who were, according to post-colonial scholar Rasheed Araeen, "still trapped in their tribal, folk, naïve and innocent worlds."[83] This perceived difference, so present in Paris in the summer of 1989, had long been evident to Morrisseau in his dealings with the Canadian art world.

In August 1989, *Globe and Mail* columnist and poet Gwendolyn MacEwen played with popular cultural references when she described her recent sighting of Morrisseau in downtown Toronto. "Brushes with Greatness:

Close Encounters of the Personal Kind" riffed on two pop culture references to describe the larger-than-life artist:

> Out of Murray's Restaurant at Bloor and Avenue Road emerged a lanky figure in blue jeans splotched with a thousand different colors of oil paints. I did a double-take; then, thunderstruck, I approached him—avatar of Thunderbird himself, greatest of our native artists.
>
> "Norval Morrisseau," I said in an awed whisper. "I am so happy to see you at last ..."
>
> "I am not Norval Morrisseau," said Norval Morrisseau.
>
> "Look," I ventured, "I'm one of your greatest admirers. I'm a writer. I've quoted you in some of my poetry."
>
> "All I want to know is where I can find a decent bacon and egg sandwich in this town," said Norval, peering over my head.[84]

The writer's witty banter suggests that the so-called art star was now too big for his britches, and had little time for "this short, white female who was wasting their time."[85] This short account plays with the shaman artist mythology, with MacEwen's description of an avatar within the context of a Hollywood alien movie reference. The alien, however, once again performatively challenges the reporter's privilege. Morrisseau has every right to be unimpressed by a writer who has written poetry about him. He prefers finding a good sandwich to spending time with a wordsmith who then uses her connections and his star power to turn this abrupt conversation into an amusing anecdote that serves her aim. He was not on display in the gallery; he was simply someone out looking for a sandwich. By refusing to engage in a conversation that the reporter demands, Morrisseau equalizes the playing field.

· · ·

In October 1990, art critic Christopher Hume wrote, "Ojibway Painter's Pointed Works Face Facts of Modern Indian Life." Hume was not referring to Morrisseau, however, but to forty-seven-year old Carl Beam. "Along with artists such as Jane Ash Poitras and Robert Houle, Beam is one of a tiny handful of native painters whose concerns go well beyond tribal myths and the way things used to be."[86] With this one sentence, Hume (like Liam Lacey's 1989 report) emphatically dismisses Morrisseau and turns his attention to Beam, the new Indigenous art sensation. Beam's work is edgy, controversial, and created using techniques that relate to new directions in conceptual and contemporary art movements of the time.

Writing in the context of the Oka Crisis, Hume states, "As the summer's events made clear, treating Indians like dirt is official government policy in Canada. That's not new, of course. But what has always surprised me is how few native artists have dealt with this in their work. Around here, most are busy producing Norval Morrisseau–inspired legend paintings. Out west and down south, they do essentially the same thing. Fortunately, there are a few exceptions."[87] And with that, Hume brings to an end Morrisseau's importance as an artist in the media. As the curators of *Magiciens de la Terre* found in their quest to find Morrisseau in 1988, he had disappeared.

Gift Giving

Given the dramatic ups and downs the media captured during the decade of the 1980s, it is a wonder Morrisseau had time to paint, but paint he did. In 1983, while the artist was riding the tide of success, he decided to do something dramatic as a way to help advance his ongoing but mostly unnoticed efforts to advocate for change in Canada's colonial handling of Indigenous peoples. He decided to create a painting and give it to the people of Canada.

It was not the first time Morrisseau had gifted a painting to the Canadian people. In 1981, in response to his 1978 Order of Canada award, Morrisseau painted a large mural, *A Separate Reality*, for the then National Museum of Man that later became a showpiece of the Canadian Museum of Civilization's First People's Hall in 2003.[88] Early in 1983 Morrisseau called then Prime Minister Pierre Trudeau with the offer to give the people of Canada another large painting. A follow-up handwritten letter, dated 19 February 1983 was sent by his agent, James P. Richards, on behalf of the artist, explaining that Morrisseau had telephoned the Prime Minister's office and that this correspondence served to formally explain his wish to offer a gift of both the mural (untitled in the letter) and a set of limited-edition porcelain plates titled *Children of Mother Earth*.[89] Morrisseau clearly and forcefully states his wishes for a formal ceremony at the Department of Indian Affairs to present the art directly to Trudeau "on or about March 14," illustrating an ease and certainty with his identity as a senior artist. The three-page letter provides rough dimensions of the painting and the need for a two-week lead time prior to the unveiling ceremony with the Prime Minister in order to finish the painting, transport it to Ottawa, re-stretch, hang, and make final details to the work. Morrisseau asks for money to cover labour, travel, and material expenses. To better explain his vision for the mural, he adds: "The

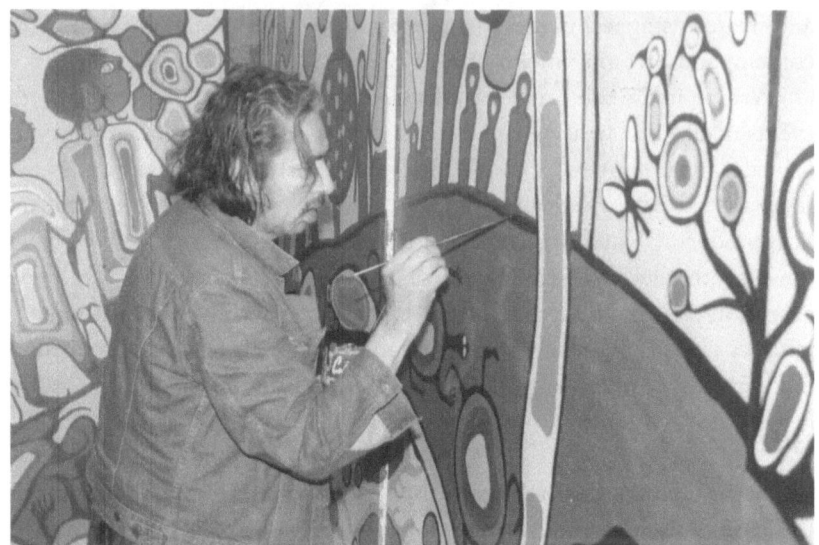

Morrisseau touches up *Androgyny* (1983) prior to the 15 April 1983 gift-giving ceremony and unveiling in the foyer of INAC headquarters in Gatineau, Quebec. Reproduced with permission of the Indigenous and Northern Affairs Canada Aboriginal Art Centre archives.

theme of the mural is A [*sic*] shaman that is Androgyne in four directions, filled with all parts of nature in Canada, thunderbeings, sacred serpents and turtles, flowers, animals, and we children of Mother Earth. PS. Butterflies and Bumble Bees, too!"[90] He also admits in the letter that he had lost his Order of Canada medal that was awarded to him, and would appreciate receiving a new one in advance of the unveiling ceremony.

Although the Prime Minister agreed to most of the terms of the gift, he did not show up for Morrisseau's unveiling of *Androgyny*. The Minister of Supply and Services, Jean-Jacques Blais, accepted the work on Trudeau's behalf. A series of photos and an internal newsletter illustrate Morrisseau's last-minute touch-ups and preparations for the ceremony at the Indian Affairs location in Hull (Gatineau). Morrisseau's envisioned plan worked and acknowledged his importance as an artist whose stature was such as an artist in Canada that he could contact the Prime Minister's office and have his wishes met.

Morrisseau offered *Androgyny* as a gift to the Canadian people with certain reciprocal expectations inherent in Anishinaabek ceremonial exchange. The Prime Minister of Canada accepted the painting from the senior artist and it was accessioned into the Indian Art collection at the Department of

Indian Affairs (INAC), the colonial branch of the government that oversaw First Nations people. Both the gifting and the painting situate ceremony as a central concept to this theoretical understanding of art.

"In Anishinaabe tradition, an offering is a gift. It's a gesture of relationship between people, animals, spirits, and other entities in the universe, given in the interests of creating ties, honoring them, or asking for assistance and direction," explain Jill Doerfler, Niigaanwewidam James Sinclair, and Heidi Kiiwetinepinesiik Stark in the introduction to *Centering Anishinaabeg Studies*, reminding readers that an offering carries with it responsibility articulated in cultural protocols.[91] Morrisseau's gift of *A Separate Reality* in 1981 demonstrates his adherence to such cultural protocols, signifying a response to the honour accorded him by the nation. Doerfler, Sinclair, and Stark reiterate that the acceptance of the offered gift also forges a bond that should be "a mutually beneficial partnership, not only for participants, but for the universe around them."[92] This ceremonial exchange is central to the narrative surrounding *Androgyny*. Morrisseau, I think, deliberately offered his painting as a gift to the Prime Minister and forcefully stated his wishes for a formal ceremony at the Department of Indian Affairs to present the art directly to the leader of the country, hoping to facilitate and inspire a different relationship for First Nations with Canada—a symbolic gesture for future change.

As a painting consigned to hanging in a government building, *Androgyny* served as a form of benign decoration, yet that was never the intent of Morrisseau, who painted a provocative work that challenged Canadian values and skewed views on gender. The site itself affected its meaning and value. The Terrasses de la Chaudière, where the work was permanently installed, is a complex of federal government offices built in 1978 as part of Prime Minister Trudeau's vision to see more government workers located in Quebec, directly across the river from Ottawa. The building complex houses about 6,500 workers and includes the headquarters of Indigenous and Northern Affairs Canada (INAC). *Androgyny* is part of the INAC Indian Art collection and therefore is cared for by this colonial arm of the Canadian government.

By virtue of Morrisseau's gifting his painting to the "People of Canada" and its acceptance into the colonial arm of the Canadian government's INAC art collection, the work of art entered into a colonial archive. Ann Laura Stoler's work on conceiving of a colonial archive as a process rather than as a static form is applicable. She argues that archival materials have not been left behind or become obsolete; instead, Stoler finds that colonial archives (in her case those of the Netherland Indies) are an "arsenal" of sorts that can be reactivated to suit new governing strategies.[93] I believe her concept of reading a colonial archive as an agential act is useful when considering Morrisseau's gift to a collection of art—an archive—administered by the INAC. The purview of hanging the work in government settings moved this work into a new milieu that was not, I think, what Morrisseau had had in mind when he offered the gift. Adding the painting to a government department's collection shifted Morrisseau's intention of gift giving to one of claiming and control, fraught with colonial power. Still, having imbued the painting with its own agency, it, like Morrisseau, performs its own version of Indigeneity as it moves through space and time.

The painting would hang in the INAC location for over twenty years. Morrisseau's effort to engage in a reciprocal gifting ceremony that implied something returned in exchange for the monumental painting was thwarted when the gift was interpreted within a different cultural frame. *Androgyny* took on new meaning during Morrisseau's retrospective exhibition. At that point, both Morrisseau and his painting were rediscovered by the art world and by the media.

CHAPTER FIVE

2006
Re-Mythologizing Mishomis

*The drunken bullshit, the weird write-ups, the people they say I
don't want to meet. I have taken my attention off people. Now
it's on Norval the shaman, the painter....*[1]

Norval Morrisseau

Newsworthiness tends to adhere to events, and therefore the media's attention span for stories is often short-lived. The media frenzy surrounding Morrisseau's life in and around 1987 slowed to a trickle once the papers lost interest in the artist's personal life and when the narrative no longer fit the sensational framing of Morrisseau's downward spiral. Cultural historian Charmaine McEachern, in her discussion of media coverage of events surrounding South Africa's Truth and Reconciliation Commission, finds that media narrativation is most often framed in moral terms, and that once the moral focus of a news event has passed, the media is no longer interested in reporting on it.[2] Media coverage of Morrisseau was spotty in the 1990s, as the aging artist slipped into obscurity only to be rediscovered when he received a retrospective at Canada's National Gallery of Ottawa in 2006.

In 1991 two exhibitions of art that included his work led to some media interest, and the tone of these stories illustrates how Morrisseau has faded from public sight. Christopher Hume, writing for the *Toronto Star*, reassures readers that Morrisseau looks as good as when he interviewed him in 1978, demonstrating a lapse in public awareness. Recalling stale but recurring media stories about the artist, Hume draws attention to Morrisseau's checkered past as he reports that Morrisseau "insists he has never been better. He's not on a bender. Not under Mafia control. Not dying in the gutters of Vancouver. In fact the artist is not only alive but well."[3] In 1999, in the Arts and Leisure section of the *Globe and Mail*, Chris Dafoe's feature on Morrisseau once again reacquainted readers with the artist in an exclusive interview titled "Such a Long Journey." Above a photograph of Norval being embraced by his friend and caregiver Gabe Vadas, a short introduction under the heading "Exclusive" prefaces the story: "Painter Norval Morrisseau blazed an artistic trail in Canada, bringing native imagery to the cultural mainstream. But his life has been marred by alcoholism, homelessness and now, Parkinson's disease. After years of silence, he talks to the *Globe and Mail* about how he's found stability with a young man and his family, and how painting still sustains him."[4] The feature, framed around a meeting between the reporter and the two men at the popular Joe Forte restaurant in downtown Vancouver, begins with a description of Morrisseau's appearance and that of Gabe Vadas. That the ailing sixty-eight-year-old sits in a wheelchair with "long-nailed fingers," "long, grey and unkempt" hair, paired with a description of the bone breastplate "hung with what appears to be a silver watch and a copper ornament" that he wears under a windbreaker, reinforces enduring desriptors. Gabe Vadas, "his Hungarian son—he is 33 and his kinship with the old man is not recognized by family or law," is described as looking at the artist with "rough affection." Dafoe describes Vadas's appearance as bearded, with "long hair and ... dressed in jeans and an old red and black checked shirt."[5] The thick description is meant to juxtapose Morrisseau and Vadas with the clientele of the restaurant, who Dafoe notes are somewhat awestruck over the presence of the artist.

After a couple of paragraphs describing Morrisseau's problems in the late 1980s and 1990s, Dafoe situates Morrisseau within his mythical narrative. "Critics have compared him to artistic giants such as Pablo Picasso and Marc Chagall," explains the reporter, adding: "One collector, Jasper art dealer Galal Helmy, went even further. I would buy Morrisseau before I would touch Picasso." The report also notes that Picasso received one of Morrisseau's works from an early patron and that his style was highly influential, spawning "countless imitators."[6] The report is like a dance as it hops from side to side, describing Morrisseau's problematic past and behaviours punctuated by alcohol and drug abuse and philandering (noting, though offering no evidence to support, that Morrisseau may have fathered as many as fourteen children), and then heralding his phenomenal success as an artist. It reads like the paradox advanced in the 1974 NFB film that presented the Morrisseau's pull between Christianity and Anishinaabe spirituality.

Don Robinson, Toronto art dealer and owner of the Kinsman Robinson Gallery that had represented the artist for the past ten years, is quoted extensively, confirming that Vadas has been a stabilizing influence and observing that "Gabe isn't highly educated and it's a difficult role to play, but Norval is definitely the better for it." Robinson, too, like Vadas, brings up the bitter issue of forgeries and mistreatment of the artist by unscrupulous "finaglers and forgers who exploited him," whom Vadas characterizes as "a lot of leeches." Morrisseau "mischievously" corrects this assessment by repositioning them as "shaman-in-training." Still, by 1999, as the reporter makes clear, copyright and exploitation were issues clouding Morrisseau's significance as an artist. The story concludes by reasserting Morrisseau's shamanistic construction: "The old Indian looked on silently, through heavy lidded eyes, as his Hungarian son talked excitedly about the mystical tales of legends and the power they possess. It is a world the old man knows well, a world that has been much kinder to him than this one."[7] Paired with this feature is a short assessment of Morrisseau's importance by *Globe and Mail* visual art critic Blake Gopnik. In this report, Morrisseau's legacy as a trailblazer is confirmed while some of the myths surrounding his artistic style are dispelled. Referencing some of the new names in Indigenous art represented in the National Gallery in 1999, including Faye Heavyshield and Dorothy Grant, Robert Houle, by then a Native studies professor at the Ontario College of Art and Design in Toronto, clarifies that the birchbark scroll imagery was an influence but specific images were not presented, nor should they be understood as modern equivalents to the scrolls. "Morrisseau argued that they were medicine—but I'm not going to hold my breath on that," states Houle as he challenges Morrisseau's own myth-building narrative about his art being spiritual medicine. Gerald McMaster, then curator of Indian art at the Canadian Museum of Civilization, adds, "Morrisseau was trying to speak to a larger audience whereas traditional objects spoke to an internal audience."[8] The Gopnik report cogently concludes by stating that Morrisseau "prompted" other Native artists to take from a number of art traditions, something mainstream artists had long done.

Included with the two feature articles are six photographs. As noted, the front-page contemporary photo of Morrisseau and Vadas commands attention and visually brings Morrisseau's importance into the present day. A smaller photograph on the front page is a reproduction of Morrisseau's monumental *Observations of the Astral World* (1990) with a note that the "2.4 metre by 5.1 metre painting has never been exhibited." This work is not discussed in the body of the essay, however. The other four photographs are found in the back of the section: a small photo of Morrisseau "Down and out in Vancouver, 1987"; a 1964 photo of the artist with his wife Harriet and their two young children, Victoria and Pierre; a picture of Morrisseau at the Tom Thomson Cabin artist residency at Kleinburg, Ontario, before his incomplete painting *Child of the Year* (1979); and finally a photo of the artist in 1962 at his historic premiere exhibition at the Pollock Gallery. The pictures are meant to visually document Morrisseau's career. The inclusion of the family photo from 1964 reconfirms the artist's racial identity, as he is wearing a beaded and fringed buckskin jacket and his son is in a traditional *tikinagan*. The juxtaposition of the 1962 photo at the Pollock Gallery with the 1990 reproduction of *Observations of the Astral World* provides an example of how Morrisseau's style changed over the course of his career, while the 1979 Kleinburg photo signals Morrisseau's success in the Canadian art world. Finally, the 1987 picture, which had been carried by a number of the Canadian dailies when it was found that Morrisseau was living on the streets in Vancouver after a recurrence of his alcoholism, reminds readers of a key feature of his mythical story—one tied closely to the tropes assigned the Imaginary Indian in Canada.

The 1999 *Globe and Mail* feature serves as a preface to the artist's twenty-first-century renaissance. Four stories surfaced in the *Globe and Mail* between 2000 and 2005 in advance of his retrospective that referred to Morrisseau tangentially, and two additional stories were penned that related to issues of authentication. A permanent collection exhibition at the Thunder Bay Art Gallery in 2000 included works by Morrisseau and was promoted in a short report in the *Globe and Mail* that celebrated the gallery's impressive Indigenous art collection. Linda Turk explains that Morrisseau "lived and worked in Thunder Bay for part of his life, and it brings a strange thrill of recognition to see the same Jack pines and ravens in his paintings that can be seen outside the gallery" but says little of substance about his art.[9] A 2004 story about Tom Hill receiving the Governor General's Award describes Morrisseau as the "archetype for native art."[10] A brief report about a $200,000 award from Ontario's Cultural Attractions fund for the McMichael Gallery's fortieth anniversary explains that much of the investment will be used to promote "a retrospective of the works of first-nations artist Norval Morrisseau." Little more is said about the artist or retrospective other than that it is being mounted by the National Gallery of Canada.

Kate Taylor's 2005 commentary in the *Globe and Mail* related to an initiative entitled "Art of This Land." The new installation incorporates Indigenous art into the historical Canadian art collection and signals a long overdue change in curatorial policy at the National Gallery of Canada that came about "quietly, slowly, without much political debate or public fanfare."[11] Taylor notes that while the gallery has organized several solo exhibitions by Inuit printmakers, Norval Morrisseau will be the "first Indian artist" to receive a retrospective at the gallery. She describes Morrisseau as a contemporary artist "who revolutionized Canadian art by painting Ojibway legends that had never been visually recorded."

In the course of a month in 2005, James Adams wrote two feature-length reports about the growing issue of fake Morrisseaus that had flooded the art market. Morrisseau hired legal counsel to set up a committee to function much like the Andy Warhol Art Authentication Board in the so-called ensuing battle over Morrisseau's art.[12] In both news stories Adams promotes Morrisseau as "Canada's most famous and influential first nations artist." In his first report Adams quotes Morrisseau's lawyer Aaron Milrad as acknowledging that his client "probably produced a lot of work to support his bad habits—works that, whatever their artistic merits, are nonetheless 'genuine' Morrisseaus."[13] In his April report Adams, who estimated the number of works by the artist at 9000, sketches the history of the allegations around fake Morrisseaus, opinions by Morrisseau and Gabe Vadas, comments by gallery owners, and how the market may be affected. Linking the story to his worth in the art market, the story concludes by observing how dealers are planning for higher prices with the upcoming retrospective.

While the *Globe and Mail* provided only a smattering of news related to Morrisseau's art, a *New York Times* arts report clearly recognized the power of Morrisseau's work. The newspaper commented on an exhibition of fifty of Morrisseau's drawings on loan from the Museum of Civilization and shown at New York City's Drawing Centre's Drawing Room in 2001, curated by Gerald McMaster and Catherine de Zeghler. Arts reporter Holland Cotter describes the show as "extraordinary" and calls the style of the drawings, many done on paper towels while Morrisseau was incarcerated in 1972–73, as "fluidly pictographic."[14] The review engages with Morrisseau's art though indirectly referencing signifiers often used in the media to describe the artist: "The results aren't ingratiating or beautiful. Like visionary works in many cultures, they're aggressive, sometimes violent, as much about fearfulness as about transcendence."[15]

Shaman Artist Retrospective

During the first decade of the twenty-first century, Morrisseau went from obscurity to a media sensation, and was rediscovered again with the announcement of a retrospective exhibition of his work at the National Gallery of Canada in Ottawa. What appeared to be a pivotal moment for Morrisseau with his 2006 retrospective resulted, in part, in stagnation because the press continued to frame him with the racialized and largely imaginary construction that it had relied on since 1962, a representation that considered his art works secondary to his "Indianness."[16]

The media had long painted Morrisseau with what Ralph Friar and Natasha Friar describe as a "permanent fictional identity," a construction fraught with colonial motivations such as assimilation, discipline, and racism.[17] Coverage of the retrospective exhibition subtly reinforced this frame, yet this time around there was a difference. Complicating the narrow colonial imaginary was the artist's rich artistic practice and his entry into the National Gallery of Canada with a retrospective exhibition, which confirmed his significance as one of Canada's great artists.

Morrisseau envisioned a future for Indigenous art based on the aesthetics and narratives inspired by Original People's art, and this made his art unique and important. The retrospective exhibition of his work complicated enduring press imagery because the breathtaking array of works assembled for the first time defied facile analysis and challenged the media's habit of focusing on the man rather than on the artwork. An interrogation of print media related to press coverage of the opening of Morrisseau's 2006 retrospective offers an opportunity to critically engage Morrisseau's vision and consider how the press responded to the startling collection of art presented.

The National Gallery's retrospective exhibition of Morrisseau's art career in October 2006 serves as a watershed moment in art historical discourse in Canada. To begin with, as the first retrospective exhibition afforded an Indigenous artist in Canada, its importance reaches historic proportions. Indigenous curator Greg Hill brought together a range of seminal works from private and public collections, curating an exhibition befitting the first entry of a southern Indigenous artist in the National Gallery.[18] A signal that Morrisseau had "made it," the National Gallery retrospective bestowed credibility by repositioning his art in convincing ways.

Though Morrisseau was a trailblazer from the early 1960s and left his mark on an Indigenous arts movement, large facets of his oeuvre had not been publicly accessible until fifty-nine representative works were assembled for the exhibition. Morrisseau was a mostly unknown or forgotten entity to the nation, and the retrospective provided opportunities to revisit his art and his mythology. While the retrospective exhibition provided Morrisseau's art with a newfound seriousness, what would happen to the imagined notion of Morrisseau—a mythology crafted in the press, art books, and documentary films in the 1960s and 1970s that endured and found its fullest form in the late 1980s?

An analysis of print media sources from two feature reports, written by the *Ottawa Citizen*'s Paul Gessell and the *Globe and Mail*'s art critic Sarah Milroy, and supporting art works help tell this story. Press reports surrounding the retrospective exhibition, in which the press rediscover this artist, demonstrate evidence of Morrisseau's work as a significant contribution to Canadian art history. The choice to award Norval Morrisseau a retrospective exhibition at the National Gallery of Canada in Ottawa opened a new dialogue on Morrisseau in the press.

For any artist, the role of a retrospective exhibition is to encompass a career in its entirety. The National Gallery's *Norval Morrisseau: Shaman Artist*, curated by Greg Hill, did something similar. Hanging Morrisseau's art in the National Gallery imbued it with what art historian Svetlana Alpers called the "museum effect."[19] The very act of hanging art in a museum setting changes the way an audience reacts to the work. If anything, the museum effect was even greater for Morrisseau because of the few works of Indigenous art on display at the National Gallery. In 1996 the gallery had purchased Anishinaabe artist Carl Beam's (1945–2005) *North American Iceberg* (1985). The large-scale work, completed on plexiglass, directly confronts colonialism and is representative of directions in contemporary Indigenous art in the 1980s and 1990s, when a new generation of artists began to create confrontational works. While Morrisseau had painted such themes in the 1970s, works by him were seldom shown in the press and were inaccessible to most Canadians.

Even before the exhibition officially opened, Morrisseau's art caught the attention of Canadians. A planned media event held prior to the opening on 3 February 2006 led to a flurry of new stories related to the exhibition in papers regionally and nationally. Many of the reports were accompanied by a photo of the ailing Morrisseau positioned in his wheelchair in front of *Androgyny*, an image widely disseminated over the wire service. *Androgyny*, the impressive mural painted by Morrisseau in 1983 as a gift to the people of Canada, had hung for the past twenty-three years in the lobby of the headquarters of the then Department of Indian Affairs and Northern Development in Gatineau, Quebec, as noted in Chapter 4.[20] While the painting had, over the years, become increasingly invisible as busy workers passed by it on a daily basis, it quickly created a new buzz in the gallery space. The news photograph of Morrisseau reunited with his gift to the people of Canada, when printed in papers across the nation, caused a sensation. It was impossible not to notice the painting's monumentality, its intense colours, defiant in its role as a backdrop, especially in juxtaposition to the ailing artist seated in his wheelchair before it.

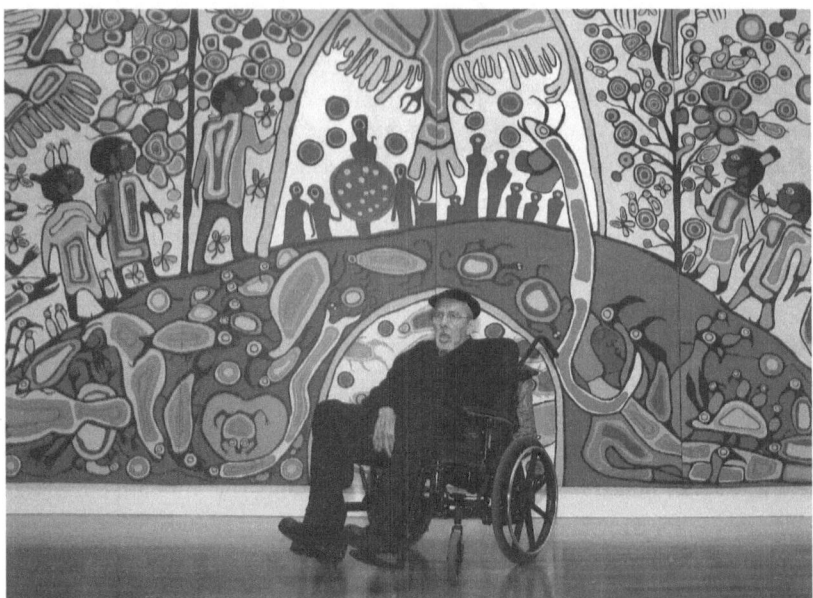

Norval Morrisseau seated in front of *Androgyny* (1983) on display at the National Gallery of Canada as part of his retrospective exhibition *Norval Morrisseau: Shaman Artist* (2006). This photo ran in the *Ottawa Citizen* with the headline, "'Copper Thunderbird' Gets His Day in the Sun." Reproduced with permission of the *Ottawa Citizen* archives.

The press photograph, visual evidence of Morrisseau and the painting installed at the National Gallery of Canada, invests the object—or is it objects?—with new meaning. Viewers of the newspaper easily conflate the photographic documentation with the art institution itself. Without having to enter the gallery space per se, the press photograph itself aids viewers/ readers in shifting the meaning of the work and thus transferring added significance to the painting. The *Ottawa Citizen* headline, for example, that ran above the large colour photograph, announces "Copper Thunderbird Gets His Day in the Sun," as it appropriates the painting's intense yellow colour as a sign of success, directly fusing *Androgyny* to the heightened status of Morrisseau's oeuvre to visually herald the artist's new-found importance.

A claiming of sorts occurs in viewing Morrisseau seated in his wheelchair before the painting. Like the art object behind him, the artist serves as an object of significance within this "virtual" gallery space. On display, caught by the camera, the "museum effect" for Morrisseau as *object* is arguably greater than that of the painting, because Canadians had long viewed Indigenous men on display through a colonial lens. Yet this objectification is different, a new value is accorded the Anishinaabe artist. Like *Androgyny*, Morrisseau himself becomes more important, because the National Gallery has claimed him as an artist for the Canadian canon of art history—he is no longer simply an Imaginary Indian. This newly constructed image of the artist also repositions art discourse surrounding Morrisseau's art.

In the actual gallery space, *Androgyny* played a key role in the exhibition. Viewers of the retrospective could not help but gasp at the overwhelming power of this work on display. With its pulsating colours and richly decorative imagery, *Androgyny* leaves a lasting impression. Locating this painting within the exhibition bolsters it, changing its meaning from its previous lobby installation. No longer a decorative accoutrement to a busy office building, Morrisseau's gift to the Canadian people finds new value in its museum setting and on the pages of Canadian newspapers.

Inserting Morrisseau and his paintings into this bastion of Canadian culture, if only for the course of the exhibition, accorded both the man and his art new respect and imbued them with a form of objectified exoticism. The press image and accompanying story manufacture and extend aspects of the museum space, changing the story of the object(s) and adding value through its sanction by the National Gallery. Unlike the powerful visual significance of the image of Morrisseau before his impressive painting, however, textual news coverage of the opening was less definitive. After the press conference organized by the National Gallery, in concert with the opening of the exhibition in Ottawa, veteran arts reporter Paul Gessell filed two reports for the *Ottawa Citizen*, the daily newspaper of the nation's capital. The *Citizen* paired the two stories with provocative headlines: "Taming Their Demons," and "An Art Pioneer Makes His Final Breakthrough."[21] A number of dailies across western Canada carried a version of Gessell's stories about the artist and the groundbreaking exhibition that was scheduled to hang until 3 April 2006, before beginning a two-year tour of other galleries. Four western papers carried edited and shortened versions of Gessell's stories.[22]

What Gessell says about Morrisseau is important because his story reached a wide Canadian audience. As noted, he penned two stories for the *Ottawa Citizen*'s final edition that day. "An Art Pioneer Makes His Final Breakthrough" ran on the front page, with a 1999 photograph of the artist provided by the National Gallery and a caption that read, "Who would be the first Native artist to be given a show akin to the exhibitions granted such 'white' Canadian artists as Tom Thomson and Emily Carr? The consensus among the Aboriginal art community was that Norval Morrisseau, seen here [in an accompanying photograph] in 1999, had to be the one."[23] This concise report conveys a sense of the importance of this exhibition within the context of the National Gallery and the Canadian art world. Gessell prophetically suggests that the show "could very well be the final nail in the coffin of institutionalized discrimination against First Nations art, or what used to be called Indian art, at the National Gallery." The arts writer has done his homework, as he charges the cultural institutions in Canada for having long exercised a form of "cultural apartheid" that could not end until the National Gallery gave a First Nations artist a "solo show akin to the kinds of exhibitions granted ... 'white' Canadian artists."[24] Quoting contemporary Aboriginal art curator from the Canadian Museum of Civilization Lee-Ann Martin as confirmation that the Indigenous art community felt Morrisseau deserved the honour of being the "first," Gessell sketches a short overview of Morrisseau's career since the sold-out exhibition at the Pollock Gallery in 1962. The *Calgary Herald* and the *Edmonton Journal* both include Gessell's provocative comment, "The exhibition could very well be the final nail in the coffin of institutionalized discrimination against First Nations Art."[25] Little in this politicized report concerns Morrisseau's art directly, as it speaks to the significance of an exhibition by an Indigenous artist more generally.

Greg Hill's retrospective catalogue *Norval Morrisseau: Shaman Artist*, published by the National Gallery of Canada in 2006, serves as a comprehensive archive of the exhibition, and includes three essays: one by Hill that positions Morrisseau's significance in Canadian art history; one by Ruth B. Phillips, who focuses on the early portion of Morrisseau's career; and an extended prose poem by Armand Garnet Ruffo that celebrates the artist's life. The catalogue also includes a list of works included, with colour reproductions, archival photographs, and a timeline of the artist's achievements. The essays focus on Morrisseau's contributions to Canadian art, positioning his significance within a larger art milieu and directly relating his achievements to his cultural heritage.

Still, while the exhibition catalogue presented interested readers complete and scholarly information regarding the artist, it was the media that reached a wider audience and therefore informed Canadians about Morrisseau and his retrospective in ways that would otherwise have been inaccessible to most of the population. Gessell's second story, an in-depth feature story in the Arts section of the *Ottawa Citizen* (with portions printed in western Canadian newspapers) offers readers a more accessible narrative about the artist and his art. "Taming Their Demons" includes six colour reproductions of Morrisseau works from the exhibition. Gessell begins "Taming" by once again striking a blow at the National Gallery. He leads with the following:

"More than an exhibit, it's an exorcism of sorts: In his upcoming solo show, the aging Norval Morrisseau escapes his image as a twisted soul conflicted by cultures, booze and sex. And the National Gallery finally, fully embraces the First Nations art it ignored for so long."[26] The term "exorcism" invoked by Gessell is a problematic one. Is he suggesting that Morrisseau is haunted by demons that require some sort of colonial cleansing? Does Gessell mean that by including Morrisseau's art in the National Gallery, his work has been assimilated into mainstream Canada's art world? Is the artist and are, by extension, other First Nations artists worthy of entry into the ivory tower because the artists have begun to act civilized, or because First Nations arts are truly of equal or greater value than much of the art present in the collection? Or does Gessell feel he can undo the media history that preceded him by recasting Morrisseau and his art within a revisionist art dialogue?

When paired with "demons," the term "exorcism" conjures up the images of primitive culture that Pearl McCarthy spoke of in her 1962 reports in the *Globe and Mail* and reinforces the Morrisseau mythology that had its roots with that first exhibition. Gessell succeeds in reactivating constructions that signify the very demons he ostensibly aims to ban in this feature report. As noted, most Canadians reading about Morrisseau in 2006 had little understanding of the artist or his biography, and thus these reports provided a significant introduction for readers. Given that Gessell finds odious the history of cultural apartheid at the National Gallery, a reader might expect to find a narrative that elevates the artist from former stereotypical press reportage. Sadly, even while Gessell writes with good intentions, he slips into a common discourse pattern.

Extracting somewhat obscure quotes from gallery dealer Jack Pollock's 1989 autobiography, Gessell resurrects details related to Pollock's initial meetings with the artist in 1962 as a way to link Morrisseau's success to mainstream actions, just as the NFB films of the early 1970s had.[27] Noting, by way of a quote, that Morrisseau was "disgusting—drunk and he had pissed his pants" and that "his house was in the middle of a garbage dump" in the first 100 words of the approximately 1,000-word essay, Gessell reinforces decidedly stereotypical constructions that overwhelm readers with a version of Morrisseau's life that had little to do with his art prowess but much to do with a negative racialized identity construction that feeds the frame of the "Imaginary Indian.[28]

While Morrisseau's personal problems have bearing on his work and his legacy, with this lead Gessell chooses to present tired stereotypes that, like the signifiers in earlier reportage, are familiar to Canadians. Both blaming the National Gallery for its 120 years of backward ways and citing curator Greg Hill's confirmation that Morrisseau is an internationally renowned artist, Gessell's two narrative strands seem incongruous. For example, the story unfolds a "long and bumpy" road to success tainted by alcohol, drugs, jail time, living on skid row, and brushes with the mob juxtaposed with evidence of Morrisseau's artistic merit. In an effort to tell the "whole truth" about the artist, Gessell's regurgitation of tropes in the opening paragraphs of this pivotal national story maintains a racialized mythology from which Morrisseau was unable to escape. Constructed in binary fashion, or as a paradox—common ways to present the Morrisseau myth—Gessell attempts to provide readers with a balanced, clinical picture of the artist to aid in this so-called exorcism. A reliance on the cross-pollinating assemblage of racial signifiers from which he cannot extricate Morrisseau leaves this feature story mired in the ooze of colonial discourse he condemns the National Gallery for reinforcing.

A number of images accompanied Gessell's text. Besides a 1974 photograph of Morrisseau painting in his studio, the *Citizen* printed five of Morrisseau's works in full colour to offer a clearer sense of Morrisseau's artistic value. It is the art that tells a refreshingly honest story—one that proclaims Morrisseau's significance as an artist. The printed works are among Morrisseau's most significant: *Self-Portrait Devoured by Demons* (1964), *The Virgin Mary* (1966), *Indian Jesus Christ* (1973), *The Gift* (1975), and *Observations of the Astral World* (c. 1992).[29] The works that accompany Gessell's article herald Morrisseau's talent and on first viewing appear to reposition the rhetoric found in the essay. However, the five paintings are chosen to support the biases in the text. The first page of the feature positions *Self-Portrait Devoured by Demons* (1964) next to the noted looming headline, "Taming Their Demons." The eye-catching painting can be viewed as an illustration of Gessell's thesis of exorcism, as the painted representation of Morrisseau stands naked on display, his body twisted and entwined by serpents, a signifier of exorcism heavily steeped in a Christian tradition. No textual discussion of the work is included, yet the image speaks to demons. Three of the pieces relate to Christian themes evoked by Gessell. Like the textual narrative, these paintings can easily be connected to a version of the Morrisseau mythology made famous in news reports and by the 1974 NFB documentary *The Paradox of Norval Morrisseau*, and reinforce the film's argument of a polarized struggle in the artist between Anishinaabe and Christian influences.[30] Gessell includes an early *Virgin Mary* from 1966 and the more provocative *Indian Jesus Christ* painted during Morrisseau's six-month incarceration in Kenora, Ontario, in 1973, as well as *The Gift* from 1975. According to Gessell, "Morrisseau was trying to integrate Christianity with Native spirituality."[31] Gessell notes that Morrisseau had originally been a Catholic, converted "to the Apostolic faith," and then in 1976 embraced Eckankar, "a New-Age religion." *Indian Jesus Christ* is described in a caption as having been painted by the artist after he was jailed for "drunk and disorderly behaviour." The main text of the story explains that painting this work was a "decidedly political act back then" but does not elaborate, adding strength to the assertion that these paintings can be "read" semiotically to reinforce Gessell's textual exorcism rather than referencing Canada's colonial legacy.[32] *The Gift*, another of Morrisseau's provocative works from the 1970s, is afforded more analysis. Gessell explains: "This 1975 painting is one of Morrisseau's most political. It shows a priest-like character handing the 'gift' of smallpox to an aboriginal adult and child. Works such as this opened the floodgates for other contemporary aboriginal artists to create politically charged works criticizing relations between native and European communities."[33] Gessell introduces the political allusions present in Morrisseau's work, though he does little to contextualize the political turn, missing an opportunity to focus on the complexities of Morrisseau's impressive oeuvre and the artist's effort to bring attention to colonialism in Canada.

Observations of the Astral World packs a punch as the banner to this two-page spread. Below the painting is a large block quote from Pollock: "He's eccentric, mad, brilliant. He's an extraordinary human being. I love him and I can't stand him … But he loves me. There's a bond between us. Amazing."[34] Gessell's reliance on testimony from Pollock adds fuel to the mythmaking that occurred early in Morrisseau's career that aided in confining the artist to a narrow racial identity. Without considering the monumental eight-by-seventeen-foot painting's significance in any way in relation to his oeuvre or to Canadian art, Gessell leaves readers to only admire a pretty picture.

A second feature article, written by Sarah Milroy and printed in the national *Globe and Mail* on 7 February 2006, also interpreted Morrisseau's retrospective exhibition for readers. The former editor of *Canadian Art* magazine, Milroy had been the art critic at the *Globe and Mail* for more than a decade when she wrote this report.[35] Under the headline "Morrisseau Has Defeated the Demons," Milroy also conjures up demons. Unlike Gessell, who pairs the terms "taming" and "exorcism" with Morrisseau's *Self-Portrait Devoured by Demons*, Milroy's feature report describes for its national readership a successful culmination of his life's work. Pairing the artist's significant painting *Misshupishu*, or *Water Spirit* (1972) with the headline's active verb construction alludes to a triumphant symbolic calming of the turbulent waters that surrounded Morrisseau's artistic career. The review spills onto page five with a secondary headline, "Visionary Spirituality on Display."

In her review, Milroy repositions the exhibition and Morrisseau in ways that complement Hill's curatorial vision in *Shaman Artist* and his attempt to revision the Morrisseau narrative. She states, "One of Canada's most treasured painters has overcome alcoholism, sexual abuse, and pandering tourist-trap drivel ... His creative brilliance deserves this moment in the sun."[36] Clearly aware of the past media rhetoric surrounding Morrisseau and his personal issues, Milroy adeptly moves beyond such descriptors, choosing instead to contextualize his work around a contemporary art discourse, recognizing a narrative more germane than a frozen-in-time story. For example, Milroy acknowledges past stereotypical constructions of Morrisseau as she suggests a new reading: "Seated in front of his huge, vividly coloured work *Androgyny*, the artist sits slumped in his wheelchair ... At his feet a swarm of photographers crouched to get their shots of the Anishinabe artist ... They were pulling out all the stops, going for the most dramatic view of the artist's weatherbeaten, crumbling frame, a figure that many might see as embodying the tragic, broken figure of the Indian in contemporary society ... In truth, behind the mask of his Parkinsonism, Morrisseau was having a great moment, long awaited, and fully savoured."[37] With this description of a frenzied and "surreal" press conference, Milroy recognizes that the "spectacle of the museum, the artist and the public is almost as fascinating as the art on display," hitting on the nub of this story, acknowledging how Morrisseau's art has often played a secondary role to a larger racial narrative.[38] Unlike Gessell, Milroy seems intent on focusing her remarks on Morrisseau's contributions to Canadian art, lauding the artist, the curator, catalogue essays, and most of all Morrisseau's "magnificent" art on display at the gallery.

Water Spirit (1972), Milroy contends, "articulates his 'visionary spirituality.' "[39] The image of Mishupishu demonstrates Morrisseau's unique visual language that features thick unifying black lines, interior segmentation, and a clear relationship to Anishinaabe oral narratives. An illustration of the final panel of Morrisseau's iconic six-panel work *Man Changing into Thunderbird* from 1977, another symbolic work, charts Morrisseau's evolution as an artist and spiritual being, his transformation into Copper Thunderbird. "In his activism," Milroy explains, "Morrisseau was a pioneer breaking new ground in a discourse that has now become a staple of Canadian cultural debate." While Milroy laments Morrisseau's turn away from the edgy art he produced in the 1970s, she admits "we should rejoice in these later paintings, light and decorative though they may sometimes be. Morrisseau, at last, is seeing the joyous side of life."[40] With respect to the term "demons" used in this art review, Milroy concludes, "One of the comforts of advancing years, surely, is that one's inner demons can finally lie down and sleep a little."

The die was cast early—long before Morrisseau's 1962 debut, when racialized and colonial discourse entered the pages of newspapers. The press, as part of Canada's colonial project, has long served as a primer for racialized discourse. Canadians adeptly read between the lines, and a story such as Gessell's January 2006 feature does not deviate far from the constructions printed after Morrisseau's 1962 debut exhibition, and sadly does little to reposition Morrisseau's story around art. Gessell and Milroy both refer to Morrisseau's so-called demons in their feature stories covering his landmark 2006 retrospective exhibition. However, Gessell attempts to perform an "exorcism" through conjuring up past descriptions of the artist and pairing works that lead the reader toward an assimilationist discourse long fused with the artist, while Milroy is content to report on Morrisseau's artistic achievements. Gessell weaves together arcane details that reinforce stereotypes already present in media discourse—Morrisseau as spectacle. Milroy, instead, acknowledges the popular cultural habit of spectacle with regard to Morrisseau—the press conference, the public, and the gallery. Though Gessell quotes Hill's refutation of the tired but long-standing claim that "the artist was incapable of reconciling 'Norval Morrisseau the Indian' and 'Norval Morrisseau the contemporary artist,'" much of the *Citizen* essay reinforces this confining rhetoric.[41] Milroy, it seems, treats this retrospective as one might expect, as a pivotal contribution to the history of Canadian art. By focusing mostly on Morrisseau's art rather than on the stereotypical tropes continually rehashed by the press throughout his career, she accomplishes what Gessell seems incapable of doing, moving beyond the tired enduring rhetoric.

While these two media reports were in no way the final word on the retrospective, together, I believe, they capture differing directions at work in Canada. Though Gessell's feature article reminded readers of the National Gallery's complacency regarding Aboriginal art in the gallery, his story fails to move beyond a long-standing racialized discourse that had haunted Morrisseau, and in this way serves only to illustrate the entrenched and pervasive force of such constructions. Milroy, however, understands that the retrospective is an acknowledgement of Morrisseau's vision for his art and his legacy for contemporary Indigenous art in Canada. Morrisseau's art reveals an expansive vision, one informed by his agency and revelation, a body of work that deserves to be considered beyond racial bounds.

Once the exhibition opened, the *Ottawa Citizen* and the *Globe and Mail* continued to weigh in on this historic exhibition. Connie Higginson-Murray filed a report a few days later, below a reproduction of Morrisseau's *Artist and Shaman between Two Worlds* (1980). She begins her report, "Norval Morrisseau is a man of extremes. He has been called outrageous, frustrating, mad, a brilliant eccentric, a drunk, and an artistic genius." The reporter gets right to the point, relying, like her colleague Gessell, on the confining "paradox" frame still recognizable by her sentence construction. Titled "'Picasso of the North,'" the article suggests, "His exposure in the 1960s to the world of Pablo Picasso is one of the main influences in his artistic style."[42] No other reference is made to the headline that is stated in quotation marks. The Picasso reference is key to the Morrisseau mythology, and Higginson-Murray makes good use of the mythic narrative.

The *Ottawa Citizen* viewed Morrisseau's retrospective as an opportunity to promote local connections. On 18 February, for example, the paper challenged its readers to "Take a Day to Explore Our Home and Native Land," offering a compilation of materials that one reporter amassed "in search of the Capital's Aboriginal spirit, past and present." Linking the national anthem with Indigeneity, the quirky report offers readers tidbits to experience historic events and contemporary experiences to build on a day's visit to the Morrisseau retrospective, such as finding out "How did the natives bypass the falls?" or "Where can I buy aboriginal items?"[43] The report suggests visits to Major's Hill Park to see the "Anishinaabe Scout, a symbol of the natives who guided French explorer Samuel de Champlain through the wilderness," Tony Hunt's totem pole in Confederation Park, and at the corner of Metcalfe and Queen, a contemporary sculpture of a "hunter stalking a deer." The Morrisseau retrospective, according to this report, fits neatly into an ethnographic view of Indigenous Canada that includes decorative accoutrements of Canadian identity, affirmations of Indigenous populations in their present as well as past existence that illustrate what Nicolas Thomas describes as a form of "cultural colonization," where "national narratives are formed by situating indigenous people in the past ... while new and flourishing settler culture otherwise dominates the landscape."[44]

The *Citizen* also printed "Painting Purchased by Chance for $8" to further round out coverage of the historic exhibition. The report featured Hank Leclair, a government photographer sent on assignment in 1959 to Red Lake to take pictures of doctors and nurses, who was introduced to Morrisseau and purchased one of his paintings for eight dollars. Leclair admits in the article that he did not think much of Morrisseau's talent, considering the purchase more of a donation to someone struggling: " 'I'm not much of an artist, but I could do the same' ... thinking at the time the drawings were like children's work."[45] The paper printed the photograph Leclair took that day of Morrisseau and a nurse looking at the painting hung outside his log cabin. It was not until the 1970s that Leclair thought about Morrisseau again when he read about his success in an airline magazine, and at that point he dug out the rolled-up painting and began to display it, despite the teasing he received from friends.

As part of a media moment at the retrospective's opening, Leclair had the opportunity to meet the artist and show him a photo of that day back in 1959. The *Citizen* was there to capture the orchestrated meeting and printed both Leclair's original photograph and a photo of the reunion in the City section of the paper. The paper makes the price of the painting the focus of this human-interest piece, pitching it like an episode from the *Antiques Roadshow* television series. Leclair's sympathetic purchase turns into a financial windfall. Reminding readers that paintings by the artist now sell for as much as $250,000, Leclair admits that he has "come to appreciate the painting's artistic value over the years" but he would potentially sell it.[46] Describing the work as a "donation to a poor man and not an investment" to a young artist "who lived in the woods" activates the Morrisseau myth as it relates to primitivism. That Morrisseau has been given a retrospective at the National Gallery, implied here, is a signal to all collectors that the price of their Morrisseau paintings has risen significantly.

A letter to the editor by Bob Jurmain published in the *Ottawa Citizen* later in February questions Gessell's and Higginson-Murray's description of Morrisseau as the "Picasso of the North." Confused by the usage and unaware of its mythology, Jurmain confesses, "I saw nothing in the show that resembled Picasso in motif, style, method, life, and certainly not the notion of 'reinvention' other than what any artist does." Jurmain instead likens Morrisseau's work to that of Vincent Van Gogh: "Both artists were self-taught and overcame incredible obstacles to produce remarkable work."[47] He also compares Morrisseau's art to that of Canadian Jack Shadbolt as he argues that if Morrisseau were French or American it would not have taken so long for him to receive national recognition by the National Gallery.

Jurmain's challenge to the *Ottawa Citizen*'s reporters was not the only letter that found fault with Gessell's coverage. On 2 February Martin Hankes-Drielsma wrote to the editors of the *Ottawa Citizen* to state that he was personally affronted by Gessell's characterization of the lack of Aboriginal art in the National Gallery as "a long history of apartheid." The author agrees that Morrisseau's exhibition was overdue. "But, 'apartheid'? Come on, Mr. Gessell, lighten up on the rhetoric ... Apartheid means something much larger, broader, deeper and worse."[48] Worse? I'm not sure things get much worse than what has occurred in colonial Canada—a place so famously divisive that the South Africans came to Canada to research the reservation system, looking for ways to establish their own apartheid system.[49] That Canadians know so little about Canada's colonial past and present is not surprising, however.

Documenting Morrisseau in the Twenty-First Century

Many of the roots of the Morrisseau myth can be found in the two NFB documentaries made in the early 1970s. These, however, were not the last time filmmakers made documentaries about the artist, and examining films from the last part of his life provides a counterpoint to the 1970s films. Three films from the early twenty-first century feature Morrisseau and offer insights into how the roots of his mythology grew.

In 2003, Dino Schiavone and Raoul McKay made the forty-six-minute long *Life and Work of the Woodland Artists*, featuring the art of the so-called Indian Group of Seven.[50] Similar to the 1973 NFB film *Colours of Pride* in that it features several of the same artists, the 2003 film borrows the convention used in *Colours* of having each of the artist's signatures written on to the screen. Stereotypical musical signifiers using panpipes and drums reinforce romantic connections to the Imaginary Indian, further connecting it to *Colours*. Unlike the 1973 film, however, this documentary situates the artists within their historical context and is important in that it discusses the aims of the Professional Native Indian Artists Incorporated (PNIAI), under the direction of Daphne Odjig, to professionalize and support contemporary Indigenous art. Morrisseau is one of the featured artists, though because of the larger focus of the film, only about four minutes of the footage is devoted to him. Descriptions by Métis artist Bob Boyer and Indigenous poet Duke Redbird offer little information about him.

A short eighteen-minute documentary made in 2007 in conjunction with Morrisseau's retrospective at the National Gallery, *Gifts from the Thunderbird* adds little to the Morrisseau narrative other than to heavily reinforce the spiritual force of Morrisseau's art.[51] The film clearly had a limited budget and for this reason it is difficult to compare it to the slick NFB productions of the 1970s. A highlight of the film is an interview with Anishinaabe poet Armand Garnet Ruffo, whose essay was included in the exhibition catalogue of *Norval Morrisseau: Shaman Artist*. Ruffo tells stories that ground discussions of Morrisseau's art, shifting away from "legend" to a more serious engagement with oral narratives. However, interviews with a viewer of the exhibition and a museum guide do little more than reinforce a frozen-in-time discourse that ensures Morrisseau's mythology remains intact. The documentary includes an extended interview with Anishinaabe artist and historian Barry Ace, in which he discusses elements of Morrisseau's art such as line, motion, and imagery. The production values are so poor in this film, however, that as Ace points to paintings in the exhibition catalogue, the glare on the page detracts from his analysis. The third documentary produced in the 2000s is noteworthy. Montreal-based filmmaker Paul Carvalho created a fifty-three-minute documentary on Morrisseau titled *A Separate Reality: The Life and Times of Norval Morrisseau*.[52] Produced in association with the Canadian Broadcasting Company (CBC), the film was aired on CBC's *Life and Times* in February 2005. Because of Morrisseau's frailty, Carvalho found creative ways to present the artist. The title recalls a mural painted by the artist in 1981 but also has larger popular culture references. It evokes the title of a wildly successful book published in 1971 by New Age guru Carlos Castaneda that featured descriptions of the teaching of a Yaqui shaman Don Juan, thus connecting the two shaman for New Age audiences.[53] Carvalho also reuses NFB footage from *The Paradox of Norval Morrisseau*, includes clips from an interview with Morrisseau discussing his plans for painting *A Separate Reality* (1981) as he worked on it on-site at the Canadian Museum of Civilization, and features early archival interviews with Jack Pollock from the CBC radio archives. A contemporary interview with Joseph and Esther Weinstein about their early encounter and subsequent friendship with Morrisseau in the Red Lake region beginning in 1958 makes it an important archive in itself.

A *Toronto Star* review of the film with the headline "Native Painter Travels to Gutter and Back" situates the documentary around Morrisseau's adopted son Gabe Vadas and the ailing Morrisseau, in what the review characterizes as a story of "The mutual redemption of the lost boy and the down-and-out Northwestern Ontario Indian."[54] A second review of the documentary printed in the *Vancouver Sun* explains that the film "sheds new light on the brilliant but tragic life of one of Canada's most cherished but inscrutable artists."[55] The description is positioned paradoxically, reinforcing the construction of Morrisseau established in *The Paradox of Norval Morrisseau*. Missing from *Paradox*, however, but featured in *Separate Reality* are details of the sexual abuse Morrisseau faced early on at residential school, offering viewers a better contextual understanding of trauma enacted by colonialism. In the *Sun*'s review of the documentary, a short description of the film's discussion of

Morrisseau's rape between the ages of eight and twelve by three priests and how it led to his drinking problems at age thirteen signals a change in how Morrisseau is understood. The film also discusses Morrisseau's homosexuality, and Carvalho is quoted in the review as saying that from the time of the artist's breakup with his wife, Harriet, "as far as I know, all of his relationships were with men."[56] Given new directions in documentary filmmaking and a lifetime to look back upon, *Separate Reality* promises a revisionist approach to documenting Morrisseau's life, reworking problematic aspects of *The Paradox of Norval Morrisseau.*

The film opens with a short but confounding minute-long sequence of an Indigenous man with a long ponytail, dressed in buckskin, and carrying a large birchbark vessel on his back, emerging from a verdant green forest to harvest the bark from a birch tree. His white collared shirt and a coifed moustache alert viewers that this contrived scene is not supposed to be a pre-contact re-creation but is staged to represent the artist as a young man. Music sets the tone, signifying a mystical experience. The director has overlaid the beginning of this scene with two combined clips of audio lifted from the 1974 *Paradox*, where Morrisseau explains: "I still believe in the ways of my people. As the Great Spirit told me, 'I will guide you and keep you every day.' I'm a born artist I guess and that was my destiny to be an artist. The only thing I know how to do is how to read and how to paint."[57] As the actor lies down on the forest floor, the camera angle looking down on him as he lifts an eagle feather and holds a rattle, a drum beats and the rattle shakes. A narrator expresses how Morrisseau's art comes from "his guts" and "from the atavistic dreams of a society that has lived for thousands of years as hunters in the north of Canada." As images from Morrisseau's paintings of water spirits share the screen with the dappled light through the forest, the narrator describes how Morrisseau painted "the authentic heritage of his people." Pan pipe music cuts in with a montage of details from his paintings, interspersed with still photographic images of Morrisseau taken from *Paradox* and the forest scene where the actor now sketches. An extended quote by curator and scholar Tom Hill, also featured in *Paradox*, overlays this image before the film cuts to contemporary footage of Hill: "He's certainly spiritual, definitely Canadian. He's brilliant. He's a painter extraordinaire. He's all of that. I think he is one of the greatest painters around."

Carvalho adds archival footage of Morrisseau painting *A Separate Reality* at the Canadian Museum of Civilization in 1981, a painting Morrisseau explains is a gift to the Canadian people in recognition of his being awarded the Order of Canada in 1978. The vast painting that hangs today in the

First People's Hall in the museum is one of Morrisseau's most impressive. A male narrator then authoritatively introduces the artist, reminding viewers of the artist's 1987 breakdown: "Norval Morrisseau, a homeless heavy drinker, rescued from self-destruction by a friend in the alleys of Vancouver." This stark statement is reminiscent of the earlier NFB film, except that the quote is followed by a contextualized clarification by Indigenous artist and scholar Jeanette Armstrong: "I can see that in order to birth the kind of art that Norval Morrisseau has given us, the gift he has given us, the incredible suffering he has gone through to present that to us." From a traditional interview shot with Armstrong in an office, the next shot moves to swirling lights in the dark. The camera steadies as viewers recognize a night scene with car lights on a busy city street, and then a shot of Gabe Vadas pushing Morrisseau in a wheelchair down a busy boulevard in the middle of a multi-lane street. Vadas pointedly reveals a key theme in the film and explains the title of the documentary: "Norval used hallucinogens very, very young but he didn't see the use for them. Alcohol was the conductor that helped him go to a separate reality." The title emerges on the screen, overlaying the two friends. In the next shot we see a silhouette of the ailing artist, bathed in a seemingly spiritual light rising in the centre and streaming through the window of his room. Then, after the silhouette shot, comes a scene of Vadas and his wife pushing Morrisseau in his wheelchair at night into the bright and inviting light of a shop.

The film continues to tell of Morrisseau's life, punctuated by dramatic re-creations that show a young boy on the shore of a lake, the boy in a canoe with his grandfather paddling, and the boy sitting on the shore in the evening as his grandfather tells him traditional stories before a campfire. One scene of the boy drawing in the beach sand on the shore recalls a scene from *Paradox*, where Morrisseau sketches a drawing in the sand. The camera pulls away from the scene to reveal a series of intricate drawings covering the beach.

It is in one of the dramatic re-creations that viewers also learn that Morrisseau was abused in residential school. This is a key departure from *Paradox* and one of the few areas of the documentary that strays from the established mythology. A scene of the boy walking away from the camera, through the darkened, empty halls of a school toward a magnetic blue light at the end of the hall sets the stage for Tom Hill to explain that Morrisseau was "raped by the priests" at residential school and how this affected his life. Vadas supports Hill's revelation: "Norval was, of course, abused in the school." Morrisseau also discussed these events in context to his receiving the Order of Canada. In the 1981 video in his explanation for painting *A*

Separate Reality that he was preparing to give to the Canadian people, he states: "First you drive me down to the pits of the bottom of hell by your missionaries and then later on you lift me up with medals." "If I never went through this bottom thing or this upward thing," explains Morrisseau, "I'd never be this great artist."[58]

In *Separate Reality*, Carvalho reinforces the Morrisseau mythology that was cast in *Paradox*. He maintains a romanticized vision using light, suggestive music and dramatic re-creations to fashion an updated image of Morrisseau. Discussions of Morrisseau's spirituality and importance as a shaman are found throughout the film. Laudatory praise is heaped on the artist but with little actual discussion of specifics. Images of his art are interjected throughout but no titles, explanations, or focused discussions support the art. It is the man Morrisseau, a larger-than-life figure the film is most interested in. Even then, however, the film presents little that is new. Its reliance on the structure, footage, and audio found in *Paradox* make this documentary more of an homage to the NFB film more than a departure from it. Three significant changes occur in this film, however. Gone is the rhetoric about assimilation that the narrator of *Paradox* continually advances. A second difference, related to assimilation, is that Morrisseau's pull between Christianity and Native spirituality is not present. Finally, and most importantly, the film acknowledges that the artist's confrontation with colonialism during his time at residential school was a destructive force in his life.

From the standpoint of the Morrisseau myth, the story stays true to earlier constructions. The sage shaman, a key element of Morrisseau's myth, remains intact in the film, especially in included footage of Morrisseau explaining his art in 1981. The footage demonstrates his own performative efforts to reinforce this identity. While it is clear from interviews with Gabe and Michelle Vadas that Morrisseau was a shaman on his own terms, heavily influenced by Eckankar, other aspects of the film promote him as a shamanistic interpreter of his Anishinaabe culture. The dramatic re-creations interspersed throughout the film echo frozen-in-time elements commensurate with stereotypical tropes found in popular culture. Unlike the many obituaries published after the artist's death, this documentary does not capitalize on Morrisseau as the "Picasso of the North," choosing instead to focus on his spiritual connection to painting.

All three of the noted documentaries produced in the 2000s owe a debt to the NFB films from the 1970s. I have screened *The Paradox of Norval Morrisseau* and *The Colours of Pride* countless times to students and public audiences. Feedback is varied, but many agree that it is the times that most influence the ways in which the artist is presented. In the 1970s Canadians were racist, so Morrisseau and his art were not engaged as they would be today. If that is the case, why do images and patterns of representation of the artist from *Paradox* continue to be reproduced in news photos, documentaries, and text? While things have changed in this country since the mid-1970s, aspects of the themes and narratives found in the early NFB films remain. Although less obvious, such references linger, haunting understandings of Morrisseau. Choices of music, leading narrations, and stereotypical signifiers eclipse discussions of the artist's work in the 1970s documentaries, and similar conventions find their way into many media reports. The Morrisseau myth is being reshaped, but recent media reports still rely on established frames to construct the artist.

Androgyny as Agent

Morrisseau's retrospective prompted a new form of social mobility for the artist's entire oeuvre and pushed all his paintings into new and upward directions in relation to taste, producing a new form of competition among the elite community of art collectors. Through a revisioning of the artist's place in Canadian art history, the public was instructed by both the National Gallery and the media that Morrisseau's art was in fact a highly collectable commodity. This change moved *Androgyny* into a new chapter of its life story also, and even though it was not "for sale" in an economic sense, culturally and politically the work took on new value, as did Morrisseau's oeuvre more generally. After the completion of the travelling retrospective exhibition in 2008, following Morrisseau's death in December 2007, *Androgyny* was immediately requested by the Queen's representative in Canada, then Governor General Michaëlle Jean. She asked that the work be hung in Rideau Hall, the Governor General's residence in Ottawa, Ontario. Shortly after, the work was installed in the ballroom in the presence of Jean with two of Morrisseau's daughters.

The Governor General's residence is the site of a wide variety of official cultural events, such as the prestigious Governor General's awards including the Order of Canada. *Androgyny* lent a new caché to the social gatherings. The otherwise staid and conservative decoration of the ballroom, with its ornate pilasters and gilded mirrors, was reinvigorated by *Androgyny*. Governor General Jean, of Haitian descent, no doubt appreciated the opportunity to reshape the ostentatious surroundings. In order to better explain the meaning of the work, Viviane Gray, then director of the Indian and Inuit Art Centre, provided an explanation of the work:

> There is a commonly held belief among the First Nations that we, as human beings, are both male and female. Norval Morrisseau's painting *Androgyny* represents a thriving and bountiful world in which all the diverse elements, including the male and female characteristics that are part of nature, are in perfect balance. *Androgyny* is Norval Morrisseau's masterpiece as it represents not only his painterly skills and brilliant use of colour but his knowledge and understanding of Ojibway cosmology. His representation of the multi-layered universe, the axis of the universe symbolized by the Thunderbird and the variety of living life forms and Manitou-spirits that inhabit the water, earth and sky zones of the universe are all characteristics of the Ojibway shaman's world view. This painting was donated to the people of Canada by the artist, Norval Morrisseau, in 1983 as an expression of his own harmony as shaman artist.[59]

On 31 October 2008 *Androgyny*'s story as object took a dramatic turn. Prime Minister Stephen Harper decided to reveal his cabinet shuffle in a press conference held at Rideau Hall in front of *Androgyny*. This calculation on the part of a shrewd politician shifted the painting's value yet again. No longer situated in the National Gallery, *Androgyny* now took on the role of sanctioning, as a sign of Indigeneity and thus a representation of Canada's Indigenous peoples, in relation to the Prime Minister's political mandate. While news reports on that day were most concerned with the makeup of Harper's cabinet, the painting was present in press photographs and footage of the event.[60]

A letter to the editor in the *Globe and Mail* the following week, entitled "Learning from a Master," confirmed that readers had noticed more than the makeup of the cabinet shuffle. Letter writer Nancy Robinson conjures up a romanticized image, writing: "What a wonderful picture on your Oct. 31 front page—the new federal cabinet under Norval Morrisseau's astounding mural *Androgyny*. Moved to the ballroom at Rideau Hall in September, the painting is described on the Governor-General's website: *Androgyny*, depicting 'the Ojibway shaman's worldview,' represents 'a thriving and bountiful world in which all the diverse elements ... are in perfect balance.' An appropriate message for the modern world that is very much out of balance."[61] The tone of this letter naively reveals the usefulness of Canada's Other, here cast within a romantic vision, pointing Canadians toward a more harmonious

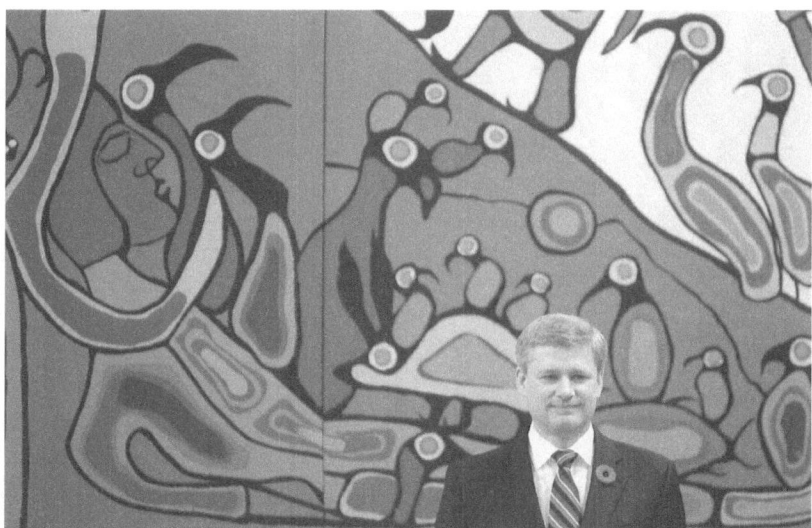

Former Canadian Prime Minister Stephen Harper stands before Morrisseau's *Androgyny* (1983) at the unveiling of his Cabinet shuffle at Rideau Hall, in Ottawa, Ontario, on 30 October 2008. This photograph is part of a number shot that day. Photo by Sean Kilpatrick, reproduced with permission of CP photo archives.

sense of cosmic and political balance. The dramatic canvas, with its so-called "shamanic worldview," resonates as a symbolic vision of inclusion and unity that only hints at Canada's colonial project.

The *Hill Times*, published in Ottawa, noted Morrisseau's painting with the headline "Morrisseau's *Androgyny* Makes Splash at GGs." "It was the unexpected guest at the swearing-in that got a lot of tongues wagging. The Julie Couillard of this occasion. It was the Norval Morrisseau at the front of the ballroom at Rideau Hall, which can only be described as stunning, exciting, intriguing and engaging. Okay distracting too."[62]

The photograph of Harper's cabinet shuffle before the "distracting" *Androgyny* takes on added significance because the Prime Minister had formally apologized to Canada's First Nations on 11 June 2008 for the Indian Residential School system. "There is no place in Canada for the attitudes that inspired the Indian residential schools system to ever prevail again," Harper said in the course of his speech.[63] *Androgyny*, then, appears to signify support for Harper as the apology was fresh in the minds of Canadians. Later, in 2009 when Harper explained at the G20 summit that Canada did not have a history of colonialism, many Indigenous peoples reconsidered Harper's apology as hollow.[64] Yet the photographic evidence of Harper and *Androgyny*

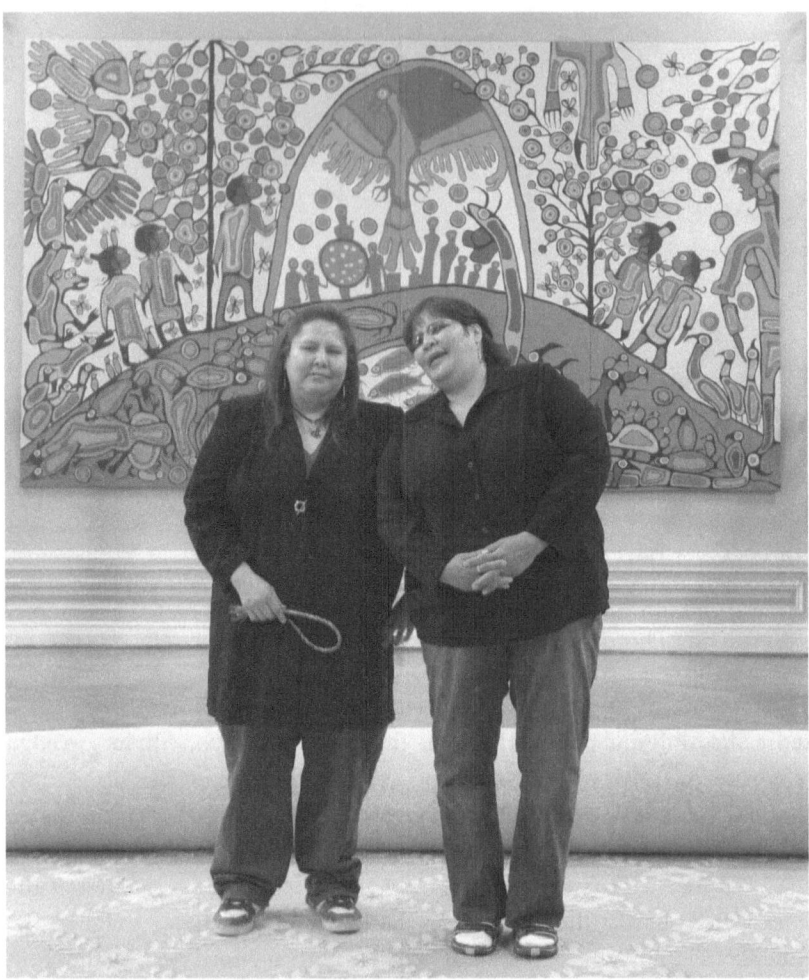

The adult daughters of Norval Morrisseau, including Lisa Morrisseau Meekis (left) and Victoria Morrisseau Kakegamic pose in front of *Androgyny* after it was installed in the ballroom at Rideau Hall, 18 September 2008. They, in addition to their other five siblings, challenged their father's will, alleging undue influence by his executor Gabor Vadas. Photo was included in news story "Norval Morrisseau's Children Sue Over Will," 30 June 2010, cbc.ca. Photo by Adrian Wyld, reproduced with permission of CP photo archives.

remains a power visual link thanks to Google images.

Androgyny, with its electric colours and overpowering size, imposes or performs Indigenous identity as it moves from site to site—from Morrisseau's studio, where the work was begun and the concept was formulated, to the Terrasses de la Chaudière, where the artist finished the work, readying it for its next chapter, when it was added to a significant archive that has grown and changed in meaning and importance. As it confronted visitors and employees it performed a role and told a story that championed the talents of Morrisseau, his effort to gain reciprocal gifts for Indigenous peoples from the Canadian government, and the different regimes of value accorded it, depending on who viewed it. The wait was long but worth it when *Androgyny* took centre stage as part of *Norval Morrisseau: Shaman Artist* in the National Gallery of Canada's retrospective exhibition. When Morrisseau reunited with *Androgyny*, both press and audiences acknowledged its new performative role.

With its move into another cultural institution, Rideau Hall, it performed yet another role—another regime of value. Claimed by a political leader, however, *Androgyny* defied Stephen Harper's efforts to manage the painting as a symbolic backdrop to a national rhetoric. *Androgyny* instead exerted its own agency, told its own story, performed Indigeneity under its own terms, much like its master, Morrisseau, had attempted to do throughout the decades since he'd entered Canada's art scene.

Androgyny made an appearance in the press again in 2010, in a photo that accompanied a story about the fact that Morrisseau's children were suing Gabe Vadas about the terms of their father's will. The photo, taken during the 2008 installation of the work at Rideau Hall, shows two of Morrisseau's daughters standing before his painting. Here, however, the photograph is utilized as a form of claiming. The news report explains that the seven children of Morrisseau had filed a lawsuit in the British Columbia Supreme Court in Vancouver in June 2010 to challenge Morrisseau's will and request that it be invalidated. The cbc.ca news story notes that court documents allege that Gabor Vadas had exercised "undue influence" over Morrisseau.

Clearly the painting *Androgyny* had begun to stand in for the artist himself, its glowing presence referencing the artist's own forceful personality. Reusing the 2008 photograph, the CBC Internet news report shifts the meaning of the work yet again. The notion of the gift takes on added significance when considering Morrisseau's estate and legacy in relation to his children. The photograph of his two daughters before one of the artist's masterpieces as it hung in the nation's Rideau Hall claims the work for the family, but also for Canada and Canadians. We all own it, after all, or so Morrisseau stated when he gave it to us all. Bringing the work together with a lawsuit about claim and ownership of copyright complicates the meaning of the painting in fresh ways.

CONCLUSION

Why am I alive? To heal you guys who're more screwed up than I am.[1]

Norval Morrisseau

Clearly media representations of Morrisseau have, over time, fashioned an imperfect portrait. Morrisseau's own efforts to redirect such frames had mixed success. In its endorsement of an imaginary figure framed sketchily as an artistic Other, and in its employment of dubious, yet not ineffective, binaries, the media persists in shaping mythologies. Morrisseau myths appear to hide as much as they reveal about him and also about Canada. They shield the colonial realities of Canadian society, hide the overtly racialized ways in which Morrisseau has been framed, and they attempt to rework narratives that have skewed understandings of Morrisseau's contributions to Canadian art.

A ready set of signifiers had long been in place in popular culture in this settler nation. Binaries, simplistic and moralizing, result in the Imaginary Indian—tropes rehashed and repackaged again and again. Complex discourses that result in the construction of the Imaginary Indian provided an assigned script for Morrisseau. Yet while the media manipulated established tropes to keenly focus on his behaviour, Morrisseau, with help from allies, friends, and art dealers, advanced his own narrative. Primitivism provided a ready vocabulary for media discussion of his art early on and played out over the decades in descriptions of Morrisseau as a recorder of legends. For others, Morrisseau's art offered exciting opportunities and new directions for considering Indigenous arts.

How Morrisseau is remembered is significant to this study and his published obituaries are all about memory and memorializing. Having resurfaced as a public figure with his 2006 retrospective, Morrisseau shortly after succumbed to Parkinson's disease and died on Thursday, 6 December 2007. His death was reported both nationally and internationally in the form of obituaries. Myths are often a vital part of obituaries. Most dailies across the nation chose to report his death by recalling the mythological moniker, Picasso of the North. Objectification through this epithet brings together a mythological conflation of Pablo Picasso's enduring mythology (e.g., artistic genius, philanderer, maverick, and self-promoter) with Canada's settler nation mythology (e.g., our true North strong and free, northern frontier, pride).[2] The *Winnipeg Free Press* freely played with the epithet that had come to define Morrisseau when its headline announced, " 'Picasso of the North' the Torchbearer for Native Art." The paper noted that his passing would not be the end of the "gritty story" of the "great Anishinaabe painter once called 'Picasso of the North.'"[3] The *Globe and Mail* also referred to Morrisseau as the "Picasso of the North," adding, "Like the great Spanish artist, he could draw spontaneously, never lifting his pencil until the image was complete."[4] This obit includes three photos; one is a still from *Paradox of Norval Morrisseau* that shows him painting next to a framed image of the Madonna and Child, and a second is a reproduction of one of his early works of art, identified with a cutline including an unidentified quote that evokes modern primitivism: "He transports us into a shadowy archetypal realm." The *Ottawa Citizen* hailed, " 'Picasso of the North' Blazed a Path That Many Young Artists Followed."[5] The Canwest newswire published the following lead: "Called 'the Picasso of the North' by Marc Chagall, Morrisseau rose to prominence in the 1960s, the first aboriginal artist to achieve success in the mainstream art world."[6] The Canadian Press wire service combined the Picasso moniker with primitivism: " 'Picasso of the North' pioneered what became known as the Woodland school of painting, which featured aboriginal pictography."[7]

Obituaries generally tend to venerate an individual, and it is not unusual for such notices to paint public figures in the best light possible, even if it means adding inaccurate information. Maria Tippett, in her deconstruction of the Bill Reid mythology, describes how this happened after the Haida artist's death: "Reading the obituaries and the tributes [to Reid] made me feel increasingly uneasy about the reporting in the press. Much of it was inaccurate."[8] While it was naive of Tippett to imagine that the press would have sketched a precise representation of Reid, her comment is a reminder that obituaries written for Morrisseau offer a snapshot of his mythological identity rather than a characterization of a true self. Descriptions of Morrisseau as both an artistic rebel and a man with a troubled past are requisite elements in most of the obituaries found in the Canadian media. Terms such as "pride" and "struggle" repeatedly surface—terms that had long been assigned to him. Such words have come to signify Indigenous artists and Indigenous peoples more generally in press reports in ways that serve as codes for difference. As identity is fashioned through text and image it is no surprise that this is reinforced in news coverage. Literary scholar Ying-Wen Yu recalls that in the afterword to Gerald Vizenor's novel *Bearheat*, Native American novelist Louis Owens cautions that imposing static definitions on Indigenous arts are "destructive, suicidal, even when the definitions appear to arise out of revered tradition."[9] Depictions of Morrisseau in his obituaries, as in other media coverage over the course of his career, tended to reinforce the romantic elements of Noble Savage stereotypes.

An obituary for Cree artist Randall Charboneau in the *Globe and Mail* in 2006 provides similar elements and shares many comparisons to the Morrisseau obituaries. Next to a large photo of Charboneau, shirtless and displaying a tattooed upper body, the story reminds the mainstream readers that prison time "where he emerged from an abyss of booze, robbery, and violence" led him to become a "gentle and spiritual artist."[10] In a story that frames state discipline as a positive antidote to his past behaviours, the *Globe and Mail* introduces Charboneau, from Missanabie Cree River First Nation, in ways that could easily be mistaken for a description of Morrisseau in its association of creativity with behavioural problems. "The Cree might say that Randall Charboneau was finally seized by a Weetigo, an evil spirit in Cree mythology that drives humans to despair. Fellow artists might speculate that he imploded under the weight of his creativity, as true artists sometimes do. Either way, Canada has lost a raw talent, one who ultimately couldn't tame his demons, despite all appearances to the contrary." The obituary adds that Charboneau's "Ojibway style" work "has invited inevitable comparisons to the work of fellow aboriginal Canadian artist Norval Morrisseau." And as with Morrisseau, it appears as though the taming of demons is a goal for Indigenous artists.

Not all of the tributes to Morrisseau were equally framed with stereotypical tropes. Phil Fontaine, then National Chief of the Assembly of First Nations, attempted to avoid confining rhetoric in his released statement to the Canada NewsWire service: "Norval Morrisseau was the key figure at the centre of an Indigenous art movement in Canada in the 1960s that broke through stereotypes, racism and discrimination in that era. He struggled to have his art shown in fine art galleries, and he succeeded. His work has been on display in the most prestigious museums in Canada and around the world. It was a tremendous breakthrough when his art was featured prominently at Expo '67 in Montreal as part of the 'Indian pavilion.'"[11]

Fontaine's message includes an acknowledgement that Morrisseau's approach was "courageous and often controversial," yet "instrumental in encouraging First Nations people to know their spirituality, history and culture in order to better understand ourselves."[12] The National Chief ignores the "Picasso of the North" label and mostly shifts his description away from personal behaviours in favour of a construction that celebrates Morrisseau's achievements as it benefitted Canada's First Nations. Fontaine concludes that Morrisseau "taught us to be proud of who we are" and "inspired countless other First Nations people to pursue a career in the arts." Laudable claims to be sure, ones Morrisseau strived for and attempted to make clear in his statements and actions. Canada's media tended not to promote this element of Morrisseau's narrative. Fontaine refreshingly offers detail about the artist that reinforce his pivotal importance in Canadian art, including his selection as the "only Canadian painter invited to participate in the *Magicians of the Earth* exhibition at the Museum of Modern Art in Paris, France."

Globe and Mail columnist John Allemang also attempted something different when he penned a poem to commemorate Morrisseau on 8 December 2007. It utilizes many of the signifiers present in the Morrisseau myth as it pokes fun at them, challenging that he was more real than the imaginary Picasso of the North myth permitted:

The life's at least the stuff of art.
You look at where he got his start—
The Anishnaabe woods and lakes
That don't provide the kind of breaks
Required to mount a one-man show
Where critics spot the next Van Gogh—
And try to calculate the odds
That he'd surpass creative frauds
Who think a spacious SoHo loft
Is what you're owed when art goes soft.
His times were hard—by birth, by choice,
By listening to the inner voice
That made him credit whisky's kicks
For all his shamanistic tricks.
But somehow, when effect met cause,
He found a way to break the laws
Which taught First Peoples that fine art
Was, much like them, a thing apart.
Picasso of the North? No way—
His native gift was everyday.[13]

In his seemingly simple 250-word poem, Allemang dismisses the Picasso epithet, characterizing Morrisseau as a unique talent.

Mud Slinging

By 8 December 2007 the *Globe and Mail* had turned its coverage from deferential to sensational with the headline, "Relatives Quarrel over Ojibwa Artist's Remains."[14] Explaining that Morrisseau is proving to be as controversial in death as he was in life, the story tells how a "family feud has broken out over what to do with his remains." At the heart of the publicized dispute was whether Gabe Vadas or Morrisseau's brother Bernard had rights to the artist's body. Vadas is reported as being conciliatory to family wishes, while Bernard Morrisseau is presented as seeking legal advice to take full control of the artist's remains. This report was the beginning of a new round of media interest in Morrisseau, this time related to litigation, forgeries, and in-fighting. In March 2008, for example, when Morrisseau was to receive a posthumous National Aboriginal lifetime achievement award, the *Globe and Mail* reported that the award would be held by the organization until the litigation around Morrisseau's remains was settled, noting that three or four of his children and his adopted son Gabor Vadas would be in attendance at the ceremony.[15] Even in death media coverage of Morrisseau centred on his unruly body.

Stories had long swirled in press reports about how Morrisseau was taken advantage of by corrupt individuals wishing to benefit from his fame. After the 1987 press coverage of the artist's crash on the streets of Vancouver, such news reports became more common. A Canada Press wire story made news picked up by even the remote *Daily News* in Prince Rupert, British Columbia as early as January 1986, for example, with a headline stating "Morrisseau Drained by Art's 'Psychic Leeches.'"[16] Describing the artist as a "national institution," the report out of Edmonton explains how the "haggard and weak" fifty-five-year old had vanished from the art scene for about three years because he was "disgusted by the 'assembly line' of the Canadian art industry." The story, which had also been reported in Canadian dailies, as noted in Chapter 4, signalled Morrisseau's frustration with trying to please dealers and collectors.

In 2005 Canadians learned from press reports that not only was Morrisseau taken advantage of but that because of fraud he was forming a committee of experts, called the Norval Morrisseau Heritage Society (NMHS), in an effort to "stanch the flood of allegedly fake Morrisseau paintings that have entered the art market in recent years."[17] The report also revealed that the Morrisseau family had hired a private investigator to track down the source of the many forgeries that had "cropped up across Canada." Morrisseau's Toronto-based counsel, Aaron Milrad, outlined some of the difficulties in authenticating the artist's works. First, Morrisseau's alcoholism and lifestyle in the 1980s, when he was selling or giving away work to support his bad habits, means that much of this work is considered "less genuine" than other works by the artist. Second, Milrad explains, "we are also affected by the first nations 'problem.'" Milrad characterizes the "problem" as "they [Native people] may have a different view of what's a Morrisseau than we do."[18] While Milrad gives no indication of what is real, the forgery story was unleashed. The following month the *Globe and Mail* printed "Paint Brawl," which offered additional drama to the ongoing forgery story, framed around the growing value of Morrisseau paintings in light of the upcoming retrospective exhibition. The story, which describes rivalries between Toronto gallery owners to sell Morrisseau works, notes that a Morrisseau painting "can sell for $35,000 or more."[19] A photograph on the second page of the story is a still taken from the NFB documentary *The Paradox of Norval Morrisseau*, showing him painting at a kitchen table, with a print of the Madonna and Child hung on the wall behind him (the same photo reproduced in his *Globe and Mail* obituary in 2007). In the film, the scene was used to establish the paradoxical relationship the artist had with Christianity; here, it helps demonstrate his painting practice as it identifies him in his makeshift studio.[20]

In early 2007 Val Ross of the *Globe and Mail* penned a story that uncovered how fake Morrisseau paintings were being sold online, and the paper printed a screen shot of a fake Morrisseau on an eBay.ca site to prove it. Milrad called it a "new wrinkle in an old scam," explaining that the NMHS and Gabe Vadas had instigated litigation to ensure that eBay would not sell fakes in the future. This endeavour, however, according to the report, cost the estate about $70,000 a year.[21] This was the start of a series of countless litigations over the authenticity of Morrisseau paintings.

Since 2007, much of the news coverage related to Morrisseau's art has been in the context of legal battles and art fakes. In his research into the Canadian print media's coverage of art fraud between 1978 and 2012, Joshua Nelson found few examples, despite suggestions by some in the media that art theft is big business in Canada.[22] In his analysis of media reports surrounding Morrisseau's victimization by forgers, Nelson was shocked to find that—rather than discuss forgery—news stories from 2007 printed in the *Ottawa Citizen* and the *Victoria Times-Colonist* often emphasized personal details such as that the artist was "an addict and/or former addict," an "ex-con," or "suffering from a neurological disorder." Nelson also noted that such stories identified Morrisseau's agent/spokesperson as a "former street person" whom the artist adopted after "abandoning his biological children."[23]

Press stories about Morrisseau fakes often note that the art is "easy" to forge, calling attention to its "primitive" style. The Saskatoon *StarPhoenix* went so far as to publish a cheeky story, "Easy Steps to Tell If Your Morrisseau Is a Forgery."[24] Suggesting that owners should "check to see if the paint is still tacky" and not to "trust any art dealer selling Morrisseau paintings from the back of a van," the article draws attention to the farcical nature of the forgery stories, playing up the many claims by collectors that they had been hoodwinked.

At least fifteen allegations of fraud have been taken up in civil court actions in Ontario since 2007. Two cases—Maggie Hatfield v. Donna Child and Artworld Inc., and Kevin Hearn v. Joseph Bertram McLeod and Maslak McLeod Gallery Inc.—elicited the most press coverage in the past few years. Because of its celebrity angle, the Kevin Hearn litigation has resulted in sustained interest. According to a *National Post* story printed in November 2012, Hearn, the keyboardist for the Canadian rock band Barenaked Ladies, launched a lawsuit against Joe McLeod and the Maslak McLeod Gallery. He alleged that *Spirit Energy of Mother Earth*, the painting he purchased in 2005 from the Toronto gallery, was a "fake." Describing the artist as "brilliant and charismatic but erratic," the *National Post* report adds that Morrisseau "struggled with alcohol and drug addiction." It concludes by stating, "There is disagreement on everything from the prevalence of fake Morrisseaus to whether the man known as the Picasso of the North was always mentally competent to make declarations about the authenticity of his own paintings."[25] This account confirms Nelson's findings of Morrisseau's victimization, as the character assassination undermines the artist's credibility. A follow-up article in the *National Post* in 2014 notes that allegations by Hearn and another celebrity, "famed Canadian tenor John McDermott," point to a never proven but "well-organized band of forgers in Thunder Bay, Ont., who have spent more than a decade churning out a lucrative supply of fakes in the style of Norval Morrisseau." Quoting their lawyer, Jonathan Sommer, the report explains, "It's important to him [Hearn] that the truth about Norval, whatever it is, is revealed." Brian Shiller, lawyer for McLeod, is given more credibility in the story as he challenges Sommer, who he says "has been making the allegation of a fraud ring for a long time now ... but no evidence has been forthcoming." The *Post* adds that another case argued by Sommer (Hatfield) "was ultimately dismissed last March in Ontario Superior Court, in part because of the perceived unreliability of Mr. Morrisseau's claims."[26] While the 2012 *National Post* story questions Morrisseau's mental state, this story goes further, dismissing claims by Sommer because of "the fact that Mr. Morrisseau was suffering from what has been reported as advanced Alzheimer's disease at the time."[27] While the *National Post* appears to side with arguments made by McLeod's lawyer, *Globe and Mail* coverage seems more sympathetic to Sommer in its story about the court ruling in the Maggie Hatfield suit in 2013. Contending that "Canadian art scene observers who have been trying to prove that the market for Norval Morrisseau paintings has been awash in fakes and forgeries for years have been dealt a major setback in a decision from the Ontario Small Claims Court," the report positions the Canadian art scene observers on the side of Sommer.[28] The story follows up on a 2012 report, also written by James Adams, that pointedly asks in the headline, "Is This a Fake?"[29] While the report concludes that the Hatfield trial demonstrates "the profound instability of the Morrisseau market" and notes that the market is now flat, neither of these two *Globe and Mail* stories attempts to undermine the credibility of Morrisseau, mostly sidestepping opportunities to rehash the stereotypical frames reinforced by the *National Post* reportage.

The news reports surrounding the forgery lawsuits and questions of authenticity continue to discuss Morrisseau in terms of his past behaviours, his contribution to art—though only in general terms—and how his lifestyle impacted his mental faculties, making him an unreliable source on even his own art. References to him as the "Picasso of the North" continue to surface. Missing from the recent press stories, however, are discussions of the part of his mythology that Morrisseau asserted himself, his shaman artist identity.

Artistic Mythologies

The history of art is chock full of mythic constructions of artists. Since the publication of *The Lives of the Most Excellent Painters, Sculptors, and Architects* by Giorgio Vasari during the Italian Renaissance, titillating tales about artists have been *de riguer*. In captivating generations of readers, Vasari's work set a course for the crafting of sensational stories about artists. Following Vasari's accounts of Michelangelo and Caravaggio, each generation and each nation has forged myths about their art stars.

Modern artists like Van Gogh and Jackson Pollock have well-developed mythologies, due in part to their tragic and brief lives, whereas Spanish painter Pablo Picasso is an artist whose long and celebrated life became the stuff of myth. Picasso and his art attracted celebrity attention—even in

Canada. When the Art Gallery of Toronto (now the Art Gallery of Ontario) hosted the *Picasso and Man* exhibition in 1964, Kay Kritzwiser reported the high attendance figures and she expected this popular show to be a record-breaker for the gallery, surpassing the popularity of the Van Gogh exhibition in 1960.[30] Perhaps to impress upon readers the celebrity culture that surrounded Picasso, the report lists a number of celebrities that were attracted to the show, including Dizzy Gillespie, Sid Caesar, and Sir Henry Lintott, British High Commissioner in Ottawa. More than thirty biographies have been written about him and countless art books featuring his art flood the art sections of bookstores. Art historian Johanna Drucker rightly views Picasso as "exemplary of the mythic modern artist."[31] Stories related to Picasso are every bit the products of creativity that his art is. The artist himself was centrally involved in his mythmaking. Picasso was a master self-promoter, a fact made evident on the Internet by the four pages of quotable quotes by the artist on Brainyquotes.com.[32] Biographers and art historians have long added to this mythology, positioning the artist as a genius, a revolutionary, and as a philanderer. In 1998, a fed-up feminist art historian Linda Nochlin wrote an essay for the *Independent* newspaper asking why we still needed the sexist Picasso myth. Wondering if it is possible to separate the "real" Picasso from the Picasso myth, Nochlin challenges readers with a revision of the myth. She contends, "It is hard to separate ... aesthetic inventiveness from the legendary misogyny of the artist, an essential element of the Picasso myth."[33] Still, Picasso mythologies live on. Recently, Argentine novelist Cesar Aira mused about whether he'd want to be Picasso or to have a Picasso, while writing about his visit to the much-anticipated reopened Picasso Museum in Paris for *New Yorker* magazine.[34] Aira decides, given the prices Picasso art commands at auction, that he'd rather have a Picasso than be him. Aira concludes that the artist was more powerful than any king or president, and this, for the writer, was too heavy a burden to bear. Though Picasso died in 1973, he continues to loom large in popular culture, not only because his artworks are worth millions but also because he lived a life that blurred fantasy and fact.

In Canada, a small crop of enduring artist mythologies has been nurtured in popular culture. Members of the Group of Seven stand as icons in Canadian art history, and Lawren Harris (1885–1970) typically functions as spokesman for the group known as creators of landscapes that have come, at least until recently, to visually define Canada. Biographer James King characterizes Harris as "a man who cultivated his internal landscape and attempted to externalize that terrain in his paintings."[35] King notes that while Harris strongly advocated for his art and the work of his contemporaries, he was a private person. As a result, the mythology that exists is framed mostly around the Group of Seven as a force that artistically represented Canada more than an individualized set of myths. So what of other Canadian artists?

After the Group of Seven, Emily Carr (1871–1945), who was aligned with the group of male painters, comes to mind as an artist who has elicited books and exhibitions that have presented and represented her role as a landscape painter, as a female artist, and as a quirky character with a pet monkey.[36] In my experience in the classroom, many students think Emily Carr was an Indigenous artist simply because she painted Indigenous imagery. Unlike her Group of Seven counterparts, Carr visited villages along the northwest coast, painting totem poles and decaying houses, at times including Indigenous peoples rather than just the empty landscapes preferred by Harris.

Art historian Mark Cheetham finds that Alex Colville (1920–2013), one of Canada's best-known artists, described as "Canada's painter laureate," has been shaped in mythological terms. A short biography of Colville who, like Morrisseau, had a career that spanned about half a century, also promoted his interests.[37] How might Colville and Morrisseau compare? On the surface it seems as though they have little in common, but deeper consideration reveals similarities between the two. Each achieved milestones in the Canadian art world as members of the Royal Canadian Academy of Art and as recipients of the Order of Canada.[38] Colville's career, like his precise and polished works, is characterized by his influence beyond his art practice. His influence in educational and political institutions remains key to his mythology. Colville, like Lawren Harris, stepped easily into the elite cultural institutions of Canada while as a female artist, Emily Carr had less of a presence.

Colville obviously never faced discussions about whether his art belonged in an ethnographic museum or an art museum because his work fits neatly within the discourse of Canadian art. There is no need to discuss racial identity nor the worthiness of having his art collected by public museums. In a 1985 *Globe and Mail* story, reporter Bill Prentice includes Colville's assured explanation of his own artistic method: "I'm always concerned in a painting or print with making the thing absolutely authentic. The universality of art springs from the particular. A painting of mine does not make life appear to be simple."[39] Colville's identity in Canadian art, like that of Lawren Harris, remains unfettered by identity politics or colonizing tropes. That is not the case, however, for Bill Reid, whose art has graced Canada's twenty-dollar bill and has commanded impressive sums for his art.

Though mainstream artists offer a comparative structure for considerations of Morrisseau's mythology, a more compelling comparison can be made between Reid and Morrisseau. Haida artist Bill Reid (1920–98) was Indigenous and, like Morrisseau, he fashioned a contemporary visual language that referenced traditional cultural narratives, and he made art from the 1960s through the 1990s. Reid's public identity also included a number of key mythological constructions.

Maria Tippett's controversial 2004 biography *Bill Reid: The Making of an Indian* takes up the task of separating myth from fact when it comes to Reid. She argues that Reid offered mainstream Canada a sanitized and therefore palatable version of Indigenous society, and concludes her investigation by stating that by the end of his life Reid had become "a linchpin between artifact and art, between salvage and revival, between art and politics, and between the Native and non-Native Communities."[40] Because Reid preserved techniques and helped to revitalize interest in northwest coast carving, he is often constructed as a liminal figure between artefact and art. Using traditional stories, Reid similarly pushed his practice in contemporary ways to integrate story with three-dimensional form. Both artists engaged in a dynamic struggle in order to actively create change in Canada with regard to Indigenous arts and culture. Like with Morrisseau, however, discussions of Reid's success as an artist fixate on identity and passive victimization rather than focusing on his artistic innovation. In this way, colonial discourse shaped myths surrounding Morrisseau and Reid, though it played out differently for each of them.

Reid, raised in Victoria, BC, reclaimed his cultural identity and his mother's Haida heritage only as an adult. Because his German-Scottish features and ancestry allowed him to pass as white, it was not until he began to publicly identify as Haida that his Indigeneity began to shape his roles. Because he was not First Nations, Reid did not attend an Indian residential school nor did he have the opportunity to grow up within his Haida cultural community. These details significantly shift the ways in which these artists are considered. Morrisseau, immersed in Anishinaabe culture from birth, benefited from that knowledge in ways that Reid missed out on. Visibly native, Morrisseau signified Indianness, meaning that media stories surrounding him melded with colonial narratives in different ways than those concerning Reid. Racial politics surrounding Reid were different but no less convoluted. A comparison of *Paradox of Norval Morrisseau* with the NFB documentary *Bill Reid*, produced in 1979, signals these variations.[41]

The NFB's disciplining gaze, central to both films, presents Reid within an assimilationist frame—part of the assimilationist efforts at play in mainstream Canadian culture in the 1970s. Footage of him receiving honours

from the Canada Council and UBC's Doctorate of Laws proclaim his success in mainstream ways. A theme of him living in two worlds is emphasized
throughout the film—not in a paradoxical way as with Morrisseau, but in
pragmatic ways. For example, when the camera follows Reid mapping out the
preliminary forms on the cedar pole he is carving for the Haida community of
Skidegate, he explains, "I'm a pretty hardheaded guy I think in a lot of ways,
yet with half my mind, I know I believe that the figures on the totem pole...
grew inside that cedar as it was growing...And the other half of my mind
tells me that is complete nonsense and romantic balderdash."[42] Later, when
Reid demonstrates the power saws he will use to carve the pole, a practice
frowned upon by community members, he shrugs it off by stating, "It gets
the job done, and that is all I'm really interested in."[43] Reid's matter-of-fact
approach is promoted in the documentary in positive ways, demonstrating
values that make him a success in mainstream Canadian culture.

In her *Globe and Mail* tribute to Reid following his death in March 1998,
art historian Charlotte Townsend Gault discussed many of the laudatory
ways the Haida artist would be remembered, situating him at "the fulcrum of
all important debates about native art and culture" and avoiding discussion of
identity politics.[44] Yet, in 2004, the *Globe* reported that acclaimed poet Robert
Bringhurst was fed up with public treatment of Reid. Bringhurst argued
that Reid had not been treated fairly in public discourse. He cited Tippett's
biography as one minor example but was most concerned with a negative
Maclean's feature published in 1999 that characterized Reid as manipulative
and maintained that Reid had exploited apprentices in the creation of his
famous works.[45] Indeed, Jane O'Hara's ten-page *Maclean's* exposé excoriates
Reid, charging that he used connections to Haida culture largely for personal
gain.[46] Much of this debate was quelled after a revisionist conference and
the follow-up laudatory publication *Bill Reid and Beyond: Expanding on
Modern Native Art* that situates Reid's success squarely within the context of
Canadian art history and Indigenous art. A number of the essays in the text
clarify his significance as a Haida artist, redirecting the discourse of racial
politics championed by the early but influential NFB documentary. Miles
Richardson, a member of the Haida nation and Chief Commissioner of the
British Columbia Treaty Commission, confirms in his essay, "Bill had his
hands and his full heart in the endeavours of the Haida Nation: He was an
ambassador for Haidaness and for the Haida Nation."[47]

Reid's artistic legacy is of course impressive and his cultural connections
are important, yet I agree with Tippett's characterization of Reid in Canadian
popular culture, an issue separate from his actual achievements. Canada's

support for assimilation, both overt and hidden, made Reid's mainstream up-bringing and visibly non-Indigenous features key elements of his mythology. For many Canadians, Reid performed the role of an acceptable, somewhat antiseptic Indigenous artist. This is not new. Think of how Canadians and the world adored Grey Owl (the masquerading British Archie Belaney) as a spokesperson for Indigenous peoples in the 1920s and 1930s. Morrisseau's treatment in popular culture differed because he did not behave nor could he pass so easily into dominant Canadian culture.

Recently Armand Garnet Ruffo released *Norval Morrisseau: Man Changing into Thunderbird*, a book of literary non-fiction that builds from the essay he penned for Morrisseau's 2006 retrospective exhibition catalogue. Ruffo describes the methods he used to tell Morrisseau's story as a form of "mythic realism," a formula he explains closely follows the structure of oral Anishinaabe narrative traditions.[48] Blending elements of traditional storytelling with episodes from Morrisseau's life, Ruffo reinforces and clarifies aspects of the artist's life as he crafts a creatively wrought biography, positioning Morrisseau within Anishinaabe ways of teaching and learning. Celebrating his mythic presence, Ruffo brings Morrisseau to life, pushing myth in fresh ways.

Ruffo accords the artist agency, describing a myriad of ways in which he actively engaged in formulating his own narratives. Combining archival research, interviews, and news coverage with both poetry and poetic prose, Morrisseau is transported into a new mythic space, one that recognizes his efforts as it also acknowledges the colonial eye that was trained upon him, spinning new mythic directions for the artist.

Man Changing into Thunderbird, the title and the concept used by others and the artist himself, refers to Morrisseau's mythic construction as Copper Thunderbird. While this is the name given to Morrisseau in a healing cer-emony in the 1950s, it also comes to shape Morrisseau in mythological terms. In Cree syllabics on his paintings, Copper Thunderbird situates the artist as authentically Indigenous and serves both primitivist and racial ends at dif-ferent times in his life. Morrisseau's monumental six-panel painting from 1977, *Man Changing into Thunderbird*, feeds the mythic construction as it intersects with his image of himself as a shaman artist and a more romantic vision of shaman from a Noble Savage perspective. A Copper Thunderbird Gallery opened in 2004 in Thunder Bay that features Woodland art and channels Morrisseau's identity. Marie Clements chose *Copper Thunderbird* as the title of her 2007 published play about the artist's life. In connection to an exhibition of Morrisseau's work, a recent symposium at First Nations

University of Canada in 2015 was also titled *Copper Thunderbird*. It acknowledged Morrisseau credibility as a shaman artist and the persisting importance
of this mythic construction.

The More Things Change...

Sure, Morrisseau won awards, received accolades, and in 2006 got to see his
retrospective exhibition at the National Gallery of Canada, but along the way
his significance as an artist was hijacked by a number of interests, much of
them precipitated by colonialism. Morrisseau was a fitting example of Gerald
Vizenor's concept of survivance because he did more than endure or survive.
In his efforts to challenge the media, in his performative actions, and by his
creative outputs, Morrisseau affected an active presence and transformed the
ways in which Canadians consider Indigenous arts. Canada's media often
disciplined and confined him, judging Morrisseau through a narrow lens
that was inserted within a larger mythic narrative, one of nation-building.
However, at times throughout his career Morrisseau unsettled the settler
nation. As early as 1962 Morrisseau demonstrated a clear understanding of
the narrow stereotypical constructions at play in popular culture in Canada
with regard to Indigenous peoples. Stating in the November 1962 *Weekend*
magazine feature, "I'm an Indian, I'm not supposed to show any emotion,"
he reveals his keen awareness of Noble Savage attributes, not to mention
illustrates his charisma and good sense of humour.[49] In Morrisseau's case,
poverty and lack of education—fixated upon by the press—appear as naturalized conditions rather than as evidence of colonialism. Yet Morrisseau's 1975
honest declaration in the *Toronto Star*, "I am tired of hearing about Norval
the drunkard," had little impact in the media that later feverishly pounced
on the artist's alcoholism-induced misfortunes in 1987.[50] The *Toronto Star*'s
Christopher Hume reported in 1991 that Morrisseau shared, "Why am I
alive? To heal you guys who're more screwed up than I am."[51] Morrisseau's
joking response reveals his enduring sense of trickster humour after thirty
years of media scrutiny.

● ● ●

The Morrisseau myth promoted by the media confirms the argument that
Canada needs its colonial Other. The nation needed Morrisseau, the artist—not in ways that other Canadian artists were championed, but to assuage
its guilt for an imperialist past and a colonial present. Putting a version of
Morrisseau on a pedestal provided Canada with an example of success—on
its own terms. That the media's mythology of Morrisseau included ongoing

examples of his problematic behaviour circulated and reinforced a stereo-typical construction that educated and disciplined Canadians. An overlay of primitivism promulgated by a Western art world reinforced this racialized discourse to stifle how Morrisseau's art was both collected and presented in galleries and in art museums. "Picasso of the North" translates most clearly into Noble Savage tropes that align Morrisseau with modern primitivism by setting him up as a counterpoint to Eurocentric notions of modern art. Even after the success of his retrospective and a renewed and revisioned interest in his art, media obituaries relied on this moniker to capture the spirit of the artist, keeping him mired in primitivist discourse.

Enduring narratives about Morrisseau's unruly behaviour haunt the mythology. His public woes, centred on alcoholism, erratic behaviours, and more recently, the added narrative of his unreliability due to his suffering from dementia, have left Canadians shaking their heads, curious about the spectacle or eager to help him *be* like everyone else. Morrisseau's insistence that living life on his terms fed his creativity was largely ignored by the media or dismissed as just another of his odd comments. His own spiritual quest so often channelled in his art, drawing from Anishinaabe, Christian, and Eckankar sources, fed his personal shaman identity but was often misun-derstood as romantic in a New Age way. As with primitivist discourse, the Noble Savage tropes that cross-pollinated and morphed in different ways in media stories remain.

From his earliest public appearances Norval Morrisseau challenged the confining narratives ascribed to him by Canada's media, yet that didn't stop the press from continually placing him in a box that had long held Canada's Indigenous Others. Morrisseau defied such simplistic framing, humorously drawing attention to his supposed stoic demeanour, voraciously studying other forms of art, astutely advocating for ways to record oral narratives and preserve knowledge held by aging elders, offering teachings to students and to government officials, and most significantly, promoting his own vision of himself as a shaman artist by painting masterworks that have no equivalent. The artist lived large, made incredible inroads in the art world as he shaped a unique visual language and advanced a form of Indigenous visual storytelling that sparked a creative movement for new generations of artists.

Performatively enacting himself as a shaman artist became a response to stereotypes used to describe him in the early 1970s. Hosting his 1978 tea party, for example, situated the artist within a narrative that combined his strong eclectic spiritual beliefs with the romantic tropes of the Noble Savage to forge a role he comfortably inhabited. That he did this within the confining space assigned him as an Imaginary Indian by Canada's media makes his efforts and successes in moulding his own version of the myth all the more impressive. Morrisseau's own shaping of himself as a shaman artist illustrates an aspect of his mythology which, while informed by countless narrative threads such as primitivism, Noble Savage tropes, and a romantic fascination with shamanism, also reveals agential change. For Morrisseau, the construction of him as Picasso of the North in the media was less apt than his own cultivated persona. He lived and he painted as Copper Thunderbird—a shape shifter who evinced change in all ways.

ACKNOWLEDGEMENTS

This book is the result of a research project that I stumbled into while I assembled resources to teach contemporary Indigenous art history in my faculty position at Saskatchewan Indian Federated College in 2001 (First Nations University of Canada). It was then that I began to consider the ways in which Morrisseau played a larger role in Canada's cultural imaginary than he did in the nation's history of art. I want to acknowledge encouragement from Bob Boyer and Kate Davis, both of whom passed away before the completion of this project. Friends, colleagues, mentors, faculty, and students at First Nations University, University of Regina, and beyond have also motivated me throughout the process. I thank also the members of the Norval Morrisseau Heritage Society for their encouragement. I thank the many librarians, archival assistants, and collections managers who provided direction and materials at institutions in Ottawa, Toronto, Montreal, and Thunder Bay.

Without generous support from the Social Sciences and Humanities Research Council, the University of Regina President's Fund, and the University of Regina's Humanities Research Institute, this text would not have been possible. I wish also to thank my research assistants Leisha Grebinski, Bridget Keating, Lydia Miliokas, Caitlyn Jean MacMillan, Caitlin Mullan, and Ashton Wiebe for the hours they spent in front of microfilm readers. I also extend my gratitude to the staff and editors at University of Manitoba Press, especially to Maureen Epp for her close attention to detail. Any errors or shortcomings are my responsibility.

My family has lived with this project for a long time and I am grateful to them for their patience. My partner Mark urged me onward, sending me down paths that helped me craft this text in unanticipated ways and I owe him more than I can say. Our two daughters Dagmar and Madelaine wholeheartedly supported me from very beginning with their infectious singing of "Norval, Norval, what's driving you?" and their inspiring zest for life. Collette, my mom, has always had my back and I want to thank her for her resolute belief in me. Finally, thank you to *all my relations* for keeping it real.

NOTES

Introduction: Discipline, Performativity, and Morrisseau

1 Paul Gessell, "Taming Their Demons," *Ottawa Citizen*, 29 January 2006, B1–4; Sarah Milroy, "Morrisseau Has Defeated the Demons," *Globe and Mail*, 7 February 2006.

2 Labels and nomenclature change over time. When Morrisseau was born and raised he was referred to as an "Indian," then he became "Native," "First Nations," and "Aboriginal"; the current preferred usage is "Indigenous." The terms Indian and Native continue to be accepted in the United States.

3 My choice of the italicized term *Indian* in this case is twofold. First, Indian was how Indigenous peoples were referred to in the press at the time Morrisseau arrived on the scene. While viewed as pejorative today, it is the legal term applied to First Nations within the Indian Act in Canada. I also use Indian in a second sense, as a reference to the stereotypical construction of the Indian that relates to a racialized monolith, as opposed to a specific Indigenous cultural group like the Anishinaabe (also known as the Ojibwe).

4 Gerald McMaster, "The Anishinaabe Artistic Consciousness," in *Before and After the Horizon: Anishinaabe Artists of the Great Lakes*, ed. David Penney and Gerald McMaster (Washington, DC: Smithsonian, 2013), 72.

5 Ibid., 74.

6 Paul Kellstedt, *The Mass Media and the Dynamics of American Racial Attitudes* (Cambridge, UK: Cambridge University Press, 2003), 5, 14.

7 Carlos E. Cortes, *The Children Are Watching: How the Media Teach about Diversity* (New York: Teachers College Press, 2000).

8 I borrow this term from Daniel Francis. See Daniel Francis, *Imaginary Indian: The Image of the Indian in Canadian Culture* (Vancouver: Arsenal Pulp Press, 1992).

9 Milroy, "Morrisseau Has Defeated the Demons.".

10 Roland Barthes, *Mythologies*, trans. Annette Lavers (New York: Noonday Press, 1975), 142–43.

11 Michel Foucault, "Method," in *Cultural Theory and Popular Culture: A Reader*, 4th ed., ed. John Storey, (Harlow: Pearson Education, 2009), 315; 318.

12 David Ljunggren, "Every G20 Nation Wants to Be Canada, Insists PM," *Reuters*, 25 September 2009, http://www.Reuters.com, 25 September 2009 (accessed 4 January 2015).

13 For examples, see Taiaiake Alfred, *Peace, Power, Righteousness: An Indigenous Manifesto* (Don Mills, ON: Oxford University Press, 1999); James Daschuk, *Clearing the Plains: Disease, Politics of Starvation, and Loss of Aboriginal Life* (Regina: University of Regina Press, 2013); Elizabeth Furniss, *The Burden of History: Colonialism and the Frontier Myth in a Rural Canadian Community* (Vancouver: University of British Columbia Press, 1999); Todd Gordon, *Imperialist Canada* (Winnipeg: Arbeiter Ring, 2010).

14 See Richard Slotkin, *Regeneration through Violence: The Mythology of the American Frontier 1600–1860* (Norman: University of Oklahoma Press, 2001).

15 Pauline Turner Strong, *American Indians and the American Imaginary: Cultural Representations Across the Centuries* (Boulder, CO: Paradigm Publishers, 2013), 4.

16 Benedict Anderson, *Imagined Communities: Reflections on the Origin and Spread of Nationalism*, new ed. (London: Verso, 2006), 6.

17 Stuart Hall, "The Question of Cultural Identity" in S. Hall, D. Held, and T. McGrew (eds.), *Modernity and Its Futures* (Oxford: Polity, 1992), 239.

18 "Is Canada's New $20 Bill 'Pornographic?'" *CBC News/Community*, http://www.cbc.ca/news/yourcommunity/2012/05/is-canadas-new-20-bill-too-pornographic.html (accessed 25 November 2012).

19 Stephen Harper, "Franklin Discovery Strengthens Canada's Arctic Sovereignty," *Globe and Mail*, 12 September 2014.

20 Gerald Vizenor, *Manifest Manners: Narratives on PostIndian Survivance* (Lincoln: University of Nebraska Press, 1994), 59–60.

21 Strong, *American Indians and the American Imaginary*, 18.

22 Mark Falcous, "The Decolonizing National Imaginary: Promotional Media Constructions During the 2005 Lions Tour of Aotearoa New Zealand," *Journal of Sport and Social Issues* 31,4 (2007): 385.

23 Nicolas Thomas, *Colonialism's Culture: Anthropology, Travel, Government* (Cambridge, UK: Polity Press), 188.

24 Terry Goldie, *Fear and Temptation: The Image of the Indigene in Canadian, Australian, and New Zealand Literatures* (Montreal: McGill-Queen's University Press, 1993), 12.

25 Paulette Regan, "Unsettling the Settler Within: Canada's Peacemaker Myth, Reconciliation, and Transformative Pathways to Decolonization" (PhD diss., University of Victoria, 2006).

26 Ken Coates, *The Marshall Decision and Native Rights* (Montreal: McGill-Queen's University Press, 2000), xiv.

27 Ibid., xv.

28 J.R. Miller, *Lethal Legacy: Current Native Controversies in Canada* (Toronto: McClelland and Stewart, 2004). See also J.R. Miller, *Compact, Contract, Covenant: Aboriginal Treaty-Making in Canada* (Toronto: University of Toronto Press, 2009); J.R. Miller, *Shingwauk's Vision: A History of Native Residential Schools* (Toronto: University of Toronto Press, 1996); J.R. Miller, *Skyscrapers Hide the Heavens: A History of Indian–White Relations in Canada* (Toronto: University of Toronto Press, 1989).

29 Nicholas Thomas, *Possessions: Indigenous Art/Colonial Culture* (London: Thames and Hudson, 1999).

30 Ibid., 15.

31 See John Corner and Dick Pels, *Media and Restyling of Politics: Consumerism, Celebrity and Cynicism.* (Beverly Hills, CA: Sage, 2003); Marianne W. Jorgensen and Louise J. Phillips, *Discourse Analysis as Theory and Method* (Beverly Hills, CA: Sage, 2003); Douglas Kellner, *Media Culture: Cultural Studies, Identity and Politics between the Modern and the Postmodern* (London: Routledge, 1995).

32 Stuart Hall, *Representation: Cultural Representations and Signifying Practices and Identities* (Beverly Hills, CA: Sage, 1997); Edward Said, *Culture and Imperialism* (New York: Vintage, 1994); Edward Said, *Covering Islam: How the Media and the Experts Determine How We See the Rest of the World* (New York: Vintage, 1997);

Edward Herman and Noam Chomsky, *Manufacturing Consent: The Political Economy of the Mass Media* (New York: Vintage, 1995); Noam Chomsky, *Media Control: The Spectacular Achievements of Propaganda* (New York: Seven Stories Press, 2008).

33   See Maxwell McCombs, *Setting the Agenda: The News Media and Public Opinion* (Cambridge, UK: Polity Press, 2004); Renita Coleman, Maxwell McCombs, Donald Shaw, and David Weaver, "Agenda Setting," in *Handbook of Journalism Studies*, ed. Karin Wal-Jorgensen and Thomas Hanizsch (New York: Routledge, 2004), 147–74.

34   The Toronto mayor in 2010 made national and international news when he was accused of hanging out with drug dealers and allegedly smoking crack cocaine. Accusations were hurled about as city of Toronto councillors and the mayor's office squared off in a public fight that ultimately led to the city councillors voting to remove some of Ford's mayoral powers when he refused to resign. See: "The Weirdest Mayoralty Ever: The Inside Story of Rob Ford's City Hall," *Toronto Life*, May 15, 2012. http://www.torontolife.com/informer/features/2012/05/15/rob-ford-the-weirdest-mayoralty-ever/3/ (accessed 15 August 2015); Ivor Tossell, "The Story Behind the Rob Ford Story" *The Walrus* March 2014. http://thewalrus.ca/the-story-behind-the-rob-ford-story/ (accessed 15 August 2015).

35   Michel Foucault, "What Is Enlightenment?" in *Ethics: Subjectivity and Truth,* The Essential Works of Foucault 1954–1984, vol. 1, ed. Paul Rabinow (London: Penguin, 2000), 317.

36   Michel Foucault, *Discipline and Punish: Birth of a Nation* (New York: Vintage, 1991), 170.

37   Teun Van Dijk, *Racism and the Press* (New York: Routledge, 1991), ix.

38   Yasmin Jiwani, *Discourses of Denial* (Vancouver: University of British Columbia Press, 2006), xx.

39   Mark Cronlund Anderson and Carmen L. Robertson, *Seeing Red: A History of Natives in Canadian Newspapers* (Winnipeg: University of Manitoba Press, 2011).

40   Lyle Dick, "Nationalism and Visual Media in Canada: The Case of Thomas Scott's Execution," *Manitoba History* 48 (Autumn/Winter 2004–5): 16.

41   Nadine Ehlers, *Racial Imperatives: Discipline, Performativity and Struggles against Subjection* (Bloomington: Indiana University Press, 2012).

42   "The Ethics of Care for the Self as a Practice of Freedom—An Interview with Michel Foucault, 1984," in *The Final Foucault*, ed. James Bernauer and David Rasmussen (Cambridge, Mass.: MIT Press, 1987), 1–20.

43   Christopher Hume, "The New Age of Indian Art," *Maclean's*, 22 January 1979, 23.

44   Barry Ace, "Artist as Shaman," *Aboriginal Curatorial Collective Archives*, December 2005, http://www.aboriginalcuratorialcollective.org/research/morriseau3.html (accessed 5 January 2007).

45   Ruth Phillips, "Morrisseau's Entrance: Negotiating Primitivism, Modernism, and Anishnaabe Tradition," in *Norval Morrisseau: Shaman Artist*, ed. Greg A. Hill (Ottawa: National Gallery of Canada, 2006), 44.

46   Greg A. Hill, ed., *Norval Morrisseau: Shaman Artist* (Ottawa: National Gallery of Canada, 2006).

47   Rob Nester notes that in early 1886, passes were issued to Indian agents in order to control movement of First Nations people. Unable to leave their reserve without a pass signed by a reserve's Indian agent, the pass system, enforced into the 1940s though never passed into legislation, monitored and disciplined free passage. Rob

Nestor, "Indian Policy and the Early Reserve Period," *Encyclopedia of Saskatchewan*, http://esask.uregina.ca/entry/indian_policy_and_the_early_reserve_period.html (accessed 4 September 2014).

48 Hill, *Shaman Artist*, 28.

49 Henning Jacobsen and Duke Redbird, dirs., *The Paradox of Norval Morrisseau*, documentary film (Montreal: National Film Board of Canada, 1974).

50 Lister Sinclair and Jack Pollock, *The Art of Norval Morrisseau* (Toronto: Methuen, 1979), 136.

51 Daschuk, *Clearing the Plains*, 127-180.

52 Ruth B. Phillips, "The Turn of the Primitive: Modernism, the Stranger and the Indigenous Artist," in *Exiles, Diasporas and Strangers*, ed. Kobena Mercer (Cambridge, MA: MIT Press, 2008), 49.

53 Collection of letters from Norval Morrisseau to Susan Ross, Thunder Bay Art Gallery archives.

54 Morrisseau, *Legends of My People: The Great Ojibway*. ed. Selwyn Dewdney (Toronto: Ryerson Press, 1965).

55 See Collection of letters between Selwyn Dewdney and Norval Morrisseau, Dewdney Papers, INAC 306065, Aboriginal Art Centre Archives, Aboriginal and Northern Development, Gatineau, Quebec.

56 Hill, *Shaman Artist*, 66.

57 See Dewdney Papers, Aboriginal Art Centre Archives, Aboriginal and Northern Development Canada, Gatineau, Quebec.

58 Quoted in Hill, *Shaman Artist*, 20.

59 Sinclair and Pollock, *The Art of Norval Morrisseau*, 17.

60 Musée de Québec, Quebec City, 1966.

61 Henning Jacobsen, dir., *The Colours of Pride*, documentary film (National Film Board of Canada, 1973); Jacobsen and Redbird, *The Paradox of Norval Morrisseau*.

62 The recent art exhibition *Seven: Professional Native Indian Artists Inc.*, curated by Michelle Lavallee, explores and showcases the achievements of the group and the seven individual artists involved in the initiative. See Michelle Lavallee, ed., *Seven: Professional Native Indian Artists Inc.* (Regina: MacKenzie Art Gallery, 2014).

63 Paul Twitchell, *Dialogues with the Master* (San Diego: Illuminated Way Press, 1970). Controversy surrounds Eckankar, which has been referred to as a cult. Religious scholar Lucy DuPertuis argues that Eckankar and over twenty other similar spiritual organizations sprung up in the United States in the 1960s and 1970s because of the influence of Sant Mat, Radhasoami, or the Divine Light Mission (DLM) tradition, the Hindu concept of charisma. Eckankar borrows liberally from the DLM for notions of illumination and light as direct symbolic paths to enlightenment. See Lucy DuPertuis, "How People Recognize Charisma: The Case of *Darshan* in *Radhasoami* and Divine Light Mission," *Sociology of Religion* 47, no. 2 (1986): 111–24.

64 Norval Morrisseau, *Norval Morrisseau: Travels to the House of Invention* (Toronto: Key Porter Books, 1997), 16.

65 Hill, *Shaman Artist*, 26.

66 Ibid.

Chapter 1: Mythmaking and Primitivism

1 Northrop Frye, *Fables of Identity: Studies in Poetic Mythology* (New York: Harcourt, Brace and World, 1963), 32.

2 Percy S. Cohen, "Theories of Myth," *Man*, n.s., 4, no. 3 (1969): 337.

3 Grace Inglis, "Morrisseau Magic Has Been Drained," *Hamilton Spectator*, 20 March 1982.

4 Peter Mason, *The Lives of Images* (London: Reaktion Books, 2001).

5 Ibid., 78.

6 Connie Higginson-Murray, " 'Picasso of the North,'" *Ottawa Citizen*, 3 February 2006, A3.

7 Bill Brown, "Copper Thunderbird: An Ojibway Who Paints His People's Past," *Weekend Magazine*, November 1962, 52–53.

8 Conversation with Dr. Fredrick Mulder, Regina, SK, 18 April 2012.

9 Ruth B. Phillips, "The Turn of the Primitive: Modernism, the Stranger and the Indigenous Artist," in *Exiles, Diasporas and Strangers*, ed. Kobena Mercer (Cambridge, MA: MIT Press, 2008), 64.

10 Joseph Weinstein, *The White Ojibway Medicine Man and Other Stories* (Bloomington, IN: iUniverse, 2009), 55.

11 James Stephens, *A Picasso in the North Country* (Thunder Bay, ON: Anishinaabe Art Gallery, 2011). Stevens attributes the "Picasso" label to Chagall (p. 3). However, on his website devoted to Norval Morrisseau, former apprentice Richie Stardreamer Sinclair challenges this claim, attributing the nickname to Jack Pollock in 1967.

12 See discussion regarding the foundation of the NFB: "Our History—The NFB Foundation," https://www.nfb.ca/historique/about-the-foundation (accessed September 2013).

13 Marshall McLuhan, *Understanding Media: The Extensions of Man* (Toronto: McGraw-Hill, 1964), 8.

14 Henning Jacobsen and Duke Redbird, dirs., *The Paradox of Norval Morrisseau*, documentary film (Montreal: National Film Board of Canada, 1974).

15 Tom Hill, "*The Paradox of Norval Morrisseau*—A Film Review," *Tawow: Canadian Indian Cultural Magazine* 4, no. 4 (1974): 3.

16 Bill Nichols, *Representing Reality* (Bloomington: Indiana University Press, 1991).

17 Norval Morrisseau spent six months in jail in 1973–74 and had only been released the day before the NFB film crew arrived in Kenora, ON, to make this film. Upon his release, Morrisseau commenced drinking heavily. The director filmed Morrisseau according to schedule. Therefore, when he appears on screen wearing his purple shirt, viewers meet an inebriated Morrisseau in several stages of drunkenness in edited segments throughout the documentary. See: Jack Pollock, *Dear M: Letters from a Gentleman of Excess* (London: McClelland and Stewart, 1989).

18 Tom Hill's lack of introduction is most likely the result of shoddy film editing, sharing footage from *Colours of Pride*. However, there is also nothing in the credits to identify his role in the film.

19 This French term refers to painting outside of one's studio, at an outdoor location. It is a painting convention first adopted by the impressionists in Western art history.

20 Claire Pajaczkowska and Lola Young, "Racism, Representation, Psychoanalysis," in *Feminism and Film*, ed. E. Ann Kaplan (Oxford: Oxford University Press, 2000), 359.

21 Philip Deloria, *Indians in Unexpected Places* (Lawrence: University Press of Kansas, 2004), 183.

22 Using a successful device first employed by the NFB in 1968 in *The Ballad of Crowfoot* (1968), the directors include an inspiring ballad, with words and music written by Aboriginal songwriters Duke Redbird and Shingoose.

23 Barthes, *Mythologies*, 95.

24 Ibid., 42.

25 Ibid.

26 Valda Blundell and Ruth B. Phillips, "If It's Not Shamanic, Is It Sham? An Examination of Media Responses to Woodland School Art," *Anthropologica*, n.s., 25, no.1 (1983): 121–23.

27 Christopher Hume, "The New Age of Indian Art," *Maclean's*, 22 January 1979, 24–28.

28 Henning Jacobsen, director, *The Colours of Pride*, documentary film (National Film Board of Canada, 1973).

29 Charlotte Townsend-Gault, "Have We Ever Been Good?" *Rebecca Belmore: The Named and Unnamed* (Vancouver: Morris and Helen Belkin Art Gallery, 2003), 17.

30 See Homi Bhabha's "Mimicry and Man" for a thorough discussion of this concept, in *Location of Culture* (London: Routledge, 1994), 86.

31 Ibid.

32 Clement Greenberg coined the term "post-painterly abstraction" for an exhibition he curated at the Los Angeles County Museum in 1964, applying it to abstract art that moves to erase subject matter and brush stroke. http://www.theartstory.org/movement-post-painterly-abstraction.htm (accessed August 10, 2015).

33 Lister Sinclair and Jack Pollock, *The Art of Norval Morrisseau* (Toronto: Methuen, 1979), 61.

34 Joy Carroll, "The Strange Success—and Failure of Norval Morrisseau," *Canadian Art* 21, no. 6 (1964): 348–50.

35 Norval Morrisseau, preface to Sinclair and Pollock, *The Art of Norval Morrisseau*, n.p.

36 Sinclair and Pollock, *The Art of Norval Morrisseau*, 13.

37 Ibid., 15.

38 Ibid., 18–21.

39 Ibid., 17.

40 Ibid.

41 Ibid., 45.

42 Ibid., 45–46.

43 Ibid. 66.

44 Stevens, *A Picasso in the North Country*, 214.

45 Ibid.

46 John Bentley Mays, "Morrisseau's Art Explores Magic Forests of the Mind," *Globe and Mail*, 9 July 1981.

47 Lister Sinclair, "Morrisseau Drawn from Life," letter to the editor, *Globe and Mail*, 11 July 1981.

48 Jack Pollock, "Norval Morrisseau," *Tawow: Canadian Indian Cultural Magazine* 4 no. 4 (1974): 5-6. *Tawow* magazine was a quarterly publication produced by the Department of Indian Affairs and Northern Development as a forum for

Indian writers and poets, begun under the auspices of the Jean Chrétien in 1970. The magazine ceased publication in 1980, according to Valeria Alia, *Un/Covering the North: News, Media, and Aboriginal People* (Vancouver: University of British Columbia Press, 1999).

49 "Myth and Symbol," *Time*, 28 September 1962.

50 Paul Duval, "Accent on Art: Primitive Art" Toronto *Telegram* 22 September 1962.

51 Leslie Dawn, *National Visions, National Blindness: Canadian Art and Identities in the 1920s* (Vancouver: University of British Columbia Press, 2006), 55–115.

52 Ibid., 108.

53 Ibid., 85.

54 Lynda Jessup, "Hard Inclusion," in *On Aboriginal Representation in the Gallery*, ed. Lynda Jessup and Shannon Bagg (Ottawa: Canadian Museum of Civilization, 2002), xv.

55 Marcia Crosby, "Construction of the Imaginary Indian," in *Beyond Wilderness: Contest and Controversy*, ed. John O'Brian and Peter White (Montreal: McGill-Queen's University Press, 2007), 219.

56 Ibid., 221.

57 Charlotte Townsend-Gault, "First Nations Culture: Who Knows What?" *Canadian Journal of Communication* 23, no. 1 (1998), http:// www.cjc-online.ca/index.php/journal/article/view/1021/927 (accessed 4 January 2015).

58 The literature surrounding the topic of primitive art and primitivism is vast and varied. I have limited this discussion to a few key texts.

59 H.W. Janson, *History of Art*, rev. ed. (New York: H.N. Abrams, 1986), 5; cited in Sally Price, *Primitive Art in Civilized Places*, 2nd ed. (Chicago: University of Chicago Press, 2001) 1.

60 Steven A. Mansbach, "The Artifice of Modern(ist) Art History," in *Exiles, Diasporas and Strangers*, ed. Kobena Mercer (Cambridge, MA: MIT Press, 2008), 96–113.

61 Price, *Primitive Art in Civilized Places*, 32.

62 Daniel J. Sherman, *French Primitivism and the Ends of Empire: 1945–1975* (Chicago: University of Chicago Press, 2011), 5.

63 Price, *Primitive Art in Civilized Places*, 130.

64 Robert Goldwater, *Primitivism in Modern Art* (1938, New York: Vintage Books, 1966); *Gauguin* (New York: H.N. Abrams, 1928).

65 Hal Foster, "The Primitive Unconscious of Modern Art," *October* 34 (Autumn, 1985): 58-70.

66 Ibid., 46.

67 Bill Anthes, *Native Moderns: American Indian Painting, 1940–1960* (Durham, NC: Duke University Press, 2006), 81.

68 Ibid., 87–88.

69 Foster, "The Primitive Unconscious of Modern Art," 51.

70 Ian McLean, "Aboriginal Modernism in Central Australia," in *Exiles, Diasporas and Strangers*, ed. Kobena Mercer (Cambridge, MA: MIT Press, 2008), 73.

71 Ibid., 74.

72 Phillips, "The Turn of the Primitive," 49.

73 Ibid., 65.

74 Ibid., 67.

75 Brian O'Doherty, "Good Job Done Quietly: The Museum of Primitive Art," *New York Times*, 24 June 1962.

76 "Indian Group Is Ready to Take Court Action in Fight Against Discrimination," *New York Times*, 11 September 1963.

77 John Canaday, "Seattle's Art Show," *New York Times*, 29 April 1962.

78 "Abstraction Seen in Indian Work," *Globe and Mail*, 13 January 1962.

79 Ibid.

80 Donavon Clemson, "The Totems Fall and an Art Dies," *Winnipeg Free Press*, 5 January 1963.

81 Ibid.

82 "All Dressed Up in Buckskin n' Beads," *Winnipeg Free Press*, 6 February 1963.

83 "Indians Angry over Fake Crafts," *Winnipeg Free Press*, 17 August 1963.

84 Leanne Pupchek, "True North: Inuit Art and the Canadian Imagination," *American Review of Canadian Studies* 31, nos. 1–2 (2001): 191.

85 Joan Sangster, " 'The Beaver' as Ideology: Constructing Images of Inuit and Native Life in Post–World War II Canada," *Anthropologica* 49, no. 2 (2007): 193.

86 Jacqueline Fry, "Contemporary Arts in Non-Western Societies," *artscanada* 28, no. 6 (December 1971/January 1972): 96–101.

87 Tom Hill, "Indian Art in Canada: A Historical Perspective," in *Norval Morrisseau and the Image Makers*, by Elizabeth McLuhan and Tom Hill (Toronto: Art Gallery of Ontario, 1984), 19.

88 Ibid., 19.

89 See Heather Igloliorte, "Influence and Instruction: James Houston, Sunuyuksuk: Eskimo Handicrafts, and the Formative Years of Contemporary Inuit Art" (PhD diss., Carleton University, 2006.)

90 Norman Vorano, "Creators: Negotiating the Art World for Over 50 Years," *Inuit Art Quarterly* 19, nos. 3/4 (Fall/Winter 2004): 9–17.

91 Kristin Potter, "James Houston, Armchair Tourism, and the Marketing of Inuit Art," in *Native American Art in the Twentieth Century: Makers, Meanings, Histories*, ed. W. Jackson Rushing III (London: Routledge, 1999), 39–56.

92 For a sober portrayal of James Houston's role in the North, see Igloliorte, "Influence and Instruction."

93 Pearl McCarthy, "Advisers a Reason for Anxiety," *Globe and Mail*, 17 March 1962, 17.

94 Ibid.

95 "The Eskimo Artists of Baffin Island," *Winnipeg Free Press*, 28 August 1962.

96 Jean Blodgett, *Kenojuak Ashevak* (Richmond Hill, ON: Firefly Books, 1985). For a discussion about the Inuit graphic arts movement see Janet Berlo, "Drawing (upon) the Past: Negotiating Identities in Inuit Graphic Arts Production," in *Unpacking Culture: Art and Commodity in Colonial and Postcolonial Worlds*, ed. Ruth B. Phillips and Christopher B. Steiner (Berkeley: University of California Press, 1999), 178–93.

97 Tom Daly, producer, *Eskimo Artist: Kenojuak*, documentary film, dir. John Feeney (Montreal: National Film Board of Canada, 1963). For further discussion of the film, see: Jay Ruby, *Picturing Culture: Explorations of Film and Anthropology* (Chicago: University of Chicago Press, 2000).

98 "Defends Eskimo Sculpture," *Winnipeg Free Press*, 31 July 1962, 7.

99 "Canadian Art Being Shown in Nairobi," *Winnipeg Free Press*, 17 November 1962.

100 CP Wire, "Eskimo Girl to Visit Ghana," *Winnipeg Free Press*, 20 December 1962.

101 Ray Sinclair, "Says Eskimo Carvings Symbolic of Canada," *Winnipeg Free Press*, 2 December 1964.

102 "By Plane, Dog Team To See Eskimo Art," *Globe and Mail*, 25 January 1964.

103 "A New View on Eskimo Art," *Globe and Mail* 29 February 1964.

104 Anita Aarons, "Evidence Beyond Dispute: Eskimo Art Still the Only Truly Canadian Art," *Globe and Mail*, 18 July 1970.

105 Ibid.

106 John Graham, "Indian Art Praised," *Winnipeg Free Press*, 4 October 1972.

107 "Myth and Symbol," *Time*, 28 September 1962, 18.

108 Nicholas Thomas, *Possessions: Indigenous Art/Colonial Culture* (New York: Thames and Hudson, 1999), 12.

109 Pollock, "Norval Morrisseau."

110 William French, "Items Exotic and Raunchy Spice Up Fall Publishing Menu," *Globe and Mail*, 17 July 1979.

Chapter 2: 1962: Morrisseau's Arrival

1 Shirley Last, "Beardmore Indian's Paintings Cause Stir," Port Arthur *News-Chronicle*, 15 August 1962.

2 "Indians 'Misunderstood' Trying to Get City Jobs," Port Arthur *News-Chronicle*, 29 January 1962.

3 Ibid.

4 Ed O'Dacre, "No. 1 Among Many Problems: Few Families Are Willing to Adopt Indian Children," Port Arthur *News-Chronicle*, 15 February 1962.

5 Pearl McCarthy, "Explorers Discover New Ideas" *Globe and Mail*, 15 August 1962, 25.

6 Ibid.

7 Ibid.

8 Ruth Phillips, "Morrisseau's 'Entrance': Negotiating Primitivism, Modernism, and Anishnaabe Tradition," in *Norval Morrisseau: Shaman Artist*, ed. Greg Hill (Ottawa, ON: National Gallery of Canada), 44. For the original source, see Pearl McCarthy, "Ojibwa Painter No Primitive," *Globe and Mail*, 15 September 1962, 14.

9 Pearl McCarthy, "Ojibwa Painter No Primitive," *Globe and Mail*, 15 September 1962, 14.

10 "A Bride for Rideau Hall," *Time* (Canadian ed.), 28 September 1962, 18.

11 "Myth and Symbol," *Time*, 28 September 1962, 18.

12 Ibid.

13 Ibid.

14 Lenore Crawford, "Self-Taught Ojibway Artist Finds Fame Overnight," *London Free Press*, 29 September 1962, 19.

15 Ibid.

16 David Cobb, "Indian Artist Earns High Praise" *Toronto Star*, 13 September 1962, 13.

17 CP Wire, "Budding Artist Discovered Twice," *Winnipeg Free Press*, 26 September 1962.

18 Paul Duval, "Accent on Art," *Toronto Telegram*, 22 September 1962. Joy Carroll, in her 1964 essay, argues that Paul Duval was the only Toronto critic to review Morrisseau's show unfavourably. Joy Carroll, "The Strange Success—And Failure of Norval Morrisseau," *Canadian Art* 94 (Nov–Dec 1964): 349.

19 Rudyard Kipling wrote a poem titled "The White Man's Burden" in 1899. In the poem the burden was related to American colonization of the Philippines, but the

term resonates more deeply in popular culture as justification for imperialism. See Rudyard Kipling, "The White Man's Burden," *McClure's* magazine 12 (Feb. 1899).

20 Duval, "Accent on Art."

21 Laura Motyl, "Ojibway Painter Recording Area's Early Legends," Fort William *Daily Times-Journal*, 20 August 1962.

22 "Morrisseau Paintings Receive High Praise," Fort William *Daily Times-Journal*, 5 September 1962.

23 "Morrisseau Described As Genius," Fort William *Daily-Times Journal*, 14 September 1962.

24 B. Cattani, "Chief of Ojibway Band Gets Mention in Book," Port Arthur *News-Chronicle*, 6 February 1962.

25 "The North is Proud," *Timmins Daily Press*, 3 October 1962.

26 Ibid.

27 Ibid.

28 Shirley Last, "Beardmore Indian's Paintings Cause Stir," Port Arthur *News-Chronicle*, 15 August 1962.

29 "Crowd Applauds Indian Ceremony," Port Arthur *News-Chronicle*, 27 August 1962.

30 *Weekend Magazine* was published from 1951 to 1977 and circulated as an insert in local newspapers across Canada. A French-language version, *Perspectives*, was also circulated and included the same photos and translated stories, beginning in 1959, but grew into a separate entity in the early 1960s. Library and Archives Canada, http://collectionscanada.gc.ca/pam_archives/index.php?fuseaction=genitem.displayItem&lang=eng&rec_nbr=616944 (accessed 22 October 2013).

31 Bill Brown, "Copper Thunderbird: An Ojibway Who Paints His People's Past," *Weekend Magazine*, 24 November 1962, 52.

32 Ibid., 52–53.

33 Ibid., 53.

34 Ibid.

35 Jack Pollock, *Dear M: Letters from a Gentleman of Excess* (Toronto: McClelland and Stewart, 1989).

36 The Thunder Bay Art Gallery Archives contains a series of letters written by Norval Morrisseau to Susan Ross between 1963 and 1966. The correspondence was donated by Susan Ross.

37 Correspondence from Norval Morrisseau to Susan Ross, 22 September 1964.

38 Dorothy Pfeiffer, "Ojibway Indian Artist," *Montreal Gazette*, 27 April 1963.

39 See Theodora Kroeber, *Ishi in Two Worlds: A Biography of the Last Wild Indian in North America* (Berkeley and Los Angeles: University of California Press, 1961).

40 Pfeiffer, "Ojibway Indian Artist."

41 Joy Carroll, "The Strange Success—and Failure of Norval Morrisseau," *Canadian Art*, 21 no.6 (1964), 349.

42 Ibid., 349.

43 Ibid.

44 Ibid., italics in the original.

45 Ibid., 350.

46 Ibid.

47 Pearl McCarthy, "Metaphysics of Indian Art," *Globe and Mail*, 21 March 1964.

48 Kay Kritzwiser, "Continuity of Life Absorbs Indian Artist," *Globe and Mail*, 27 January 1965.

49 Kay Kritzwiser, "Self Support Termed Indian Goal" *Globe and Mail*, 11 February 1965.

50 "Norval Morrisseau and the Myths of the Ojibway," *Montreal Gazette*, 3 December 1966.

51 Ibid.

52 Herbert T. Schwarz, "The Art of Norval Morrisseau," in *Eskimo Sculpture and Eskimo Prints and Paintings of Norval Morrisseau* (Montreal: Galerie Cartier, 1968).

53 Selwyn Dewdney, preface to Norval Morrisseau, *Legends of My People: The Great Ojibway* (Toronto: Ryerson Press, 1965), x.

54 Ibid.

55 Ibid., xv.

56 Ibid., xxi.

57 "Proud Indian," *Ottawa Citizen*, 21 August 1965.

58 Selwyn Dewdney Correspondence Fonds, DIAND, ADAS, 306065, 7 June 1960 BS.

59 Barry Ace, "Norval Morrisseau: Artist as Shaman," *Aboriginal Curatorial Collective Archives* (December 2005), http://www.aboriginalcuratorialcollective.org/research/morriseau3.html (accessed 5 January 2007), 3.

60 Carroll, "The Strange Success," 350.

61 Letter from Norval Morrisseau to Selwyn Dewdney, 12 January 1962, Dewdney Papers, Indian Art Archives, Department of Indian Affairs and Northern Development, 306065-25 A-J.

62 Letter from Norval Morrisseau to Selwyn Dewdney, 6 January 1964, Red Lake, ON, Dewdney Papers, Indian Art Archives, Department of Indian Affairs and Northern Development, 306065-63-A-5.

63 Ibid.

64 Ibid.

65 "Plan Art Centre for Reserve," *Globe and Mail*, 11 May 1964.

66 John Graham, "Unusual Quality in Indian Work," *Winnipeg Free Press*, 3 December 1968.

67 Ibid.

68 J.R. Stevens, "Paintings Recreate Ojibwa Past," *Winnipeg Free Press*, 7 December 1968.

69 Mark Cronlund Anderson and Carmen Robertson, *Seeing Red: A History of Natives in Canadian Newspapers* (Winnipeg: University of Manitoba Press, 2011), 155–72.

70 Carroll, "The Strange Success," 349.

71 Morrisseau, *Legends of My People*, 78.

72 Ibid., 81.

73 "Murals by Indian Artists Eyed for Expo Pavilion," *Winnipeg Free Press*, 27 September 1966.

74 Ruth B. Phillips with Sherry Brydon, " 'Arrow of Truth': The Indians of Canada Pavilion at Expo 67," in Ruth B. Phillips, *Museum Pieces: Toward the Indigenization of Canadian Museums* (Montreal: McGill-Queen's University Press, 2011), 29.

75 Ibid., 33–35.

76 Ibid., 37.

77 Quoted in Lister Sinclair and Jack Pollock, *The Art of Norval Morrisseau* (Toronto: Methuen, 1979), 30.

78 Ibid., 32.

79 Greg Hill, *Norval Morrisseau: Shaman Artist*, 23.

80 Sherry Brydon, "The Indians of Canada Pavilion at Expo 67," *American Indian Arts Magazine* 22, no. 3 (Summer 1997): 60.

81 David Staples, "Artist Alex Janvier," *Edmonton Journal*, 31 January 1988.

82 Tom Hill, "A Retrospective of Indian Art," *The Native Perspective* 3, no. 2 (1978): 36.

83 Sinclair and Pollock, *The Art of Norval Morrisseau*, 32.

84 "100-Foot-High Teepee to Mark Indians of Canada Expo Pavilion," *Globe and Mail*, 12 August 1966.

85 Leslie Millin, "Indians Spend Expo Cash to Tell of Poor Deal," *Globe and Mail*, 7 April 1967.

86 Ibid.

87 "Indian Pavilion Tries Not to be Restful," *Globe and Mail*, 1 May 1967.

88 "A Record of Failure," *Globe and Mail*, 24 June 1967.

89 "Another Indian Report," *Globe and Mail*, 29 July 1967.

Chapter 3: 1970s: The Shaman Arrives

1 Gary Michael Dault, "Ojibway Artist May Soon Find He's Turned into a Living Legend," *Toronto Star*, 28 August 1975.

2 Kay Kritzwiser, "$2500 Top Price at Sotheby Auction," *Globe and Mail*, 27 May 1970.

3 Zena Cherry, "Canada's Expo Shop Sells 'Eskimo' Works Made in Japan," *Globe and Mail*, 15 June 1970.

4 "40 Indians and Eskimos Bring Their Culture to a New Side of the Mariposa Folk Festival," *Globe and Mail*, 22 July 1970.

5 *Winnipeg Free Press*, 10 June 1972.

6 Ibid.

7 Kay Kritzwiser, "Some Proof Native Pride's Well Placed," *Globe and Mail*, 12 February 1972.

8 Kay Kritzwiser, "Proud Native Heritage," *Globe and Mail*, 15 February 1974.

9 Wayne Edmonstone, "Indian Artist Clings to Legend," *Toronto Star*, 3 November 1972.

10 Ibid.

11 Joan Sutton, "Amid Pain—A Mystic Vision," *Toronto Sun*, 2 October 1974.

12 Lenore Crawford, "Self-Taught Ojibway Artist Finds Fame Overnight," *London Free Press*, 29 September 1962, 19.

13 Sutton, "Amid Pain—A Mystic Vision."

14 Dault, "Ojibway Artist May Soon Find He's Turned into a Living Legend."

15 Ibid.

16 Christopher Hume, "The New Age of Indian Art," *Maclean's*, 22 January 1979, 26.

17 Arnie Hakala, "Norval Morrisseau Isn't Afraid Now He's Back in Tune With Nature," *Toronto Star*, 24 December 1977.

18 James Purdie, "Indian Art Gets Its Due in New McMichael Gallery," *Globe and Mail*, 15 November 1975.

19 Ibid.

20 Jon Anderson, "Fierce Clarity and Sophistication," *Time*, 25 August 1975, 10–11.

21 Ibid., 10.

22 Ibid., 11.

23 Kay Kritzwiser, "ROM Acquires 11 Works by Ojibway," *Globe and Mail*, 29 May 1972.

24 Jacqueline Fry, *Treaty Numbers 23, 287, 1171: Three Indian Painters of the Prairies*, exhibition catalogue (Winnipeg: The Winnipeg Art Gallery, 1972).

25 John Graham, "Indian Art Praised," *Winnipeg Free Press*, 4 October 1972.

26 Ibid.

27 Kay Kritzwiser, "At The Galleries: Sea and Sky, People and Indian Pride," *Globe and Mail*, 24 November 1973.

28 Jack Pollock, "Norval Morrisseau," *Tawow: Canadian Indian Cultural Magazine* 4, no. 4 (1974): 6.

29 James Purdie, "New Assurance, Maturity in Native Art," *Globe and Mail*, 1 March 1975.

30 Roger Bainbridge, "The Rebirth of A Proud Tradition," *Kingston Whig-Standard*, 3 October 1975.

31 William MacIvar, "Indian Art, Tradition and Modern," *Globe and Mail*, 4 June 1974.

32 Ibid.

33 Peter White, "Shilling Takes Indian Art beyond the Old Images," *Globe and Mail*, 15 September 1976.

34 James Purdie, "The Renaissance of Indian Art From Traditional Tribal Tales to Universal Images," *Globe and Mail*, 27 August 1977.

35 Lister Sinclair and Jack Pollock, *The Art of Norval Morrisseau* (Toronto: Methuen, 1979), 114.

36 James Purdie, "At The Galleries: An Old Man Reincarnated?," *Globe and Mail*, 10 December 1977.

37 Purdie, "Indian Art Gets Its Due."

38 Kay Kritzwiser, "Robert Houle: A Native Artist with a Weakness for Mondrian," *Globe and Mail*, 21 July 1978, 11.

39 Ibid.

40 Hume, "The New Age of Indian Art," 21.

41 Ibid., 24.

42 Ibid.

43 James Purdie, "Out of the Doldrums Into An Exciting Fall," *Globe and Mail*, 29 July 1978.

44 James Purdie, "Gallery Reviews," *Globe and Mail*, 3 February 1979.

45 Ibid.

46 James Purdie, "At The Galleries: Kane's Record Priceless, Romantic Too," *Globe and Mail*, 22 January 1977.

47 Ibid.

48 Kritzwiser, "At The Galleries: Sea and Sky, People and Indian Pride."

49 James Purdie, "At the Galleries: A Battle for a Name over a Number," *Globe and Mail*, 4 February 1978.

50 Ibid.

51 Ibid.

52 Ibid.

53 Ibid.

54 Ibid.

55 Leonard Marcoe, "Morrisseau Prints Outrank His Paintings," *Winnipeg Free Press*, 24 March 1979.

56 James Purdie, "New Morrisseau Works Show He's Settled Inner Conflict," *Globe and Mail*, 19 August 1975.

57 James Purdie, "At the Galleries: Traditional Value Systems Challenged," *Globe and Mail*, 3 July 1976.

58 James Purdie, "At the Galleries: Heroic Battle Deserves a Spot in History," *Globe and Mail*, 4 March 1978.

59 Sinclair and Pollock, *The Art of Norval Morrisseau*, 35

60 Richard Baker, personal interview with author on 4 May 2012.

61 Ibid., 37.

62 Ibid.

63 Robin Green, "FYI: This Party Would Put a Dream to Shame," *Globe* and *Mail*, 29 June 1978, 8.

64 Sinclair and Pollock, *Art of Norval Morrisseau*, 29.

65 Kay Kritzwiser, "Robert Houle."

66 Greg Hill, *Norval Morrisseau: Shaman Artist* (Ottawa: National Gallery of Canada, 2006).

67 Sinclair and Pollock, *Art of Norval Morrisseau*, 38–39; 44.

68 Green, "FYI: This Party Would Put a Dream to Shame."

69 Ibid.

70 Gilbert Oskaboose, letter to the editor, *Globe and Mail*, 6 July 1978.

71 Jack Pollock, "Indian Tradition," letter to the editor, *Globe and Mail*, 8 July 1978.

72 Ibid.

73 Hume, "The New Age of Indian Art," 21–25.

74 Ibid., 23.

75 Ibid.

76 Norval Morrisseau, *Man Changing into Thunderbird*. 1977. Acrylic on canvas. Six panels, 153.5 x 125.7 cm each panel. Private collection, on loan to the Art Gallery of Ontario, Toronto.

77 Gary Michael Dault, "Painter Gives Canadians a Masterpiece," *Toronto Star*, 29 August 1977, D5.

Chapter 4: 1980s: An Inruly International Art Star

1   Grace Inglis, "Morrisseau Magic Has Been Drained," *Hamilton Spectator*, 20 March 1982.

2   Stephen Godfrey, "'Now Is The Magic Moment I Start Again.' No Regrets, No Booze," *Globe and Mail*, 6 June 1987.

3   Art Perry, "It's Sham Rather Than Shamanism," *Vancouver Province*, 1 May 1980.

4   Vanda Blundell and Ruth B. Phillips, "If It's Not Shamanic, Is It Sham? An Examination of Media Responses to Woodland School Art," *Anthropologica* 25, no. 1 (1983): 117–32.

5   Perry, "It's Sham Rather Than Shamanism."
6   Susan Himel and Elaine Lambert, "Exhibit Heralds Native Art Auction," *Globe and Mail*, 15 January 1981.
7   John Bentley Mays, "There's Nothing Sentimental About Indian Art at Brignall's," *Globe and Mail*, 6 December 1985.
8   Gary Waddell, "Manitoulin Islanders Find Roots in Art," *Globe and Mail*, 22 October 1980.
9   Quoted in Carole Corbeil, "Beyond 'Culture Apartheid': Art-Making as an Act of Personal and Political Exorcism," *Globe and Mail*, 19 April 1986.
10 Ibid.
11 Ian Mulgrew, "Natives Selling Artifacts to Pay for Trip to London," *Globe and Mail*, 3 October 1981.
12 John Bentley Mays, "Morrisseau's Art Explores Magic Forests of the Mind," *Globe and Mail*, 9 July 1981.
13 Ibid.
14 Ibid.
15 Inglis, "Morrisseau Magic Has Been Drained."
16 Kay Kritzwiser, "Rapport with the Spirit: Creating Woodland Art: The Clean Quality of a Piece of Birchbark," *Globe and Mail*, 4 January 1982.
17 Ibid.
18 Todd Sherman, "Saulteaux Carvers Re-Create Tribal Past," *Winnipeg Free Press*, 21 August 1980.
19 Ibid.
20 Cecil Rosner, "Carvers Notching Up Successes," *Winnipeg Free Press*, 20 March 1984.
21 "Craftsmen Carve a Living Out of Soapstone in Canada's Far North," *Winnipeg Free Press*, 11 August 1984.
22 Bob Lowery, "Native Art Form Kept Alive," *Winnipeg Free Press*, 3 June 1983.
23 Bob Lowery, "Artist's Plight Gnaws at McGonigal," *Winnipeg Free Press*, 14 February 1983.
24 Randy Turner, "Museum Preserves Indian Past," *Winnipeg Free Press*, 5 May 1988.
25 Ibid.
26 Betty Zyvatkauskas, "Woodland Indians Keep Past Alive," *Winnipeg Free Press*, 23 February 1985.
27 Ibid.
28 "Indian Artist Is Non-Traditional," *Regina Leader Post*, 24 May 1983.
29 Ibid.
30 Kay Kritzwiser, "Exhibit Encourages Native Artists to Abandon 'Heritage' Stereotypes," *Globe and Mail*, 13 October 1981.
31 Ibid.
32 Canadian Press Wire, "Large New Indian Exhibit Features Objects As Art, Not Artifacts," *Winnipeg Free Press*, 14 April 1984.
33 Ibid.
34 Kay Kritzwiser, "'They Are Not Doing Beaded Moccasins,'" *Globe and Mail*, 23 February 1984.
35 Ibid.

36 Ibid.

37 Nancy Baele, "Woodland Art Knock-Out Show," *Ottawa Citizen*, 17 March 1984.

38 "The Image Makers—An Examination of the Woodland School," *Arts West* 9, no. 4 (April 1984): 18.

39 John Bentley Mays, "Ottawa Exhibition a First: Native Art at Rideau Hall Capital Idea for a Showing," *Globe and Mail*, 27 May 1983.

40 "Political Speech Puts Damper on Mood At Indian Art Exhibit," *Regina Leader Post*, 22 March 1984.

41 Gwen Dambrofsky, "Artist Seeks Strength in Indian Spiritualism," *Globe and Mail*, 25 January 1986.

42 Ibid.

43 Canadian Press Wire, "Drink of Tequila Started Painter on Road to Despair," *Globe and Mail*, 11 May 1987.

44 Canadian Press Wire, "Artist Sells Quickies for Price of Booze," *Ottawa Citizen*, 11 May 1987.

45 Miro Cernetig, "Native Artist Roaming City Trading His Art for a Bottle," *Vancouver Sun*, 11 May 1987.

46 Canadian Press Wire, "Morrisseau Hits the Bottle, Wanders the Streets," *Montreal Gazette*, 11 May 1987.

47 Canadian Press Wire, "Street Life Suits Morrisseau," *Globe and Mail*, 12 May 1987.

48 "Artist 'Dry Again,'" *Vancouver Province*, 12 May 1987.

49 Canadian Press Wire, "Morrisseau Says He's Quit Drinking," *Edmonton Journal*, 12 May 1987.

50 Robert Sarti, "Native Artist Leaves Street Scene: Morrisseau Says He'll Sober Up, Return to Work," *Vancouver Sun*, 12 May 1987.

51 "Artist Taken to Hospital," *Vancouver Sun*, 13 May 1987.

52 Canadian Press Wire, "Morrisseau Tottering on Brink," *Windsor Star*, 14 May 1987.

53 Canadian Press Wire, "Artist Sells Quickies for Price of Booze," *Ottawa Citizen*, 11 May 1987.

54 Karen Webb, "Famed Native Artist on Skid Row," *The National* (Toronto: CBC News, Media Tapes and Transcripts), 11 May 1987, 10:00 pm.

55 Ibid.

56 Denny Boyd, "Black Dog Stalking the Star of This Fast Four-Act Tragedy," *Vancouver Sun*, 14 May 1987.

57 Canadian Press Wire, "Morrisseau Tottering on Brink."

58 Cernetig, "Native Artist Roaming City."

59 Canadian Press Wire, "Artist Sells Quickies for Price of Booze."

60 Sarti, "Native Artist Leaves Street Scene."

61 Ibid.

62 Godfrey, "'Now Is The Magic Moment I Start Again.' No Regrets, No Booze."

63 Canadian Press Wire "Street Life Suits Morrisseau."

64 Ibid.

65 Cernetig, "Native Artist Roaming City."

66 Canadian Press Wire, "Morrisseau Says He's Quit Drinking," *Edmonton Journal*, 12 May 1987.

67 Ibid.

68 Catherine Hopwood, letter to the editor, *Globe and Mail*, 20 May 1987.

69 Donald Clement, "Art and Anguish," letter to the editor, *Globe and Mail*, 27 May 1987.

70 Canadian Press Wire, "Renewed Interest in Indian's Art," *Toronto Star*, 22 May 1987.

71 John Bentley Mays, "Old Favorites Retain Appeal At Auction of Canadian Art," *Globe and Mail*, 14 May 1987.

72 Godfrey, "'Now Is The Magic Moment I Start Again.' No Regrets, No Booze."

73 Canadian Press Wire, "Morrisseau Returns, Ready to Paint," *Globe and Mail*, 22 September 1987.

74 Ivan Karp, "Another Perspective: How Museums Define Other Cultures," *American Art* 5, nos. 1/2 (Winter/Spring 1991): 13.

75 Ibid.

76 Norman Kleeblatt, "Identity Roller Coaster," *Art Journal* 64, no. 1 (Spring 2005): 61.

77 Benjamin Buchloh and Jean-Hubert Martin, "Interview," *Third Text* 6 (Spring 1989): 19–28; and Hans Belting, *Art History after Modernism*, trans. Caroline Saltzwedel and Mitch Cohen (Chicago: University of Chicago Press, 2003), 67–68.

78 Jean-Hubert Martin, *Magiciens de la Terre*, exhibition catalogue (Paris: Éditions du Centre Pompidou, 1989), 203.

79 Ibid.

80 Liam Lacey, "Exhibit Challenges Ideas About Native Art," *Globe and Mail*, 13 July 1989.

81 Jean-Louis Ferrier, "Exposition: Paris: Pour Tout," *Le Point* 874 (19 June 1989): 14–16.

82 "Il avait, me disait-on, disparu de la circulation et restait introuvable." René Viau, "Les Magiciens de la Terre: Vers un champ 'mondial' d'investigation?" *Parachute* 55 (July 1989): 17.

83 Rasheed Araeen, "The New Beginning: Beyond Postcolonial Cultural Theory and Identity Politics," *Third Text* 50 (Spring 2000): 13.

84 Gwendolyn MacEwen, "Brushes with Greatness: Close Encounters of the Personal Kind," *Globe and Mail*, 26 August 1989.

85 Ibid.

86 Christopher Hume, "Ojibway Painter's Pointed Works Face Facts of Modern Indian Life," *Toronto Star*, 26 October 1990.

87 Ibid.

88 The museum has undergone a number of name changes. From 1910 to 1986 it was the National Museum of Canada and then was renamed the Canadian Museum of Civilization (1986-2013) until it became the National Museum of History in December 2013. Olive Dickason, "First People's Hall: A Walk Through a Rich History," *The Canadian Historical Review*, vol. 85,2 (2004): 357-360.

89 Correspondence from James P. Richards on behalf of Norval Morrisseau to Tom Axworthy, Secretary to Prime Minister Pierre Trudeau, 19 February 1983, Indian Art Centre archives, Androgny 1 pdf.

90 Ibid.

91 Jill Doerfler, Niigaanwewidam James Sinclair, and Heidi Kiiwetinepinesiik Stark, eds., *Centering Anishinaabeg Studies: Understanding the World through Stories* (East Lansing, MI: Michigan State University Press, 2013), xv.

92 Ibid.

93 Ann Laura Stoler, *Along the Archival Grain: Epistemic Anxieties and Colonial Common Sense* (Princeton, NJ: Princeton University Press, 2010), 3.

Chapter 5: 2006: Re-Mythologizing Mishomis

1 Nancy Baele, "Ojibwa Artist Holds Strong Belief in the Healing Power of Color," *Ottawa Citizen,* 5 May 1991.

2 Charmaine McEachern, *Narratives of Nation Media, Memory and Representation in the Making of the New South Africa* (New York: Nova, 2002).

3 Christopher Hume, "Morrisseau's New Colors Dazzle," *Toronto Star,* 7 May 1991.

4 Chris Dafoe, "Such a Long Journey," *Globe and Mail,* 10 April 1999, C-1.

5 Ibid.

6 Ibid., C-15.

7 Ibid.

8 Blake Gopnik, "He Broke a Taboo—More Power to Him," *Globe and Mail,* 10 April 1999, C15.

9 Linda Turk, "Thunder Bay Gallery Glories in the Works of Native Artists," *Globe and Mail,* 14 July 2000.

10 "A Champion of Native Artists," *Globe and Mail,* 15 May 2004.

11 Kate Taylor, "It's Official: Native Art Is Real, No Artifact," *Globe and Mail,* 4 May 2005, R3.

12 James Adams, "Morrisseau Moves to Authenticate Art: Committee Created to Vet the Works of the Now-Ailing Artist," *Globe and Mail* 23 March 2005; James Adams, "Paint Brawl," *Globe and Mail,* 23 April 2005, R1.

13 Adams, "Morrisseau Moves to Authenticate Art."

14 Holland Cotter, "Art in Review; Draw and Tell—The Transformative Lines of Norval Morrisseau/Copper Thunderbird," *New York Times,* 16 March 2001, E37.

15 Ibid.

16 As noted in the case of Bill Reid, this was a common issue for Indigenous artists in Canada. See Maria Tippett, *Bill Reid: The Making of an Indian* (Toronto: Random House, 2011).

17 Ralph E. Friar and Natasha A. Friar, *The Only Good Indian … The Hollywood Gospel* (New York: Drama Book Specialists, 1972), 2.

18 Greg Hill, *Norval Morrisseau: Shaman Artist* (Ottawa: National Gallery of Canada, 2006). In 2002 the National Gallery of Canada mounted a retrospective exhibition of Inuit artist Kenojuak Ashevak and had earlier in 1996 showcased the work of Pitseolak Ashoona. In 1992 the National Gallery created a permanent gallery to house its Inuit collection.

19 Svetlana Alpers, "The Museum as a Way of Seeing," in *Exhibiting Culture: The Poetics and Politics of Museum Display,* ed. Ivan Karp and Steven Lavine (Washington, DC: Smithsonian Institution Press, 1991), 25–32.

20 Norval Morrisseau, *Androgyny* (1983), acrylic on canvas, 365.7 X 152.4 cm., Indian Affairs Canada Collection accession number 306400.

21 Paul Gessell, "Taming Their Demons," *Ottawa Citizen,* 29 January 2006, B1–4; and Paul Gessell, "An Art Pioneer Makes His Final Breakthrough," *Ottawa Citizen,* 29 January 2006, A1.

22 Papers that published Gessell's story included "Morrisseau Fathered Neo-Aboriginal Art," Victoria *Times-Colonist,* 29 January 2006, 2; "Island Artist Brings End to Cultural Apartheid," Victoria *Times-Colonist,* 29 January 2006, 1; "Morrisseau Makes Mark: First Solo Show by a First Nations Artist," Vancouver *Province,* 29 January 2006, 28; "Shaman Artist Ends Canada's Cultural Apartheid,"

Edmonton Journal, 29 January 2006, 3; "Native Artists Finally Win over National Gallery," *Calgary Herald*, 29 January 2006, 3.

23 Gessell, "An Art Pioneer."

24 Ibid.

25 See *Calgary Herald*, 29 January 2006, 3; *Edmonton Journal*, 29 January 2006, 3; and Gessell, "An Art Pioneer."

26 Gessell, "Taming Their Demons."

27 See Jack Pollock, *Dear M: Letters from a Gentleman of Excess* (Toronto: McClelland and Stewart, 1989).

28 Gessell, "Taming Their Demons."

29 This selection of works was made from the press kit assembled by the National Gallery for the exhibition. Media outlets could choose from a pre-selected group of works from the exhibition to easily obtain copyright approval and rights for publication. Gessell, "Taming Their Demons."

30 Carmen Robertson, "The Reel Norval Morrisseau: An Analysis of The National Film Board of Canada's *Paradox of Norval Morrisseau*," *International Journal of Learning* 11 (Fall 2005): 315–21.

31 Gessell, "Taming Their Demons."

32 Ibid.

33 Ibid.

34 Ibid.

35 Milroy has written controversial reviews of First Nations art exhibitions, including the Art Gallery of Ontario's 2009 *Remix: New Modernities in a Post-Indian World* show, where she questions the need for such an exhibition at all. Sarah Milroy, "Are We Past the Age of an Aboriginal Art Show?" Review of *Remix: New Modernities in a Post-Indian World*, *Globe and Mail*, 22 April 2009.

36 Sarah Milroy, "Morrisseau Has Defeated the Demons," *Globe and Mail*, 7 February 2006, R1, R5.

37 Ibid., R1.

38 Ibid.

39 Ibid.

40 Ibid.

41 Gessell, "Taming Their Demons," B1–4.

42 Connie Higginson-Murray, " 'Picasso of the North,'" *Ottawa Citizen*, 3 February 2006, A3.

43 Peter Johansen, "Take a Day to Explore Our Home and Native Land," *Ottawa Citizen*, 18 February 2006, L7.

44 Nicholas Thomas, *Possessions: Indigenous Art/Colonial Culture* (London: Thames and Hudson, 1999), 109.

45 Joel Kom, "Painting Purchased by Chance for $8 Now Highly Valued Aboriginal Art," *Ottawa Citizen*, 3 February 2006, D1–2.

46 Ibid., D2.

47 Bob Jurmain, "Morrisseau a Van Gogh of the North," letter to the editor, *Ottawa Citizen*, 20 February 2006, A9.

48 Martin Hankes-Drielsma, " 'Apartheid' Spoils Good News about Art Show," letter to the editor, *Ottawa Citizen*, 2 February 2006, A11.

49 Educator Shannon Thunderbird reminded Canadians during the Truth and Reconciliation process that South Africa had looked to Canada's Indian Act for guidance in setting up their system of apartheid. See "Canada and South Africa Share a Dark Past," Radio Canada International, http://www.rcinet.ca/english/archives/column/the-link-africa/TruthandReconciliationCanadaSouthAfricaResidentialSchoolsAbuses/ (accessed 3 April 2014).

50 Dino Schiavone and Raoul McKay, dirs., *The Life and Work of the Woodland Artists*, documentary film (Vancouver: Moving Images Distribution, 2003).

51 *Gifts from the Thunderbird: The Life and Art of Norval Morrisseau*, documentary film (Tuza Productions, 2007).

52 Paul Carvalho, dir., *Separate Reality: The Life and Times of Norval Morrisseau*, documentary film (Montreal: Perception Films, 2005).

53 According to "The Dark Legacy of Carlos Castaneda," (Salon.com, 12 April 2007), Castaneda's *Separate Reality* sold 10,000 copies in 2006. See Carlos Castaneda, *A Separate Reality: Further Conversations with Don Juan* (New York: Simon and Schuster, 1971).

54 Judy Stoffman, "Native Painter Travels to Gutter and Back," *Toronto Star*, 23 February 2005, F1.

55 Yvonne Zacharias, "A Portrait of Norval Morrisseau," *Vancouver Sun*, 24 February 2005.

56 Ibid.

57 Carvalho, *A Separate Reality*.

58 "Norval Morrisseau — How to express appreciation." Video clip of unidentified footage, 1981. https://www.youtube.com/watch?v=RxOXXEI2jGE (accessed 12 October 2015).

59 Viviane Gray, Indian and Inuit Art Centre, Indian and Northern Affairs Canada, 2008.

60 Harper increased his cabinet to thirty-eight members from thirty-one, and had eleven women in cabinet, up from seven previously. CBC.ca, 30 October 2008, http://www.cbc.ca/news/canada/harper-shuffles-cabinet-to-create-right-team-for-these-times-1.706956

61 Nancy Robinson, "Learning from a Master," *Globe and Mail*, 3 November 2008, 14.

62 "Morrisseau's *Androgyny* Makes Splash at GGs," *Hill Times*, 3 November 2008.

63 For Harper's full speech, see "Statement of Apology to Former Students of Indian Residential Schools," 11 June 2008, http://www.aadnc-aandc.gc.ca/eng/1100100015644/1100100015649 (accessed 4 April 2014).

64 Colleen Simard, "Harper Drops the 'C-bomb' on G20," *Winnipeg Free Press*, 3 October 2009.

Conclusion

1 Reprinted quote by Norval Morrisseau from Christopher Hume, "Morrisseau's New Colors Dazzle," *Toronto Star*, 7 May 1991 in Randy Kennedy, "Norval Morrisseau, Native Canadian Artist, Is Dead." *New York Times* 8 December 2007.

2 The North conjures up many different connotations. In literature the North has been seen as a Leviathan or an object of fear—fear of nature. For a deeper discussion read "True North Strong and Free," in Rob Shields, *Places on the Margin: Alternative Geographies of Modernity* (London: Routledge, 1991), 162-198.

3 Peter Goddard, " 'Picasso of the North' the Torchbearer for Native Art," *Winnipeg Free Press*, 6 December 2007.

4   Donn Downey, "Prolific and Brilliant Ojibwa Painter Was Called 'the Picasso of the North,'" *Globe and Mail*, 5 December 2007.

5   "'Picasso of the North' Blazed a Path That Many Young Artists Followed," *Ottawa Citizen*, 8 December 2007.

6   "Iconic Painter Norval Morrisseau Dead at 75," Canwest News, 5 December 2007, http://search.proquest.com/docview/461244517?accountid=13480 (accessed 2 February 2015).

7   Mike Fuhrmann, "Norval Morrisseau Praised for Giving Native Artists 'New Visual Language,'" Canadian Press, 6 December 2007, http://search.proquest.com/docview/360040698?accountid=13480 (accessed 2 March 2014).

8   Maria Tippett, *Bill Reid: The Making of an Indian* (Toronto: Random House, 2011), 3.

9   Ying-Wen Yu, "Playing Indian: Manifest Manners, Simulation and Pastiche," in *Survivance: Narratives of Native Presence*, ed. Gerald Vizenor (Lincoln: University of Nebraska Press, 2008), 95.

10   Ron Csillag, "Randall Charboneau, Artist 1964-2006," *Globe and Mail*, 2 December 2006.

11   "Statement by Assembly of First Nations National Chief Phil Fontaine on the Passing of Renowned Ojibway Artist Norval Morrisseau," Canada NewsWire, 4 December 2007. http://search.proquest.com/docview/455400672?accountid=13480.

12   Ibid.

13   John Allemang, "Norval Morrisseau (1931–2007)," *Globe and Mail*, 8 December 2007, http://search.proquest.com/docview/383381135?accountid=13480 (accessed 2 March 2014).

14   James Adams, "Relatives Quarrel over Ojibwa Artist's Remains," *Globe and Mail*, 8 December 2007, A1.

15   James Adams, "National Aboriginal Achievement Awards Lifetime Trophy: Morrisseau Medal on Hold Pending Legal Ruling," *Globe and Mail*, 6 Mar 2008, R1.

16   Canadian Press Wire, "Morrisseau Drained by Art's 'Psychic Leeches.'" Prince Rupert *Daily News*, 24 January 1986.

17   James Adams, "Morrisseau Moves to Authenticate Art," *Globe and Mail*, 23 March 2005, R1–3.

18   Ibid., R 3.

19   James Adams, "Paint Brawl," *Globe and Mail*, 23 April 2005.

20   Ibid. The description for the photograph erroneously describes the image as deriving from the CBC documentary *Separate Reality: The Life and Times of Norval Morrisseau*.

21   Val Ross, "Old Art Scam Surfaces Online," *Globe and Mail*, 14 February 2007.

22   Joshua Nelson, "Framing the Picture: The Canadian Print Media's Construction of an Atypical Crime—Art Fraud—and Its Victims, 1978–2012" (MA thesis, University of Guelph, 2013), 94.

23   Ibid., 161.

24   Les MacPherson, "Easy Steps to Tell If Your Morrisseau Is a Forgery," Saskatoon *StarPhoenix*, 10 November 2012, A3.

25   Jacquie Miller, "Barenaked Ladies' Keyboardist Kevin Hearn Sues Toronto Gallery for Morrisseau Forgery," *National Post*, 5 November 2012, http://arts.nationalpost.com/2012/11/05 (accessed 14 February 2014).

26 Tristan Hopper, "Art Forging Ring Alleged in Lawsuit Leaves Authenticity of Works by Aboriginal Artist Norval Morrisseau in Question," *National Post*, 3 February 2014.

27 Ibid.

28 James Adams, "Court Rules Morrisseau Painting Is Authentic," *Globe and Mail*, 3 April 2013.

29 James Adams, "Is This a Fake?" *Globe and Mail*, 4 June 2012.

30 Kay Kritzwiser, "Picasso at the Post in Gallery Stakes," *Globe and Mail*, 15 February 1964.

31 Johanna Drucker, *Theorizing Modernism: Visual Art and the Critical Tradition* (New York: Columbia University Press, 1996), 119.

32 See: http://www.brainyquote.com/search_results.html?q=picasso&pg=4 (accessed August 1, 2015).

33 Linda Nochlin, "Why the World Needs the Myth of Picasso," *The Independent*, 5 December 1998.

34 Cesar Aira, "Picasso," *The New Yorker*, 11 August 2014, http://www.newyorker.com/magazine/2014/08/11/picasso (accessed 12 July 2014).

35 James King, *Inward Journey: The Life of Lawren Harris* (Toronto: Thomas Allen, 2012).

36 Jo Ellen Bogart and Maxwell Newhouse, *Emily Carr: At the Edge of the World* (Plattsburg, NY: Tundra Books, 2003); Marcia Crosby, in *Beyond Wilderness: Contest and Controversy*, ed. John O'Brian and Peter White (Montreal: McGill-Queen's University Press, 2007), 219–22; Lewis DeSoto, *Extraordinary Canadians: Emily Carr. A Penguin Lives Biography* (London: Penguin, 2008); Edythe Hembroff-Schleicher, *Emily Carr: The Untold Story* (Surrey, BC: Hancock House, 1978); Doris Shadbolt, *The Art of Emily Carr* (North Vancouver: Douglas and McIntyre, 1979); Maria Tippett, *Emily Carr: A Biography* (Vancouver: House of Anansi Press, 2006).

37 Mark Cheetham, *Alex Colville: The Observer Observed* (Toronto: ECW Press, 1994).

38 In addition, each received honorary degrees (Morrisseau was given his by McMaster University, and Colville received seven honorary degrees from a variety of universities in central and eastern Canada). Each had their art displayed on the cover of *Maclean's* magazine, and each had a retrospective exhibition—Colville in 1983, Morrisseau in 2006. Colville had his first solo exhibition in St. John, New Brunswick, in 1951—eleven years before Morrisseau's.

39 Bill Prentice, "Out of the Gallery and into the Living Room," *Globe and Mail*, 6 July 1985.

40 Maria Tippett, *Bill Reid: The Making of an Indian* (Toronto: Vintage Canada, 2004), 279.

41 Jack Long (dir.), *Bill Reid* (National Film Board of Canada, 1979, 27 min).

42 Ibid.

43 Ibid.

44 Charlotte Townsend Gault, "The Raven and Bill Reid," *Globe and Mail*, 28 March 1998.

45 Alexandra Gill, "A Friend Rallies around Bill Reid," *Globe and Mail*, 6 February 2004.

46 Jane O'Hara, "Trade Secrets: Haida Artist Bill Reid Was a National Icon. But From 1980 on, Suffering from the Debilitating Effects of Disease, He Relied on Others to Produce His Work," *Maclean's* 112, 42 (October 18, 1999): 20.

47 Miles Richardson, "On Its Own Terms," in *Bill Reid and Beyond: Expanding on Modern Native Art*, Karen Duffek and Charlotte Townsend-Gault, eds. (Vancouver: Douglas & McIntyre, 2004), 25.

48 Conversation with Armand Ruffo, 6 February 2015. See also Armand Garnet Ruffo, *Norval Morrisseau: Man Changing into Thunderbird* (Madeira Park, BC: Douglas and McIntrye, 2014).

49 Ibid., 53.

50 Gary Michael Dault, "Ojibway Artist May Soon Find He's Turned into a Living Legend," *Toronto Star*, 28 August 1975.

51 Christopher Hume, "Morrisseau's New Colors Dazzle," *Toronto Star*, 7 May 1991.

BIBLIOGRAPHY

Ace, Barry. "Artist as Shaman." *Aboriginal Curatorial Collective Archives*, December 2005. http://www.aboriginalcuratorialcollective.org/research/morriseau3.html. (accessed 5 January 2007).

Ahmed, Sara. *Differences That Matter: Feminist Theory and Postmodernism*. Cambridge, UK: Cambridge University Press, 1998.

———. *Queer Phenomenology: Orientations, Objects, Others*. Durham, NC: Duke University Press, 2006.

———. *Strange Encounters: Embodied Others in Post-Coloniality*. London: Routledge, 2000.

Aira, Cesar. "Picasso," *The New Yorker*, 11 August 2014. http://www.newyorker.com/magazine/2014/08/11/picasso (accessed 12 July 2014).

Alfred, Taiaiake. *Peace, Power, Righteousness: An Indigenous Manifesto*. Don Mills, ON: Oxford University Press, 1999.

Alia, Valerie. *Un/Covering the North: News, Media, and Aboriginal Peoples*. Vancouver: University of British Columbia Press, 1999.

Alpers, Svetlana. "The Museum as a Way of Seeing." In *Exhibiting Culture: The Poetics and Politics of Museum Display*, edited by Ivan Karp and Steven Lavine, 25–32. Washington, DC: Smithsonian Institution Press, 1991.

Anderson, Benedict. *Imagined Communities: Reflections on the Origin and Spread of Nationalism*. 1983. New edition. New York: Verso, 2006.

Anderson, Mark Cronlund, and Carmen Robertson. *Seeing Red: A History of Natives in Canadian Newspapers*. Winnipeg: University of Manitoba Press, 2011.

Anthes, Bill. *Native Moderns: American Indian Painting, 1940–1960*. Durham, NC: Duke University Press, 2006.

Appiah, Kwame Anthony. *The Ethics of Identity*. Princeton, NJ: Princeton University Press, 2005.

Araeen, Rasheed. "The New Beginning: Beyond Postcolonial Cultural Theory and Identity Politics." *Third Text* 50 (Spring 2000): 3–20.

Barthes, Roland. *Mythologies*. Translated by Annette Lavers. New York: Noonday Press, 1975.

Belting, Hans. *Art History after Modernism*. Translated by Caroline Saltzwedel and Mitch Cohen. Chicago: University of Chicago Press, 2003.

Berlo, Janet. "Drawing (upon) the Past: Negotiating Identities in Inuit Graphic Arts Production." In *Unpacking Culture: Art and Commodity in Colonial and Postcolonial Worlds*, edited by Ruth B. Phillips and Christopher B. Steiner, 178–93. Berkeley: University of California Press, 1999.

Bhabha, Homi. *Location of Culture*. London: Routledge, 1994.

Blodgett, Jean. *Kenojuak Ashevak*. Richmond Hill, ON: Firefly Books, 1985.

Blundell, Vanda, and Ruth B. Phillips. "If It's Not Shamanic, Is It Sham? An Examination of Media Responses to Woodland School Art." *Anthropologica* 25, no. 1 (1983): 117–32.

Bogart, Jo Ellen, and Maxwell Newhouse. *Emily Carr: At the Edge of the World*. Plattsburg, NY: Tundra Books, 2003.

Brydon, Sherry. "The Indians of Canada Pavilion at Expo 67." *American Indian Arts Magazine* 22, no. 3 (Summer 1997): 54–66.

Buchloh, Benjamin, and Jean-Hubert Martin. "Interview." *Third Text* 6 (Spring 1989): 19–28.

Carroll, Joy. "The Strange Success—And Failure of Norval Morrisseau." *Canadian Art* 21, no. 6 (1964): 348–50.

Carter, Julian B. *The Heart of Whiteness: Normal Sexuality and Race in America*. Durham, NC: Duke University Press, 2007.

Carvalho, Paul, director. *Separate Reality: The Life and Times of Norval Morrisseau*. Documentary film. Montreal: Perception Films, 2005.

Castaneda, Carlos. *A Separate Reality: Further Conversations with Don Juan*. New York: Simon and Schuster, 1971.

Cheetham, Mark. *Alex Colville: The Observer Observed*. Toronto: ECW Press, 1994.

Chomsky, Noam. *Media Control: The Spectacular Achievements of Propaganda*. New York: Seven Stories Press, 2008.

Clements, Marie. *Copper Thunderbird*. Vancouver: Talonbooks, 2007.

Coates, Ken. *The Marshall Decision and Native Rights*. Montreal: McGill-Queen's University Press, 2000.

Cohen, Percy S. "Theories of Myth." *Man*, n.s., 4, no. 3 (1969): 337–53.

Coleman, Renita, Maxwell McCombs, Donald Shaw, and David Weaver. "Agenda Setting." In *Handbook of Journalism Studies*, edited by Karin Wal-Jorgensen and Thomas Hanizsch, 147–74. New York: Routledge, 2004.

Corner, John, and Dick Pels. *Media and Restyling of Politics: Consumerism, Celebrity and Cynicism*. Beverly Hills, CA: Sage, 2003.

Cortes, Carlos E. *The Children Are Watching: How the Media Teach about Diversity*. New York: Teachers College Press, 2000.

Coward, John M. *The Newspaper Indian, Native American Identity in the Press, 1820–90*. Urbana: Illinois University Press, 1999.

Crosby, Marcia. "Construction of the Imaginary Indian." In *Beyond Wilderness: Contest and Controversy*, ed. John O'Brian and Peter White, 219–22. Montreal: McGill-Queen's University Press, 2007. Originally published in *Vancouver Anthology: The Institutional Politics of Art*, edited by Stan Douglas, 267–68, 275–79, 287–90. Vancouver: Talonbooks, 1991.

Daly, Tom, producer. *Eskimo Artist: Kenojuak*. Directed by John Feeney. Documentary film. Montreal: National Film Board of Canada, 1963.

Daschuk, James. *Clearing the Plains: Disease, Politics of Starvation and Loss of Aboriginal Life*. Regina: University of Regina Press, 2013.

Dawn, Leslie. *National Visions, National Blindness: Canadian Art and Identities in the 1920s*. Vancouver: University of British Columbia Press, 2006.

Deloria, Philip. *Indians in Unexpected Places*. Lawrence: University of Kansas, 2004.

DeSoto, Lewis. *Extraordinary Canadians: Emily Carr*. A Penguin Lives Biography. London: Penguin, 2008.

Dewdney, Selwyn, and Kenneth E. Kidd. *Indian Rock Paintings of the Great Lakes*. Toronto: University of Toronto, 1967.

Dick, Lyle. "Nationalism and Visual Media in Canada: The Case of Thomas Scott's Execution." *Manitoba History* 48 (Autumn/Winter 2004–5): 2–18.

Dickason, Olive Patricia. "First People's Hall: A Walk Through a Rich History," *The Canadian Historical Review*, vol. 85,2 (2004): 357–360.

———. *Canada's First Nations: A History of Founding Peoples from Earliest Times*. Norman: University of Oklahoma Press, 1992.

Doerfler, Jill, James Niigaanwewidam Sinclair, and Heidi Kiiwetinepinesiik Stark, eds. *Centering Anishinaabeg Studies: Understanding the World through Stories*. East Lansing, MI: Michigan State University Press, 2013.

Drucker, Johanna. *Theorizing Modernism: Visual Art and the Critical Tradition*. New York: Columbia University Press, 1996.

Duffek, Karen, and Charlotte Townsend Gault, eds. *Bill Reid and Beyond*. Vancouver: Douglas and McIntyre, 2004.

DuPertuis, Lucy. "How People Recognize Charisma: The Case of *Darshan* in *Radhasoami* and Divine Light Mission." *Sociology of Religion* 47, no. 2 (1986): 111–24.

Dyer, Richard. *White: Essays on Race and Culture*. London: Routledge, 1997.

Ehlers, Nadine. *Racial Imperatives: Discipline, Performativity and Struggles against Subjection*. Bloomington: Indiana University Press, 2012.

Emberley, Laura. *Defamiliarizing the Aboriginal: Cultural Practices and Decolonization in Canada*. Toronto: University of Toronto Press, 2007.

Erdrich, Louise. *Books and Islands in Ojibwe Country*. Washington, DC: National Geographic Press, 2003.

Falcous, Mark. "The Decolonizing National Imaginary: Promotional Media Constructions During the 2005 Lions Tour of Aotearoa New Zealand." *Journal of Sport and Social Issues* 31, 4 (November 2007): 374–389.

Fanon, Franz. *Black Skin, White Masks*. Translated by Charles Lam Markham. New York: Grove Press, 1967.

———. *The Wretched of the Earth*. New York: Grove Press, 1963.

Ferrier, Jean-Louis. "Exposition: Paris: Pour Tout." *Le Point* 874 (19 June 1989): 14–16.

Foster, Hal. "The Primitive Unconscious of Modern Art." *October* 34 (Autumn, 1985): 45–70.

Foucault, Michel. *Discipline & Punish: Birth of the Prison*. Translated by Alan Shendan. New York: Vintage, 1991.

———. "The Ethic of Care for the Self as a Practice of Freedom—An Interview with Michel Foucault, 1984." In *The Final Foucault*, edited by James Bernauer and David Rasmussen, 1–20. Cambridge, MA: MIT Press, 1987.

———. "What Is Enlightenment?" In *Ethics: Subjectivity and Truth*. Essential Works of Foucault, 1954–1984, vol. 1, edited by Paul Rabinow, 303–20. London: Penguin, 2000.

———. "Method." In *Cultural Theory and Popular Culture: A Reader*, 4ᵗʰ ed., edited by John Storey, 313–19. Harlow: Pearson Education, 2009.

Francis, Daniel. *Imaginary Indian: The Image of the Indian in Canadian Culture.* Vancouver: Arsenal Pulp Press, 1992.

Friar, Ralph E., and Natasha A. Friar. *The Only Good Indian ... The Hollywood Gospel.* New York: Drama Book Specialists, 1972.

Fry, Jacqueline. "Contemporary Arts in Non-Western Societies." *artscanada* 28, no. 6 (December 1971/January 1972): 96–101.

———. *Treaty Numbers 23, 287, 1171: Three Indian Painters of the Prairies.* Exhibition catalogue. Winnipeg: The Winnipeg Art Gallery, 1972.

Frye, Northrop. *Fables of Identity: Studies in Poetic Mythology.* New York: Harcourt, Brace and World, 1963.

Furniss, Elizabeth. *The Burden of History: Colonialism and the Frontier Myth in a Rural Canadian Community.* Vancouver: University of British Columbia Press, 1999.

Gifts from the Thunderbird: The Life and Art of Norval Morrisseau. Documentary film. Tuza Productions, 2007.

Goldie, Terry. *Fear and Temptation: The Image of the Indigene in Canadian, Australian, and New Zealand Literatures.* Montreal: McGill-Queen's University Press, 1993.

Goldwater, Robert. *Primitivism in Modern Art.* 1938. New York: Vintage Books, 1966.

———. *Gauguin.* New York: H.N. Abrams, 1928.

Gordon, Todd. *Imperialist Canada.* Winnipeg: Arbeiter Ring, 2010.

Graburn, Nelson. "The Discovery of Inuit Art: James A. Houston—Animateur." *Inuit Art Quarterly* 2, no. 2 (1987): 3–5.

Hall, Stuart, ed. *Representation: Cultural Representations and Signifying Practices.* Beverly Hills, CA: Sage, 1997.

———. "The Question of Cultural Identity." In *Modernity and Its Futures,* edited by S. Hall, D. Held, and T. McGrew. 273–327. Oxford: Polity, 1992.

Harding, Robert. "Historical Representations of Aboriginal People in the Canadian News Media." *Discourse and Society* 17, no. 2 (2006): 205–35.

Hembroff-Schleicher, Edythe. *Emily Carr: The Untold Story.* Surrey, BC: Hancock House, 1978.

Henry, Frances, and Carol Tator. *Discourses of Domination: Racial Bias in the English Language Press.* Toronto: University of Toronto Press, 2002.

———. *Racial Profiling in Canada.* Toronto: University of Toronto Press, 2006.

Herman, Edward, and Noam Chomsky. *Manufacturing Consent: The Political Economy of the Mass Media.* New York: Vintage, 1995.

Hill, Greg. *Norval Morrisseau: Shaman Artist.* Ottawa: National Gallery of Canada, 2006.

Hill, Ronald Paul. "Blackfellas and Whitefellas: Aboriginal Land Rights, the Mabo Decision, and the Meaning of Land." *Human Rights Quarterly* 17, no. 2 (May 1995): 303–22.

Hill, Tom. "Indian Art in Canada: A Historical Perspective." In *Norval Morrisseau and the Image Makers,* by Elizabeth McLuhan and Tom Hill, 11–27. Toronto: Art Gallery of Ontario, 1984.

———. "*The Paradox of Norval Morrisseau*—A Film Review." *Tawow: Canadian Indian Cultural Magazine* 4, no. 4 (1974): 1–4.

————. "A Retrospective of Indian Art." *The Native Perspective* 3, no. 2 (1978): 31–90.

Igloliorte, Heather. "The Image Makers—An Examination of the Woodland School." *Arts West* 9, no. 4 (April 1984): [chap. 5 n.40].

Iseke-Barnes, Judy, and Vivian Michelle Jimenez Estrada. "Art This Way: Decolonizing Art with Arthur Renwick." *Canadian Journal of Native Studies* 28, no. 1 (2008): 1–32.

Jacobsen, Henning, director. *The Colours of Pride*. Documentary film. National Film Board of Canada, 1973.

Jacobsen, Henning, and Duke Redbird, directors. *The Paradox of Norval Morrisseau*. Documentary film. Montreal: National Film Board of Canada, 1974.

Jameson, Fredric. *Postmodernism: The Cultural Logic of Late Capitalism*. Durham, NC: Duke University Press, 2003.

Jessup, Lynda. "Hard Inclusion." In *On Aboriginal Representation in the Gallery*, edited by Lynda Jessup and Shannon Bagg. Ottawa: Canadian Museum of Civilization, 2002.

Jiwani, Yasmin. *Discourses of Denial*. Vancouver: University of British Columbia Press, 2006.

Johnson, E. Patrick. *Appropriating Blackness: Performance and the Politics of Authenticity*. Durham, NC: Duke University Press, 2003.

Jorgensen, Marianne W., and Louise J. Phillips. *Discourse Analysis as Theory and Method*. Beverly Hills, CA: Sage, 2003.

Karp, Ivan. "Another Perspective: How Museums Define Other Cultures." *American Art* 5, nos. 1/2 (Winter/Spring 1991): 10–15.

Kellner, Douglas. *Media Culture: Cultural Studies, Identity and Politics between the Modern and the Postmodern*. London: Routledge, 1995.

Kellstedt, Paul. *The Mass Media and the Dynamics of American Racial Attitudes*. Cambridge, UK: Cambridge University Press, 2003.

King, James. *Inward Journey: The Life of Lawren Harris*. Toronto: Thomas Allen, 2012.

Kipling, Rudyard. "The White Man's Burden." *McClure's Magazine* 12 (February 1899).

Kleeblatt, Norman. "Identity Roller Coaster." *Art Journal* 64, no. 1 (Spring 2005): 61–63.

Kroeber, Theodora. *Ishi in Two Worlds: A Biography of the Last Wild Indian in North America*. Berkeley and Los Angeles: University of California Press, 1961.

Lavallee, Michelle, ed. *Seven: Professional Native Indian Artists Inc.* Regina: MacKenzie Gallery, 2014.

Long, Jack (dir.). *Bill Reid*. National Film Board of Canada, 1979, 27 min.

Lutkehaus, Nancy, and Jenny Cool. "Paradigms Lost and Found: The 'Crisis of Representation' and Visual Anthropology." In *Collecting Visible Evidence*, edited by Jane M. Gaines and Michael Renov, 116–39. Minneapolis: University of Minnesota Press, 1999.

Mackey, Eva. *The House of Difference: Cultural Politics and National Identity in Canada*. New York: Routledge, 1999.

Mansbach, Steven A. "The Artifice of Modern(ist) Art History." In *Exiles, Diasporas and Strangers*, edited by Kobena Mercer, 96–113. Cambridge, MA: MIT Press, 2008.

Martin, Jean-Hubert. *Magiciens de la Terre*. Exhibition catalogue. Paris: Éditions du Centre Pompidou, 1989.

Mason, Peter. *The Lives of Images*. London: Reaktion Books, 2001.

McClean, Ian. "Aboriginal Modernism in Central Australia." In *Exiles, Diasporas and Strangers*, ed. Kobena Mercer, 72–95. Cambridge, MA: MIT Press, 2008.

McCombs, Maxwell. *Setting the Agenda: The News Media and Public Opinion*. Cambridge, UK: Polity Press, 2004.

McEachern, Charmaine. *Narratives of Nation Media, Memory and Representation in the Making of the New South Africa*. New York: Nova, 2002.

McLuhan, Marshall. *Understanding Media: The Extensions of Man*. Toronto: McGraw-Hill, 1964.

McMaster, Gerald. "The Anishinaabe Artistic Consciousness." In *Before and After the Horizon: Anishinaabe Artists of the Great Lakes*, edited by David Penney and Gerald McMaster, 71–105. Washington, DC: Smithsonian, 2013.

McNab, David. "A Brief History of the Denial of Indigenous Rights in Canada." In *A History of Human Rights in Canada: Essential Issues*, edited by Janet Miron, 99–115. Toronto: Canadian Scholar's Press, 2009.

McWhorter, Ladelle. *Bodies and Pleasures: Foucault and the Politics of Sexual Normalization*. Bloomington: University of Indiana Press, 1999.

———. "Practicing Practicing." In *Feminism and the Final Foucault*, edited by Dianna Taylor and Karen Vintges, 143–62. Urbana: University of Illinois Press, 2004.

Miller, J.R. *Compact, Contract, Covenant: Aboriginal Treaty-Making in Canada*. Toronto: University of Toronto Press, 2009.

———. *Lethal Legacy: Current Native Controversies in Canada*. Toronto: McClelland and Stewart, 2004.

———. *Shingwauk's Vision: A History of Native Residential Schools*. Toronto: University of Toronto Press, 1996.

———. *Skyscrapers Hide the Heavens: A History of Indian–White Relations in Canada*. Toronto: University of Toronto Press, 1989.

Miller, Mary Jane. *Outside Looking In: Viewing First Nations Peoples in Canadian Dramatic Television Series*. Montreal: McGill-Queen's University Press, 2008.

Morrisseau, Norval. *Legends of My People: The Great Ojibway*, edited by Selwyn Dewdney. Toronto: Ryerson Press, 1965.

———. *Norval Morrisseau: Travels to the House of Invention*. Toronto: Key Porter Books, 1997.

Nelson, Joshua. "Framing the Picture: The Canadian Print Media's Construction of an Atypical Crime—Art Fraud—and Its Victims, 1978–2012." MA thesis, University of Guelph, 2013.

Nestor, Rob. "Indian Policy and the Early Reserve Period." *Encyclopedia of Saskatchewan*. http://esask.uregina.ca/entry/indian_policy_and_the_early_reserve_period.html (accessed 4 September 2014).

Nichols, Bill. *Representing Reality*. Bloomington, IN: Indiana University Press, 1991.

O'Brian, John, ed. *Clement Greenberg: The Collected Essays and Criticism*, vols. 1–4. Chicago: University of Chicago Press, 1988–95.

Pajaczkowska, Claire, and Lola Young. "Racism, Representation, Psychoanalysis." In *Feminism and Film*, edited by E. Ann Kaplan, 356–74. Oxford: Oxford University Press, 2000.

Penney, David and Gerald McMaster, eds. *Before and After the Horizon: Anishinaabe Artists of the Great Lakes*. Washington, DC: Smithsonian, 2013.

Phillips, Ruth B. "Morrisseau's 'Entrance': Negotiating Primitivism, Modernism, and Anishnaabe Tradition." In *Norval Morrisseau: Shaman Artist*, edited by Greg Hill, 42–77. Ottawa: National Gallery of Canada, 2006.

———. "The Turn of the Primitive: Modernism, the Stranger and the Indigenous Artist." In *Exiles, Diasporas and Strangers*, edited by Kobena Mercer, 46–71. Cambridge, MA: MIT Press, 2008.

Phillips, Ruth B., with Sherry Brydon. " 'Arrow of Truth': The Indians of Canada Pavilion at Expo 67." In *Museum Pieces: Toward the Indigenization of Canadian Museums*, by Ruth B. Phillips, 27–47. McGill-Queen's University Press, 2011.

Phillips, Ruth, and Christopher Steiner, eds. *Unpacking Culture: Art and Commodity in Colonial and Postcolonial Worlds*. Berkeley: University of California Press, 1999.

Pollock, Jack. *Dear M: Letters from a Gentleman of Excess*. London: McClelland and Stewart, 1989.

———. "Norval Morrisseau." *Tawow: Canadian Indian Cultural Magazine* 4, no. 4 (1974): 5–6.

Potter, Kristen. "James Houston, Armchair Tourism and the Marketing of Inuit Art." *Native American Art in the Twentieth Century*, edited by Jackson Rushing III, 39–57. New York: Routledge, 1999.

Price, Sally. *Primitive Art in Civilized Places*. 2nd edition. Chicago: University of Chicago Press, 2001.

Pupchek, Leanne. "True North: Inuit Art and the Canadian Imagination." *American Review of Canadian Studies* 31, nos. 1–2 (2001): 191–208.

Razack, Sherene, ed. *Race, Space, and the Law: Unmapping a White Settler Society*. Toronto: Between the Lines, 2002.

Regan, Paulette. "Unsettling the Settler Within: Canada's Peacemaker Myth, Reconciliation, and Transformative Pathways to Decolonization." PhD diss., University of Victoria, 2009.

Rickard, Jolene. "Sovereignty: A Line in the Sand." *Aperture* 39 (Spring 1995): 50–59.

Robertson, Carmen. "The Reel Norval Morrisseau: An Analysis of the National Film Board of Canada's *Paradox of Norval Morrisseau*." *International Journal of Learning* 11 (Fall 2005): 315–21.

———. "Thunderbirds and Concepts of Transformation in the Art of Norval Morrisseau." *Journal of Canadian Art History* 33, no. 2 (2012): 53–70.

———. "Mishomis in Black and White: Reconciling Press Images of an Indigenous Artist." In *Tecumseh's Vision: Indigenous Borders After the War of 1812*, ed. Paul Emile McNab, David McNab, and Ute Lischke. 109–134. Winnipeg: Aboriginal Issues Press, 2015.

Ruby, Jay. *Picturing Culture: Explorations of Film and Anthropology*. Chicago: University of Chicago Press, 2000.

Ruffo, Armand Garnet. *Norval Morrisseau: Man Changing into Thunderbird*. Madeira Park, BC: Douglas and McIntyre, 2014.

———. *The Thunderbird Poems*. Madeira Park, BC: Harbour Publishing, 2015.

Said, Edward. *Covering Islam: How the Media and the Experts Determine How We See the Rest of the World*. New York: Vintage, 1997.

———. *Culture and Imperialism*. New York: Vintage, 1994.

Sangster, Joan. " 'The Beaver' as Ideology: Constructing Images of Inuit and Native Life in Post–World War II Canada." *Anthropologica* 49, no. 2 (2007): 191–209.

Schiavone, Dino, and Raoul McKay, directors. *The Life and Work of the Woodland Artists*. Documentary film. Vancouver: Moving Images Distribution, 2003.

Schwarz, Herbert T. "The Art of Norval Morrisseau." In *Eskimo Sculpture and Eskimo Prints and Paintings of Norval Morrisseau*. Montreal: Galerie Cartier, 1968.

Sedgwick, Eve Kosofsky. *Touching Feeling: Affect, Pedagogy, Performativity*. Durham, NC: Duke University Press, 2003.

Shadbolt, Doris. *The Art of Emily Carr*. North Vancouver: Douglas and McIntyre, 1979.

Sherman, Daniel J. *French Primitivism and the Ends of Empire: 1945–1975*. Chicago: University of Chicago Press, 2011.

Shields, Rob. *Places on the Margin: Alternative Geographies of Modernity*. London: Routledge, 1991.

Sinclair, Lister, and Jack Pollock. *The Art of Norval Morrisseau*. Toronto: Methuen, 1979.

Slotkin, Richard. *Regeneration through Violence: The Mythology of the American Frontier 1600–1860*. Norman: University of Oklahoma Press, 2001.

Smith, Paul Chaat. *Everything You Know About Indians Is Wrong*. Minneapolis: University of Minnesota Press, 2009.

Stevens, James. *A Picasso in the North Country*. Thunder Bay: Anishinaabe Art Gallery, 2011.

Stoler, Laura Ann. *Along the Archival Grain: Epistemic Anxieties and Colonial Common Sense*. Princeton, NJ: Princeton University Press, 2013.

Strong, Pauline Turner. *American Indians and the American Imaginary: Cultural Representations Across the Centuries*. Boulder, CO: Paradigm Publishers, 2013.

Szuchewycz, Bhodan. "Re-Pressing Racism: The Denial of Racism in the Canadian Press." *Canadian Journal of Communication* 25, no. 4 (2000): 497–515.

Thobani, Sunera. *Exalted Subjects: Studies in the Making of Race and Nation in Canada*. Toronto: University of Toronto Press, 2007.

Thomas, Nicholas. *Possessions: Indigenous Art/Colonial Culture*. London: Thames and Hudson, 1999.

———. *Colonialism's Culture: Anthropology, Travel, Government*. Cambridge: Polity.

Tippett, Maria. *Bill Reid: The Making of an Indian*. Toronto: Random House, 2011.

———. *Emily Carr: A Biography*. Vancouver: House of Anansi Press, 2006.

Townsend-Gault, Charlotte. "First Nations Culture: Who Knows What?" *Canadian Journal of Communication* 23, no. 1 (1998). http:// www.cjc-online.ca/index.php/ journal/article/view/1021/927 (accessed 4 January 2015).

———. "Have We Ever Been Good?" In *Rebecca Belmore: The Named and Unnamed*, 9–50. Vancouver: Morris and Helen Belkin Art Gallery, 2003.

Twitchell, Paul. *Dialogues with the Master*. San Diego: Illuminated Way Press, 1970.

Valaskakis, Gail Guthrie. *Indian Country: Essays on Contemporary Native Culture.* Waterloo, ON: Wilfrid Laurier Press, 2005.

Van Dijk, Teun. *Racism and the Press.* New York: Routledge, 1991.

Viau, René. "Les Magiciens de la Terre: Vers un champ 'mondial' d'investigation?" *Parachute* 55 (July 1989): 17–18.

Vizenor, Gerald. *Manifest Manners: Narratives on PostIndian Survivance.* Lincoln: University of Nebraska Press, 1994.

———, ed. *Survivance: Narratives of Native Presence.* Lincoln: University of Nebraska Press, 2008.

Vorano, Norman. "Creators: Negotiating the Art World for Over 50 Years." *Inuit Art Quarterly* 19, nos. 3/4 (Fall/Winter 2004): 9–17.

Walcott, Rinaldo. *Black Like Who? Writing Black Canada.* 2nd ed. Toronto: Insomniac Press, 2003.

———, ed. *Rude: Contemporary Black Canadian Cultural Criticism.* Toronto: Insomniac Press, 2000.

Weinstein, Joseph. *The White Ojibway Medicine Man and Other Stories.* Bloomington, IN: iUniverse, 2009.

Wiegman, Robyn. *American Anatomies: Theorizing Race and Gender.* Durham, NC: Duke University Press, 1995.

Yu, Ying-Wen. "Playing Indian: Manifest Manners, Simulation, and Pastiche." In *Survivance: Narratives of Native Presence,* edited by Gerald Vizenor, 89–102. Lincoln: University of Nebraska Press, 2008.

INDEX